T0319747

Money, Financial Instability and Stabilization Policy

Money, Financial Instability and Stabilization Policy

Edited by

L. Randall Wray

Professor of Economics and Research Director, Center for Full Employment and Price Stability, University of Missouri, Kansas City, US

Mathew Forstater

Associate Professor of Economics and Director, Center for Full Employment and Price Stability, University of Missouri, Kansas City, US

Edward Elgar
Cheltenham, UK • Northampton, MA, USA

Published by
Edward Elgar Publishing Limited
Glensanda House
Montpellier Parade
Cheltenham
Glos GL50 1UA
UK

Edward Elgar Publishing, Inc.
136 West Street
Suite 202
Northampton
Massachusetts 01060
USA

A catalogue record for this book
is available from the British Library

ISBN-13: 978 1 84542 474 9
ISBN-10: 1 84542 474 3

Typeset by Manton Typesetters, Louth, Lincolnshire, UK
Printed and bound in Great Britain by MPG Books Ltd, Bodmin, Cornwall

Contents

Contributors   vii
Preface   ix

Introduction   1

1 Negative net resource transfers as a Minskyian hedge profile and
   the stability of the international financial system   11
   Jan A. Kregel

2 Monetary and social relationships   22
   Charles A.E. Goodhart

3 System dynamics of interest rate effects on aggregate demand   37
   Linwood Tauheed and L. Randall Wray

4 Credibility versus confidence in monetary policy   58
   Edwin le Heron and Emmanuel Carre

5 Understanding the link among uncertainty, instability and
   institutions, and the need for stabilization policies: towards a
   synthesis between Post Keynesian and Institutional Economics   85
   Slim Thabet

6 Saving, asset-price inflation and debt-induced deflation   104
   Michael Hudson

7 Unit roots in macroeconomic time series and stabilization policies: a
   Post Keynesian interpretation   125
   Gilberto A. Libanio

8 Mark-up determinants and effectiveness of open market operations
   in an oligopsonistic banking sector: the Mexican case   141
   Noemí Levy and Guadalupe Mántey

9   The Washington Consensus and (non-)development   171
    Hansjörg Herr and Jan Priewe

10 Competition, low profit margin, low inflation and economic
    stagnation   192
    Arturo Huerta

11 Foundering after floating? Exchange rate management and the
    Mexican stock market, 1995–2001   208
    Jesús Muñoz and P. Nicholas Snowden

12 The evolution of financial systems: the development of the new
    member states of the European Union   231
    Elisabeth Springler

Index   257

Contributors

Emmanuel Carre is Lecturer at the IEP (Institute of Political Sciences) in Bordeaux, France.

Mathew Forstater is Associate Professor of Economics and Director of the Center for Full Employment and Price Stability at the University of Missouri–Kansas City, Kansas City, Missouri, US.

Charles A.E. Goodhart is Professor at the London School of Economics and Deputy Director of the Financial Markets Group in London, UK.

Hansjörg Herr is Professor of Economics at FHW Berlin (Berlin School of Economics) and FHTW Berlin (University of Applied Sciences) respectively, Berlin, Germany.

Michael Hudson is Distinguished Research Professor in the Department of Economics at the University of Missouri–Kansas City, Kansas City, Missouri, US, and is president of the Institute for the Study of Long-Term Economic Trends (ISLET) in New York City and London.

Arturo Huerta is Professor of Economics at the Economic Faculty of the National University of Mexico, Mexico City.

Jan A. Kregel is Chief of Policy Analysis and Development at the Financing for Development Office in the United Nations Department of Economic and Social Affairs.

Edwin le Heron is Professor at the IEP (Institute of Political Sciences) in Bordeaux, France and President of the ADEK: French Association for the Development of Keynesian Studies.

Noemí Levy is Professor of Monetary Economics at the National Autonomous University of Mexico.

Gilberto A. Libanio is Professor of Economics at the Federal University of Minas Gerais, Brazil and Doctoral Candidate in Economics at the University of Notre Dame, Notre Dame, Indiana, US.

Guadalupe Mántey is Professor of Monetary Economics at the National Autonomous University of Mexico.

Jesús Muñoz is Business Professor in the Economics Department at Universidad Intercontinental, Mexico City, Mexico.

Jan Priewe is Professor of Economics at FHW Berlin (Berlin School of Economics) and FHTW Berlin (University of Applied Sciences) respectively, Berlin, Germany.

P. Nicholas Snowden is Senior Lecturer in the Department of Economics at Lancaster University Management School, Lancaster, UK.

Elisabeth Springler is Assistant Professor of Economics at the Vienna University of Economics and Business Administration, Vienna, Austria.

Linwood Tauheed is Visiting Professor of Economics and Black Studies at the University of Missouri–Kansas City, Kansas City, Missouri, US.

Slim Thabet is Professor of Economics at the University of Amiens, France.

L. Randall Wray is Professor of Economics and the Director of Research at the Center for Full Employment and Price Stability at the University of Missouri–Kansas City and a Senior Scholar at the Levy Economics Institute, New York, US.

Preface

This volume presents a selection of papers presented at the Eighth International Post Keynesian Workshop, organized by Paul Davidson, Jan Kregel, Mathew Forstater and L. Randall Wray, and held at the University of Missouri–Kansas City (UMKC) in June 2004. The workshop was jointly sponsored by the *Journal of Post Keynesian Economics*, UMKC's Center for Full Employment and Price Stability, and the Economics Department of UMKC. The workshop carried on the long tradition begun in the 1980s by Jan Kregel, Piero Garegnani and Sergio Paranello with workshops originally held in Trieste, Italy, continued by Paul Davidson at the University of Tennessee–Knoxville, and currently held at UMKC biannually. In its current form, the workshop begins with a week-long Post Keynesian Summer School, staffed by approximately 20 prominent Post Keynesian faculty from the US and abroad, and is attended by more than 70 graduate students and post-graduates from all over the world. The workshop ends with a four-day conference that brings together approximately 120 international heterodox scholars from universities, governments and private organizations.

The papers included in this volume were carefully selected to present an overview of the latest research on monetary theory and policy, financial markets and financial instability coming out of the Post Keynesian school of thought. Obviously, these represent only a small fraction of the interesting papers that were presented at the 23 panels organized for the conference. Rather than trying to provide a sampling of the range of topics covered, we chose to include papers related to a theme that has long interested Post Keynesian scholars: money and instability. Still, the papers collected here do provide an indication of the wide-ranging interests and of the truly international scope of Post Keynesian research. The first half of this volume is more theoretical, while the second half of the volume includes papers that are either more empirical or more focused on specific concerns.

The editors would like to thank in particular Louise and Paul Davidson for their help in every aspect of the planning and organization of the workshop. Jan Kregel took time off from his busy schedule to help in planning the workshop, and he also taught in the Summer School and gave one of the keynote presentations at the conference. Likewise, we thank Charles Goodhart for giving the other keynote talk, and for teaching in the summer school. We thank presenters at the Eighth International Post-Keynesian Workshop: Victor Acevedo Valerio, Ricardo Aguado, Antoni J. Alves, Jr, Morteza H. Ardebili, Nursel Aydiner, Michelle Baddeley, Robert A. Blecker, David Bunting, Leonardo Burlamaqui, Alcino F. Camara Neto, Paul P. Chirstensen, Octavio A.C. Conceicao, Eugenia Correa, Jerry Courvisanos, Paul Davidson, Paul Downward, Gary Dymski, Steven Fazzari, Jesus Felipe, Fernando Ferrari-Filho, Giuseppe Fontana, Mathew Forstater, Rumen Gechev, Oliver Giovannoni, Alicia Giron G., Inacio Guerberoff, Mark Hayes, Eckhard Hein, Edwin le Heron, Hansjörg Herr, Hubert Hieke, Richard P. Holt, Michael Hudson, Arturo Huerta, Frederico G. Jayme, Gustavo Junca, James Juniper, Fadhel Kaboub, Daniel Kostzer, Theodore T. Koutsobinas, Jan A. Kregel, Frederic Lee, Mauro B. Lemos, Noemi Levy, Gilberto A. Libanio, Guadalupe Mántey, John S.L. McCombie, Doug Meador, Andrew Mearman, Antonio J.A. Meirelles, Aslam Mohamed, Basil Moore, Tracy Mott, Kazuo Murakoshi, Lenin Navarro Chavez, Francisco Oliveira, Ozlem Onaran, Jose Luis Oreiro, Adolfo Orive, Etelberto Ortiz C., Thomas I. Palley, Alain Parguez, Luiz-Fernando de Paula, Esteban Perez Caldentey, Karl Petrick, Marc-Andre Pigeon, Steven Pressman, Jan Priewe, Cladio Puty, Michael Radzicki, Arslan M. Razmi, Ingrid Rima, Mark Roberts, Claudio Sardoni, Thorsten Schulten, Brendan Sheehan, John Smithin, Rogerio Sobreira, Elisabeth Springler, Otto Steiger, Gilberto Tadeu-Lima, Linwood Tauheed, Pavlina Tcherneva, Slim Thabet, Zdravka Todorova, Achim Truger, Eric Tymoigne, Bernard Vallageas, Eric Vasseur, Leonardo Vera, Matias Vernango, Jim Webb, L. Randall Wray and Tsuyoshi Yasuhara.

Staff, faculty and students of UMKC's Economics Department and CFEPS also played an important role in helping to make the workshop possible. In particular, we thank Pavlina Tcherneva, Kelly Pinkham, Jennifer Harris, James Sturgeon, Fred Lee, Dorothy Hawkins and Joelle LeClaire. The editors also thank Shakuntala Das, Fadhel Kaboub and Mehdi Guirat for help in soliciting the papers included in this volume, and Natalia Sourbeck and Heather Starzynski for excellent editorial assistance in preparation of the manuscript. We also thank Alla Semenova for preparing the index.

Finally, and most importantly, we thank the contributors to this volume for providing such a strong set of papers and for keeping to a tight deadline.

L. Randall Wray
Mathew Forstater

Introduction

L. Randall Wray and Mathew Forstater

Post Keynesian literature has long been associated with the study of money, financial markets, and financial instability. Indeed, this is perhaps the area to which Post Keynesians have made the greatest contributions. Paul Davidson's *Money and the Real World* revived interest in Keynes's contributions to monetary theory, putting money back into 'Keynesian' economics. Indeed, it is ironic that most of the post-war research associated with Keynes's name (whether of the neoclassical synthesis orthodoxy or even of the Cambridge heterodoxy) relegated the role of money to the background. Davidson emphasized the 'Chapter 17' version of Keynes, in which money plays a crucial role in the economy owing to its peculiar characteristics and to the nature of decision making in conditions of uncertainty. This was, of course, the theme of contemporaneous work by Jan Kregel, who contrasted Keynes's methodology ('shifting equilibrium') to that of orthodoxy. Since the early 1980s, there have been major advances made to the Post Keynesian approach to money, in particular the development of Basil Moore's horizontalism, the refinement of the Italian–French circuit approach, and the revival of the Knapp–Keynes chartalist approach. Many of the papers collected here draw on these traditions in the Post Keynesian literature to inform their thinking on money and monetary policy. In particular, the paper by Thabet as well as the paper by Springler, concern recent Post Keynesian approaches to money.

The economist whose name is most intimately associated with the Post Keynesian focus on financial institutions and financial instability is Hyman Minsky. While his early work can probably be identified more closely with the institutionalists than with the Keynesians of the 1950s and 1960s, he gradually incorporated the economics of Keynes within his vision of an economy operating with complex financial relations. Long before financial instability (re)appeared in the developed capitalist economies, Minsky explained why such systems are inherently unstable using his 'financial theory of investment and investment theory of the cycle'. Although in his view it would be impossible to eliminate instability, he did lay out the conditions that would tend to enhance stability, or at least postpone the instability that would inevitably arise in economies that managed to prevent 'it' (another great depression) from happening again. There is no question that Minsky's thoughts have had the greatest influence on Post Keynesian research into domestic financial instability in developed nations, and many researchers have carried Minsky's analysis to the field of international financial instability. Examples in this volume of research inspired by Minsky include most importantly the paper by Kregel, as well as the papers by Huerta, by Hudson and by Muñoz and Snowden.

It is of course well-known that Keynes participated in the discussions that would reform the international financial system in the post-war world. While his 'bancor' plan would not be adopted, the Bretton Woods system did help to bring a long period of relative international stability based on a dollar–gold standard. With the breakdown of that system in the early 1970s, the international monetary system has taken on something of a Tower of Babel form, with experiments in floating currencies, dirty float, fixed exchange rates, currency boards, monetary unions and dollarization. The result has been a series of international currency and financial crises – and a case could be made that these are becoming more frequent and increasingly severe. Davidson has revived and updated the Keynes plan for a post-Bretton Woods era. Many Post Keynesians have followed Davidson's lead in calling for a return to some sort of fixed exchange rate system. It is not always clear whether these Post Keynesians would endorse a 'go-it-alone' strategy that is not consistent with Keynes's own bancor plan, but at least some seem to support Europe's monetary union (while rejecting Maastricht criteria). Others have called for floating exchange rates, perhaps only as a 'second best' politically feasible alternative to Keynes's bancor plan, which is seen as highly improbable for political reasons. At least a few argue for floating rates as 'first best' because they preserve fiscal and monetary policy independence, with Goodhart's critique of European monetary union on the basis of chartalist theory serving as perhaps the best example. Authors in this volume that take up international stability while addressing problems with the international monetary arrangements include, in addition to Kregel and Goodhart, the papers by Herr and Priewe, by Huerta, and by Muñoz and Snowden.

In the remainder of this introduction, we will briefly summarize the most important contributions of the papers collected in this volume.

In Chapter 1, Jan Kregel argues that the international financial system has evolved since the breakdown of the Bretton Woods system in a manner that increases instability and the risk of financial crises. Further, the primary international institution created in the post-war period to contain international instability, the IMF, has changed its operating procedure so that it contributes to instability. Under the fixed exchange rate system of the Bretton Woods era, IMF lending was largely undertaken on a short-term basis to support exchange rate stability. As a condition of such 'bridging loans', countries had to deflate to generate surpluses on external accounts to earn foreign exchange to service the debt to the IMF. In this period, private international lending was relatively unimportant. However, after the 1970s, private bank loans and portfolio flows came to dominate international finance, permitting sustained imbalances in external accounts. After the US and UK experiments in monetarism, interest rates rose sharply on large outstanding foreign currency-denominated external debt (especially dollar debt). Private international institutions reduced lending to developing country borrowers with external earnings insufficient to service debt. Thus the IMF found a new role as it provided short-term adjustment lending to prevent international default. Effectively, the IMF became a guarantor of creditworthiness and enforcer of adjustment policies that came to be known as the 'Washington Consensus'. In the context of large and growing international financial flows, IMF lending was far too small to maintain international stability, so it had to recruit private lenders by providing a 'seal of approval' that the country's policies were on the right track. The problem is that external debt would continue to grow, putting developing nations into a 'Ponzi' finance situation in which external earnings are not sufficient to cover net capital factor services. At the same time, the adjustment policies almost guarantee slow domestic growth and, given nearly global adoption of demand constraints, a deflationary bias is built into the international system. The US has become the market of 'last resort', but has perhaps also succumbed to Ponzi finance. Kregel suggests that analysts should return to Domar's stability conditions and to Keynes's Clearing Union to find a path out of this dilemma.

Charles Goodhart's chapter examines the deficiencies of many of the contemporary macroeconomic models, especially their treatment of money and their neglect of the role of government. He does note, however, that the old 'exogenous' money approach of the ISLM models – in which the central bank controls the money supply – has been replaced in many models with the recognition that central banks actually set interest rates endogenously in response to perceived economic developments. Still, he finds much of the literature on central bank attempts to fool the public to be silly and welcomes recent models that include more realistic behaviour of central banks that use interest rates to target inflation. He would like to see more serious work on wage and price stickiness and on policy lags to obtain a better match with what he takes to be actual real-world experience. He is also sceptical of representative agent models that presume complete financial markets for it is not clear why such economies would use money. Further, he suggests that, rather than blind adoption of rational expectations, the expectations-generating process should be time-variant and endogenous, subject to inertia, hysteresis and initial conditions. Goodhart is particularly impressed with the work of Shubik, which embraces incomplete financial markets, default, heterogenous agents and regulatory policy. This is a precondition to studying systemic financial stability issues such as contagion and the role that government can play. Finally, Goodhart devotes the second half of his chapter to macro policy stabilization issues, addressing in particular the euro and the Growth and Stability Pact. As he has argued elsewhere, the attempt to divorce fiscal and monetary policy is the main flaw of the euro system. Because most economic theory still locates the origins of money in barter and attributes its evolution to the search for transactions costs reducing media of exchange, it is not able to model the role of government in the monetary system. Relatedly, Goodhart believes that economists have paid far too little attention to legal and governance systems and hence to the important role played by government in economic growth.

The chapter by Tauheed and Wray explores the conventional wisdom that monetary policy should raise interest rates to dampen demand, slow the economy and thus restrain inflation. It demonstrates that, on plausible assumptions, raising interest rates could actually stimulate aggregate demand through debt service payments made by government on its outstanding debt. This is more likely if private sector indebtedness is small, if private spending is not very interest-rate elastic, if interest rates are high and if government debt is large (above 50 per cent) relative to GDP. Thus it is shown that, if monetary policy tries to fight inflationary pressures that could be fuelled by large government deficits, this could generate destabilizing feedback effects: the high interest rates would increase budget deficits (as interest payments on government debt would rise) and thereby increase private sector income and wealth, leading to ever-rising private demand. Similarly, in recession, lowering interest rates could actually depress demand by reducing government interest payments. Such a scenario could be relevant to the case of Japan by the end of the 1990s, when the overnight interest rate was kept at zero in the face of depressed private sector spending. Given the very large government budget deficits and government debt-to-GDP ratios above 100 per cent, it is possible that raising rates would actually be stimulative.

In a very interesting analysis (Chapter 4), Edwin Le Heron and Emmanuel Carre argue that the evolution of monetary policy in the post-war period can best be understood by distinguishing between a *confidence* strategy and a *credibility* strategy. While debate over monetary policy formation has traditionally taken the form of rules versus discretion, the authors argue that such an approach sheds little light on central bank behaviour, especially over the past 25 years. Rather, policy has evolved from behaviour designed to increase credibility to one that is focused on building confidence. The old monetarist strategy based on a constant growth rate of money rule really was designed to build credibility: the central bank says what it does and does what it says. Further, this strategy was based on 'common knowledge' of the 'natural laws' of the economy. By respecting the universal truth that inflation is always and everywhere the result of too much money, the central bank could control inflation by controlling money growth. Even as the old-style monetarism morphed into new classical economics, the commitment to rules built credibility by avoiding surprises.

However, the consensus about the link between money growth and inflation broke down over the 1980s, leading to uncertainty about the natural laws (if they exist at all) guiding the economy. Hence monetary policy became to some extent rudderless. While many analysts and some central banks have adopted inflation targets, Chairman Greenspan of the Fed has rejected these as inflexible. Rather, the Fed has adopted a strategy of building confidence by communicating its understanding and policy intentions while taking into account expectations of markets so as to avoid surprises. Thus the Fed announces its likely policy changes far in advance and only moves once markets appear to expect action. By creating a common understanding of economic performance, even while admitting that the economy is complex and the future unknowable, Greenspan is still able to garner the confidence of markets. Hence Le Heron and Carre see in Greenspan's Fed a return to Keynes's philosophy, no doubt a position that many American Post Keynesians will view as provocative.

In the next chapter, Slim Thabet draws out the links between Post Keynesian research and one version of Institutionalism: the original Institutional economics (OIE) associated with Veblen, as opposed to the new Institutional economics (NIE) associated with North and Williamson that he believes is more consistent with orthodoxy. Of course, Post Keynesians are well known for their preoccupation with the importance of time, irreversibility and decision making under conditions of uncertainty, but what is less recognized is the study of institutions created to deal with uncertainty. After first summarizing the implications of accepting fundamental uncertainty into models of the economy, Thabet moves on to an analysis of the institutions that have been created to constrain instability in a non-ergodic world. Of course, money is the major institution of capitalist economies and has been extensively studied by Post Keynesians as well as by economists working in the OIE tradition. Thabet also examines the links among legal contracts, especially forward contracts, banking institutions and money, noting the natural affinity between the ideas of Keynes and those of Commons. The chapter also discusses the reaction of OIE 'New Dealers' to Keynes's *General Theory*, which provided a theoretical basis for the new institutions that were developed to usher in 'the age of Keynes'. Many post-war economists explicitly linked OIE and Keynes's theory in their own work: they included Eichner, Dillard, Galbraith, Cornwall and most importantly, Minsky. However, Thabet argues that OIE could benefit by paying greater attention to Post Keynesian work on uncertainty even as Post Keynesians could benefit through analysis of real-world institutions.

Michael Hudson's contribution (Chapter 6) examines the rapid growth of debt and financial savings that is a characteristic of post-war capitalist economies. This chapter recalls Minsky's description of the current stage of capitalism as the 'money manager' epoch, with huge flows of 'managed' or 'institutionalized' money chasing returns. Hudson argues that much of the savings and debt is created to finance purchase of real estate, stocks and bonds, rather than to finance tangible investment that would increase employment. Indeed, it is the potential for making high returns through speculative purchases of financial assets that turns attention away from the potential profitability of investing in means of production. This argument, of course, also recalls Keynes's Chapter 12 from the *General Theory*, that speculation could come to dominate 'enterprise'. Higher saving propensities can bid up financial asset prices, but do not increase *net savings*, defined as savings above debt. Rather, most growth of savings is equal to growth of debt. According to Hudson, a modern economy is composed of two quite distinct systems. The first, and largest, is that of land, monopoly rights and financial claims that yield *rentier* income in the form of interest, financial fees, rents and monopoly gains. The other, much smaller, system produces goods and services using labour and capital goods; profits here are very much smaller than the *rentier* proceeds. Indeed, purely financial transactions each day are greater than the annual national income. Hudson notes that the US savings rate has steadily fallen over the post-war period, and has actually been negative since the late 1990s; however, the economy has never been more 'flush' with savings and credit. That is, while net savings are below zero, gross savings are soaring as debt-financed purchases of financial assets and real estate fuel *rentier* income. Hence today's economy should be seen as a financial bubble, with asset-price inflation running apace even as commodity prices stagnate and labour's spending power falls. Hudson closely examines the growth of the 'FIRE' (financial, insurance and real estate) sector and links this to stagnation of the 'real' economy due to depressed effective demand. Earnings in the FIRE sector should be seen as transfers rather than as factor payments, effectively a diversion of revenues to a separate circular flow from the system that yields *rentier* income, little of which will be spent on output from the productive sphere. The productive sphere, in turn is hobbled by an increasing debt burden and rising transfer payments to *rentiers*. Hudson argues that something similar brought down the Roman Empire and wonders how much longer today's financial bubbles can keep expanding. Because economies cannot grow as fast as debt – which grows at least as fast as the compound interest rate – a financial crisis is likely. While government can be expected to intervene to guarantee debt, Hudson doubts that such a policy can be successful in the long run.

Gilberto Libanio notes that Post Keynesians accept long-run non-neutrality of money, cumulative causation, non-stationarity and time-dependency, and persistent effects of policy changes. At the same time, mainstream economists such as those who embrace the real business cycle approach have been searching time series data for existence of unit roots, which are taken to indicate non-stationary processes that follow a random walk. Libanio argues that evidence that many time series do exhibit unit roots could be taken to support the Post Keynesian position: that is, that such data confirm Keynesian theory rather than real business cycle theory. After first describing tests for unit roots, the chapter lays out how these have been used to confirm real business cycle theory. It is important to recognize the role that underlying assumptions play in these interpretations, such as the usual orthodox presumption that money is neutral. Libanio moves on to a useful summary of mainstream critiques of real business cycle models, particularly by New Keynesians, some of whom deny that the evidence actually can confirm the existence of unit roots. In the second half of the chapter, Libanio examines the implications of unit roots for Post Keynesian economics. He argues that unit roots can support the possibility of persistent involuntary unemployment owing to path dependence, hysteresis in labour markets and long-run non-neutrality of money. Indeed, theories in which demand constraints operate to constrain growth, or in which there are multiple equilibria (as in Keynes's 'general' model in which full employment is only one of many possible points of equilibrium) are consistent with existence of unit roots. Hence Chapter 7 reinterprets the empirical findings of real business cycle theorists using a different set of assumptions more in line with Keynes's theory. The primary real business cycle findings were non-stationarity, persistence of 'shocks' and time-dependent variance that approaches infinity as the forecast horizon increases, but all of these are consistent with the Post Keynesian paradigm. Capitalist economies operate in historical time: economic events are time-dependent and have persistent effects on the trajectory of the economy. Further, non-stationarity is a sufficient (although not necessary) condition for non-ergodicity, while non-ergodic systems need not have a long-run statistical average about which the system will fluctuate. Keynes's model of 'shifting equilibrium' is an alternative to the real business cycle 'random walk with drift' interpretation of time series data that do not exhibit mean reversion. Finally, while money endogeneity is used in the real business cycle model to ensure super-neutrality of money (only real variables matter), Post Keynesians reject such a dichotomy and emphasize that money always matters.

Noemí Levy and Guadalupe Mántey argue that commercial banks have oligopsonistic power in their domestic deposit market, and that in this market structure the loan rate is not systematically affected by central bank rates. Instead, they argue, the spread is determined by the interest elasticity of deposit demand, liability management and the banking sector balance sheet structure. After a review of the horizontalist, structuralist and asymmetric expectations approaches to short-term interest rate linkages found among endogenous money theorists, the authors turn to their alternative explanation. They then investigate the causal linkages between short-term interest rates in Mexico, where there is considerable banking oligopsony due to barriers to competition between public and private short-term financial assets. The chapter introduces a VAR (vector autoregression) model to attempt to disentangle the causal linkages between short-term interest rates in Mexico. The results of three cointegration and error-correction models obtained for the loan rate, the Treasury bill rate, and the interbank rate support their hypothesis of the existence of oligopsony in the Mexican bank deposit market and the compensatory role of deposit interest rates in determining loan rates. Levy and Mántey conclude that in nations where the institutional framework enhances deposit market oligopsony, the spread between loan and deposit rates may be so large that central banks are unable to influence credit market conditions by means of open market operations. They recommend that, under such circumstances, monetary authorities return to direct controls on credit expansion as a means of influencing aggregate demand.

In Chapter 9, Hansjörg Herr and Jan Priewe critique the Washington Consensus framework for macroeconomic policy and development and offer a sketch of an alternative approach to macroeconomic policy for developing countries. After laying out the main features of the Washington Consensus, the authors offer their critical appraisal. As is well known, this approach, typified by the policies promoted by the IMF and World Bank, focuses on 'sound money' policies and improvements in resource allocation that are believed to be linked to productivity growth. Recommendations thus include privatization and improvement of property rights, 'getting the prices right', increased competition, deregulation, 'free trade', tax cuts and cuts in government spending, government budget balancing and avoidance of large current account deficits. The authors focus on six macroeconomic themes in their critique of the Washington Consensus: inflation analysis and stabilization policy, exchange rate regimes, capital account liberalization v. controls, current account deficits and external debt, dollarization, and the domestic financial system. They then contrast a typical regime of underdevelopment and repressed growth with an alternative growth scenario. Regarding the former, they emphasize the problems of increasing external debt (denominated in foreign currency). The key to the alternative positive growth scenario, they argue, is the creation of an accepted high-quality national currency. Finally, Herr and Priewe consider three different approaches to addressing the problems created when all nations strive for a current account surplus: global competition, international clearing union, and current account deficits for the most developed countries.

Arturo Huerta examines the impact of financial liberalization on developing countries and especially those in Latin America. Given the poor productive, financial and macroeconomic conditions in these countries, free movement of capital intended to attract foreign funds has increasingly relied on the implementation of restrictive monetary and fiscal polices in order to maintain stable exchange rates and low inflation. Huerta contends that the primacy of these two policy objectives (price and exchange rate stability) has brought counterproductive results. He first looks at the effect of inflation-reducing policies on firms' profit margins, investment activities and internal financing and argues that the loss of competitiveness of domestic producers vis-à-vis imports has further eroded their financial positions and ability to raise capital for investment. Furthermore, low domestic demand, appreciated exchange rates and the increasing presence of imports in the domestic market propagate increased foreign indebtedness and decreased ability to fulfil cash commitments. The cumulative effect of these problems generates economic stagnation, which deepens the process of deindustrialization and reduced global competitiveness. Huerta points out that public policy is deficient in tackling these conditions. Governments are willing neither to devalue exchange rates to improve the competitiveness of domestic production nor to boost countercyclical spending to put a floor on falling demand. Huerta's chapter provides an inquiry into the unsustainable processes generated by the manner in which financial liberalization has occurred in Latin America.

In Chapter 11, on exchange rates and the Mexican stock market, Jesús Muñoz and P. Nicholas Snowden examine the disappointing contribution of equity finance in the recovery from the first of the sequence of emerging market financial crises experienced in the 1990s: the 'Tequila' crisis beginning in December 1994. The authors begin by demonstrating the marginal contribution of Bolsa Mexicana de Valores (the Mexican stock market, or BMV) to the financial needs of a growing economy. They argue that, in addition to institutional deficiencies, other systematic influences were acting on the demand for equities. In particular, they examine the relationship between equity returns and fluctuations in the value of the peso, especially in the period following 1997. Muñoz and Snowden conclude that equity stakes in indebted firms are likely to be of limited appeal to domestic investors under a regime of managed floating rates. The quandary they identify is that, while firms may wish to retire debt through the proceeds of new issues, domestic investors may only emerge after the debt exposure has been substantially reduced. The monetary policies Mexico used to attempt to stabilize the movements of the floating exchange rate amplified the impact on share prices, and thus the high interest rates thought to be necessary to 'defend' the peso also damaged the prospects for heavily indebted firms. The authors conclude that market reforms geared toward foreign investment may help support share prices and improve the prospects for a shift from debt towards equity.

In the final chapter, Elisabeth Springler examines the evolution of the financial system in eight of the ten new member states of the European Union. The countries under investigation are Estonia, the Czech Republic, Hungary, Latvia, Lithuania, Slovenia and Slovakia, nations with virtually non-existent financial systems prior to the late 1980s and their transition to a market economy. The purpose of the chapter is to delineate the mode of development of the financial sector observed in these countries, and thereby evaluate the prospects for future growth and continued economic convergence to the EU15 block. Springler utilizes the 'five-stage setting of banking evolution' advanced by Chick (1992) and

Chick and Dow (1988), to argue that most of the new member states have completed all but the last phase of banking development. In addition, she classifies the mode of development into 'bank-based' or 'market-based' financial systems, arguing that the latter, rooted in substantial market liberalization, lead to relative instability, while the former provide the right foundation for future economic development. Springler concludes that Hungary, Lithuania and Poland have developed a very strong bank-based financial system, while in the Czech Republic and Latvia this model is somewhat weaker but still quite advanced. In Slovakia and Slovenia, however, market-based financial systems seem to be the predominant mode of financial evolution while the bank-based systems are considerably weaker. After studying the remarkable transformation in the financial system after the banking crises that plagued all of these countries in the mid-1990s, Springler concludes, via a quantitative and qualitative analysis, that all new members states (Slovenia to a lesser extent) have the condition to promote further economic development and integration into the European Union.

1. Negative net resource transfers as a Minskyian hedge profile and the stability of the international financial system

Jan A. Kregel[1]

FROM IMF EXCHANGE RATE STABILIZATION POLICY TO IMF INTERNATIONAL STABILITY POLICY

The response of official financial institutions to the 1980s debt crisis produced an important change in the impact of their support to developing countries for adjustment to external imbalances. Before the breakdown of the Bretton Woods fixed exchange rate system, IMF lending was to support exchange rate stability. Countries could draw against their quota funds to meet external claims on domestic residents at its par rate (or at the newly agreed par rate) if they had insufficient foreign exchange earnings. In exchange the country agreed to adjust domestic economic policies to eliminate fundamental disequilibrium and bring a return to external balance. The policies that were the condition of the lending had as their basic objective the creation of an external surplus that would allow the support to be repaid within a relatively short period.[2]

The causes of the external imbalances were usually identified as excess domestic absorption due to a fiscal imbalance created by excess government spending, or exchange rate overvaluation due to a domestic inflation differential created by excess government spending. As a result the policies sought to reduce absorption by reducing domestic incomes. This was achieved by creating a fiscal budget surplus supported by monetary restriction. If the excess demand had also produced an inflation differential, an exchange rate adjustment sought to change relative prices of traded goods to restore international competitiveness. The adjustment lending was close to what are called 'bridging loans' that allow the borrower short-term funding until a more permanent financing solution can be found. In the case of IMF adjustment lending the funds were to allow the borrower to maintain external commitments at the existing, or the newly devalued, exchange rate for the period required to bring the external account back into surplus. The surpluses thus become the more permanent financing solution that allowed the bridge loan to be repaid to the IMF. The typical adjustment period was expected to be relatively short, the size of the funds required relatively modest and the interest rates charged concessional, with the IMF the sole major creditor. In this system, large debt stocks could not be built up or maintained on a permanent basis.

After the breakdown of the fixed-rate international financial system in the early 1970s the need for IMF adjustment lending to support stable exchange rates disappeared. In theory, under flexible exchange rates central banks no longer needed to hold exchange reserves since adjustment to external imbalances would take place through the impact of appropriate market adjustment of exchange rates producing changes in the relative prices of tradable and non-tradable goods.

However, the breakdown of the Bretton Woods system of stable exchange rates brought with it a fundamental change in international financial markets. From a system that had been based on official capital flows and limited foreign direct investment flows, overseen by the Bretton Woods institutions, private bank loans and portfolio flows came to dominate in the 1970s. The large imbalances generated by the external disequilibria of the petroleum and non-petroleum producing countries were intermediated through private banks lending internationally, usually through syndicated loans without any policy conditionality aimed at eliminating them. The increased availability of private financing made it possible for countries to undergo external disequilibrium for more extended periods without recourse to the IMF or to the policy conditions attached to official lending. But it also meant that the sustained imbalances created increasing stocks of external indebtedness dominated in foreign currencies.

At the same time, since imbalances were created by a good with low price elasticity (0.1), priced in dollars, the relative price adjustment that was to be produced by flexibility in exchange rates was slow to operate. However, when exchange rates did adjust this made the domestic costs of petroleum imports even higher and increased the domestic costs of debt service. This was not a problem as long as the dollar was weak and international interest rates were low. Indeed, for much of the 1970s real rates were negative, supported by the expansion in international lending due to the expansion of the euro–dollar market. But in the aftermath of the tightening of US monetary policy in October 1979, and the recession that followed, many developing country borrowers had insufficient foreign exchange earnings to meet their increased debt service as interest rates rose on their dollar-denominated bank loans. The result was a sharp decline in the willingness of foreign lenders to continue to roll over existing loans.

Thus, in need of foreign exchange that they could no longer borrow from private lenders, countries again looked to the IMF to provide short-term adjustment lending and the Fund found a new role, now as guarantor for the policies to be applied by developing countries to assure private lenders of their credit-worthiness. In the words of its new Managing Director, Rodrigo de Rato, 'The shift to a system in which member countries choose their own exchange rate regimes brought a new mandate for the Fund to exercise firm surveillance over members' exchange rate policies, and their macroeconomic policies more broadly, in order to ensure the effective operation of the international monetary system.'[3]

But, in a world of flexible exchange rates dominated by private capital flows, the external disequilibria facing countries were more the result of volatility in private capital inflows and interest rates making it impossible to meet their debt service than of excessive domestic absorption making it impossible to finance their deficit on goods and services trade. It also meant that, when capital inflows stopped, countries could have repayment commitments on principal that ex-ceeded both their existing foreign exchange reserves and the amounts that the Fund could officially lend. In this case failure to achieve sufficient short term funding did not mean failing to meet the existing parity, for, under flexible rates, this was not the concern. However, it was possible that the imbalance was suf-ficient to cause a country to have to suspend convertibility and close foreign exchange markets as the excess demand for foreign currency drove the exchange rate to zero. Since the amounts that the Fund could officially lend were designed to meet the much lower amounts associated with temporary trade imbalances, they were insufficient to meet the amounts of the excess demand for foreign exchange. To keep foreign exchange markets open it thus became necessary for the Fund to find ways to supplement its own resources. In addition to lending beyond official quota limits, this was done by associating other official lenders, such as the BIRD and regional development banks, as well as governments in mobilizing the resources necessary to meet the capital outflows at a positive exchange rate. But, in these conditions, the only way to preserve convertibility and open foreign exchange markets was to convince foreign lenders to continue to lend. From the point of view of IMF stabilization policy it thus became as important to restore borrowing countries' access to private capital markets as correcting their trade imbalance. As a result the conditions that the Fund re-quired of countries seeking support shifted to include policies to convince private lenders to continue to lend to countries in disequilibrium.

However, the objective of policy, to generate the foreign exchange earnings necessary to meet outstanding commitments, remained the same, only in the new circumstances this included the necessity to convince creditors to partici-pate in debt restructuring programmes and to continue to lend to distressed borrowers. The introduction of tight fiscal and monetary policy that had been used to reduce absorption was now viewed as the appropriate policy to convince foreign lenders to continue to provide the capital inflows that would allow the borrower to repay the Fund and other official lenders and to provide sufficient additional inflows to allow existing creditors to exit if they so desired. Thus, even though the Fund's resources were insufficient to meet the borrower's full financing needs, the existence of a Fund lending programme was considered to provide the guarantee of recovery that would convince private lenders to re-structure existing debt and for new lenders to commit fresh funds to insolvent countries that allowed them to keep exchange markets open. In the words of the IMF's Deputy Director, 'the "seal of approval" provided by IMF lending also reassures investors and donors that a country's economic policies are on the right track, and helps to generate additional financing from these sources. This means, of course, that the Fund has to be careful to maintain its credibility: if we lose that credibility, by lending in support of inadequate policies, such cata-lytic, complementary support would not be forthcoming.'[4] This view echoes that of the IMF's own Independent Evaluation Office: 'creditors ... tended to link increasing parts of their financing flows to the existence of an IMF lending arrangement acting as a "seal of approval" on recipient country policies'.[5]

Rather than providing bridging finance, under its new mandate the Fund was providing an implicit guarantee, through the conditionality on its lending pro-grammes and their surveillance, to external creditors concerning the probability of repayment. It was this new role in providing a 'seal of approval' that created an implicit moral hazard that was reinforced by the various IMF rescue packages provided to countries experiencing financial crisis after the Mexican declaration of default in 1982.

But there was an additional dimension to this new approach: to the extent that a Fund lending programme succeeded in convincing the private sector to continue to lend, it implied that the debt would not be reduced, it would only be refinanced by allowing new lenders to bail out old lenders.[6] For this to be the case it also implied that the borrowing countries' domestic policies would be more or less permanently governed by IMF surveillance and conditionality, creating the need for a much more prolonged commitment of IMF funds.[7] From being a temporary lender of bridging funds in support of a short-term adjustment programme the IMF became the permanent supplier of 'seal of approval' con-ditional loans that ensured the viability of long-term debt rollover and debt service. This in effect meant virtually permanent restrictive fiscal policies and tight monetary policies to ensure external borrowing to finance debt service.

The result has been a wide divergence between the financial performance of indebted developing countries and their real performance in terms of real per capital income growth and employment. Under the initial IMF mandate, growth rates and inflation rates tended to be higher than under the new mandate. How-ever, under the new mandate, while most countries have been able to reduce extremely high inflation rates and to create primary fiscal surpluses and external surpluses to allow them to regain access to private international capital markets, these conditions have been associated with low domestic demand growth, high real interest rates and appreciation of real exchange rates that have produced disappointing real growth performance.

THE IMF 'SEAL OF APPROVAL' AND NEGATIVE NET RESOURCE FLOWS

Part of this lack of real growth has been due to the fact that, despite the success of these policies in ensuring countries are able to attract substantial net capital inflows (in 2003, the net private financial inflow of $93 billion to developing countries was the highest level since the Asian financial crisis), when these flows are adjusted for net capital factor service payments and financial outflows, including increases in foreign reserve holdings, the figure becomes a net resource outflow of nearly $280 billion. This figure, more commonly known as the net transfer of resources, is the approximate counterpart of the balance of goods and services trade.[8] A negative value means that developing countries have reduced the domestic resources available to finance their own development and placed them at the disposition of developed countries.

Under the IMF's new mandate, negative net resource transfers characterized most of the 1980s in Latin American countries recovering from the 1982 debt crisis under IMF adjustment programmes. They have again been negative in every year since 1997. This pattern of financial flows reflects the cost of the IMF 'seal of approval' in the form of policies to restrict demand that produce a surplus on trade in goods and services that is not sufficient to cover the negative net capital factor services balance due to the servicing of the existing debt stock. As a result countries continue to depend on new external private capital inflows to remain current on their external payments commitments. And, to maintain the Fund 'seal of approval' to ensure these flows, it requires continued policies of monetary restraint, high real interest rates and primary fiscal surpluses that make return to rapid domestic growth difficult.

As noted above, negative net resource transfers are usually considered to have a negative impact on domestic growth since they represent the export of real goods and services, reducing the resources available for domestic consumption and investment, and lowering real per capita incomes. However, it is important to distinguish between the impact of the negative transfers and the policies that cause them. It might be more correct to note that policies that reduce domestic demand will in general have a negative impact on domestic growth and employment.

At the same time, this means that the transfer of real resources abroad may be part of a rational development plan if they are the result of policies to support domestic income growth and increased domestic savings. In such conditions it is possible to maximize domestic per capita incomes by investing resources abroad if the returns are higher than from using them at home. The possible benefits to growth from negative net resource flows arise from the fact that they create claims on foreigners that can be used to acquire foreign assets that will produce additional foreign claims. Alternatively, the foreign claims can be used to extinguish foreign liabilities, which reduces debt service. Both reduce the size of negative net resource flows.

The importance of domestic policy and the use of net resource outflows may be seen in the behaviour of Asian economies in the aftermath of the 1997 financial crisis compared to the experience in Latin America after the 1982 debt crisis in that region. Many crisis-stricken economies in the Asian region have used negative net resource transfers – averaging well over $100 billion per year for the region as a whole since the crisis – to reduce their private sector liabilities to foreigners and have started to use their negative net resource flows to make foreign investments. In Latin America, on the other hand, the increase in claims on foreigners during the 1980s was used primarily to cover debt service and to repay arrears. In Asia, the rise in net exports has allowed repayment of IMF lending and the possibility of using expansionary domestic policies so that economic growth and domestic savings rates have increased, while in Latin America the net outward transfer of resources has been the result of continued compression of domestic expenditure and continued implementation of IMF conditionality on domestic policy that brought the lost decade of declining per capita incomes and falling savings rates.

This is a comparison between the behaviour of Asia and Latin America, suggesting that the former policy provides the potential for higher growth. However, this conclusion must be approached with caution. In particular this is because, rather than being invested in productive activities abroad, the counterpart to strengthened commercial account positions and rising net private capital flows in the Asian region was an accumulation of international foreign exchange reserves in the order of $364 billion in 2003.

The accumulation of reserves has been mainly in low-risk and comparatively low-yield government securities of developed countries, primarily the US. Not only do these purchases reflect the net transfer of resources from developing to developed countries, they are a major component of the financing of the increasingly large external account imbalances of the United States. But more importantly, just as the holding of any liquid asset has a cost, these reserve holdings represent an investment which has a negative return. This is the result of the attempt by central banks to maintain control over domestic monetary conditions by sterilizing the financial inflows that are the counterpart of the real resource transfers. It is often thought that sterilization is an optional decision, but it is not.[9] In the absence of sterilization the net foreign earnings of domestic residents will be converted into domestic bank reserves which will either provide the basis for additional lending by the banking system or, since they represent a net increase in supply of bank reserves to the banking system as a whole, will drive the rate on interbank lending to zero. Thus, if the central bank wishes to retain control over its domestic monetary aggregates or its policy interest rate, sterilization is required. Since sterilization requires issuing a domestic claim in exchange for the foreign claim, and since the domestic claim will in virtually all cases carry an interest rate higher than the rate paid on short-term investments in the US dollar or the euro, this represents an investment with negative carry: the rate of interest paid to fund the foreign reserve position is greater than the rate of interest earned on the position. This translates into lower central bank earnings and a higher fiscal deficit since such earnings are usually transferred to the Treasury. Reserves thus not only represent a negative transfer of resources, they have a negative impact on growth if the government is pursuing a fixed fiscal target since fiscal expenditures will have to be cut to offset the decline in central bank earnings' contribution to fiscal resources.

However, it is clear that for many developing countries the costs of holding large international reserve balances are more than offset by the benefits they perceive from being able to use them to smooth sharp reversals in private capital flows and to provide a guarantee of solvency. These liquidity balances may thus be seen as the alternative to the IMF 'seal of approval' in an active Fund borrowing arrangement and conditionalities on domestic policy. Clearly, comparing the growth performance of the Asian economies who emerged as rapidly as possible from Fund programmes with the performance of Latin American economies who have been subject to IMF 'seal of approval' programmes virtually continuously since the 1982 debt crisis, the relative cost is much lower for the former.

NEGATIVE NET RESOURCE FLOWS AS A FORM OF HEDGE FINANCE

It is also possible to view the build-up of foreign exchange reserves in Asia as a form of hedge against capital flow reversal to ensure domestic and external stability. This can be done by making reference to the analysis of Hyman Minsky on financial instability. Minsky defines a debt repayment profile based on the balance sheet position of a private firm with income-generating capital investments on the asset side financed by liabilities carrying cash payment commitments on the liability side. The repayment profiles classify the relation between the future debt service flows generated by the liabilities and the expected future income flows from operating the capital assets. The most conservative financing profile – hedge finance – is one in which in every future period the firm has a large cushion of expected cash flow receipts over debt service even in the presence of an 'external shock' such as a chance rise in interest costs or decline in sales or prices or increases in wage costs. The firm with a 'hedge' financing profile is thus virtually a risk-free borrower. [10]

But a capitalist system is one in which firms borrow to finance investment and thus a majority of firms employ what Minsky calls a 'speculative' profile in which cash flows in some periods may not be sufficient to meet payments commitments in some future periods, but over the life of the investment project the firm will have earnings excesses that enable it to make good any shortfall – in the language of managerial finance, the net present value of the investment is positive.

The third profile arises when some unexpected and unforeseen shock occurs to a firm with a speculative financing profile and makes it impossible to meet current or future cash commitments – the net present value of the investment being financed by the lender becomes negative since its liabilities could not be met by liquidating its assets at their current fair market value: the firm is insolvent. To stay current on its commitments and remain in operation the firm has to attract new lending to pay what it owes in debt service each period. It thus has to convince the original lender to increase the size of the existing loan, or get new loans from other lenders, even though it has little prospect of being able to service its existing loans, unless it is successful in getting additional funding in the future.

The profiles provide a ranking of the potential for a financial crisis of the borrower and the impact on the lender when there is a change in external factors, such as interest rates. A hedge profile requires the largest changes in receipts or commitments to become a speculative profile, while a firm that starts out in speculative financing may take on a Ponzi financing profile with a much smaller variation in internal or external conditions since its margin of safety represented by the excess of expected receipts over certain commitments is lower.

We can transfer this framework to the international context by noting that countries also borrow and lend and have external earnings generated by net exports and cash commitments generated by debt servicing created by net capital inflows. The former is roughly the balance on goods and non-factor services plus net labour earnings from abroad and remittances from emigrants, while the latter is composed of the net balance on capital factor services. Thus a hedge profile for a country would be one in which it has a sufficiently large surplus on goods and services and other non-capital factor service earnings that it will always be a large multiple of its debt service commitments. This definition fits a country with a large negative net transfer of resources. The cost of holding the financial counterpart represented by the negative net carry represents the cost of the hedge against a random external event causing a failure to meet external payments or a withdrawal of foreign assets. Alternatively, it represents the cost of avoiding the acquisition of an IMF 'seal of approval'.

On the other hand, the Latin American economies in the 1980s can be represented by a Ponzi financing scheme. They did not have a sufficiently large cushion of negative net transfers and thus had to purchase insurance in the form of an IMF 'seal of approval' to convince lenders to continue to lend to them even though there was little real evidence of any ability to repay debt. The cost of this insurance was the difference between potential growth and the actual lost decade of growth in the 1980s and appears far higher than the cost of holding excess reserves. It is paradoxical that the IMF was originally to provide a low-cost source of adjustment financing based on the principle of pooling of resources through the quota system.

DOES HEDGE FINANCE PROVIDE DOMESTIC AND GLOBAL STABILITY?

As a result of the reduced costs that appear to attach to the strategy of being a 'hedge' country, most developing countries are now trying to emulate this strategy in order to increase financial stability. However, in an interdependent international trade and financial system it is not clear that this is a viable policy for all developing countries and whether it has a positive impact on global stability.

The first question can be answered by reference to historical precedent. In the immediate post-war period the US had a large external trade surplus and some economists suggested that it could be permanent, creating a situation of dollar scarcity. Others argued that it could provide the basis for generating the demand necessary to keep the US from returning to the recession of the 1930s.[11] As noted above, the trade balance is roughly the counterpart of what we have been calling the net transfer of resources and is balanced by the capital account plus the capital services account. Maintaining a constant trade surplus (or a constant trade surplus as a share of national income) requires an equivalent capital outflow (or share of income), given exchange rates. However, the increasing foreign lending that is required generates a return flow of debt service payments that produce a surplus on the capital factor services balance. In the absence of any change in the absolute amount of capital outflows the trade surplus thus has to fall to accommodate the increased factor services balance without exchange rate adjustment.

One possible solution would be for foreign lending to rise each year by an amount sufficient to cover the increasing debt service payments. Now, instead of the trade balance, and the positive impact on demand, disappearing, capital outflows would have to increase without limit. Evsey Domar provided an answer[12] to whether this process could be sustained: as long as capital outflows increase at a rate equal to the rate of interest received in debt service from the rest of the world on the outstanding loans, the rising inflows on factor service account are just offset by the rising capital outflows and there is no net impact on the trade balance and thus on demand. On the other hand, if interest rates are higher than the rate of increase in foreign lending the policy becomes self-defeating and the trade balance eventually becomes negative to offset the rising net capital service inflows. Eventually the continually rising factor service flows would turn the trade balance negative and the negative net resources flows positive.

Thus the sustainability of the hedge profile is similar to the problem analysed by Domar: it can only work if the rate of interest on foreign assets is equal to or below the rate of increase of the negative net transfers. As long as the foreign assets acquired are highly liquid, with low interest rates, the more likely it is that the policy can be maintained.

However, with respect to the stability of the financial system, it is interesting to note that the Domar conditions for a sustained long-term development strategy based on external financing, on sustained positive net resource transfers, are the precise equivalent of the conditions required for a successful Ponzi financing scheme. As long as the rate of increase in inflows from new investors in a pyramid or Ponzi scheme is equal to or greater than the rate of interest paid to existing investors in the scheme, there is no difficulty in maintaining the payments promised to prior investors in the scheme. However, no such scheme in history has ever been successful: they are bound to fail, eventually, because of the increasing size of the net debt stock of the operator of the scheme. On the other hand, if the rate of interest on foreign lending is greater than the rate of increase of foreign lending, then the system is absolutely unstable and cannot be sustained on even a short-term basis.

In the present case, it is the US that is the counterpart of the Asian developing countries accumulating dollar claims, so it is the US that is operating the Ponzi scheme. Any move to increase interest rates on US dollar claims thus increases the fragility of the scheme because it means that the US has to increase the rate of increase of its foreign borrowing and, by implication, the rate of increase in its trade deficit. On the other hand, any action to bring about a rapid reversal of the US deficit, or a contraction in US growth, would quickly counter Domar's stability conditions and make the system locally unstable, negating the hedge protection of developing countries with large negative net resource transfers invested in dollar claims.

Thus, while the hedge country strategy may provide liquidity protection for a single country, as Keynes warned, there is no such thing as liquidity for the system as a whole, and there is no such thing as a perfect hedge in an interdependent international trading and financial system. The provision of global liquidity requires a global institution based on symmetrical adjustment through automatic provision of liquidity such as proposed in Keynes's Clearing Union.

NOTES

1. UN Financing for Development Office. The views expressed here are the personal views of the author and do not represent the official or unofficial position of the United Nations on these issues.
2. In the discussions at Bretton Woods Keynes had argued against conditions on drawing from the Fund and programme conditionality was only introduced somewhat later in a 1952 Amendment to the Articles of Agreement. See A. Buira, 'An Analysis of IMF Conditionality', in A. Buira (ed.), *Challenges to the World Bank and IMF*, London: Anthem Press, 2003, pp. 82–5.
3. 'The IMF at 60: Evolving Role, Current Challenges', remarks by Rodrigo de Rato, Managing Director of the International Monetary Fund at the Breakfast Meeting with the Council on Foreign Relations New York, 20 September 2004 (http://www.imf.org/external/np/speeches/2004/092004.htm).
4. Remarks by Agustín Carstens, Deputy Managing Director, International Monetary Fund, at the WCC–World Bank–IMF High-Level Encounter, Geneva, 22 October 2004 (http://www.imf.org/external/np/speeches/2004/102204a.htm).
5. Independent Evaluation Office, 'Evaluation of Prolonged Use of IMF Resources', Washington, DC: International Monetary Fund, 2002, ISBN 1-58906-205-1.
6. For example in the solution to the Latin American crisis provided by the Brady Bonds, bank loans were repaid by selling bonded debt to institutional investors.
7. Indeed, the Report on Prolonged Use of IMF Resources (see note 5 above) notes that the increased commitment period for IMF funding programmes was in part due to a shift from its traditional balance of payments lending to developed country borrowers to lending to developing country borrowers.
8. An annexe to the United Nations Secretary General's Report on the Net Transfer of Resources for 1996 (A/49/309) makes a distinction in 'The concept of net transfer' between 'transfer on an expenditure basis' and 'transfer on a financial basis', defining the former as the payments balance on goods, non-factor services and labour factor services earnings such as remittances, and the latter, which attempts to distinguish changes in foreign currency reserves from other financial flows, as the net flow of all financial assets less changes in reserves. The figures reported here are on an expenditure basis.
9. See L.R. Wray, *Understanding Modern Money*, ch. 5, Cheltenham, UK and Lyme, USA: Edward Elgar, 1998.
10. Minsky formulated these profiles as part of his financial instability hypothesis based on the idea that financial crises are endogenous events inevitably generated by periods of financial stability. See, for example, Hyman Minsky, *Stabilizing and Unstable Economy*, Twentieth Century Fund Reports, New Haven: Yale University Press, 1990.
11. It also provided conservatives with a more acceptable alternative policy for full employment than the Keynesian proposals for deficit financing.
12. Evsey Domar, 'The Effect of *Foreign* Investments on the Balance of Payments', *American Economic Review*, vol. 40, Dec. 1950, pp. 805–26.

2. Monetary and social relationships

Charles A.E. Goodhart

INTRODUCTION

The social sciences are much more complex than the physical sciences. Not only are experiments generally easier to undertake in the physical sciences, but also the subject matter of any such studies in the social sciences, we individuals, respond and change our own behaviour in the light of those same economic experiments. Moreover, human behaviour is both variable and reactive, especially in response to major regime changes. So, any attempt to depict the economic macro system has to involve models which are gross simplifications of underlying reality.

How best then to simplify our macro models? It is such macro models which will be the main subject of my discussion. When we macroeconomists started building solvable models at the outset of the computer age, some 40 or so years ago, we generally aimed at getting a detailed and comprehensive structure of the economy, on a sector-by-sector, equation-by-equation basis, using national income statistical categories, and this led to large computable macro models, often with 50 or more equations. Amongst the resulting problems, however, were that the optimizing, so-called 'micro foundations' were weak, if not non-existent. Expectations, when considered at all, were often inconsistent with the model's own workings; and some of the implications of such large models were difficult to discern and, when worked out, often totally implausible.

All this led to the Lucasian revolution, whereby macro models had to have 'rigorous', optimizing, micro foundations, often based on so-called 'rational' expectations. This, in turn, led to a degree of mathematical and analytical complexity. In order to continue with these more complex models, the effective solution was to simplify the initial structure of the model to allow it to support the heavier analytical superstructure. Thus a surprisingly large proportion of the models currently used for policy analysis (though not, thanks be, for forecasting), in the macromonetary field have been thinned down to three equations, an IS curve, an AS (Phillips) curve and a Taylor reaction function; two players, central bank and private sector; and two assets, money and short-dated riskless debt.

I shall spend much of the first half of this chapter arguing that in many respects the Lucasian revolution has transferred the focus of implausibility, often downright nonsense, from the implications of the solutions of the models to their initial structural assumptions. And one of the key deficiencies of such macro models, including those used for analysis of longer-term developments, such as growth or optimal currency areas, is that all the action takes place in the private sector, so that the key role of government is frequently unrecognized. This will be the main topic of the second half of my chapter.

THE STRUCTURAL BASIS OF MACRO MODELS

Let me start, however, with an important subfield where the analysis has, instead, improved. When I started doing economics some 45 years ago now, one of the key building blocks of macroeconomics was the LM curve. The assumed process was that the Central Bank would inject high-powered base money into the system; this would then be translated into growth in the monetary aggregate(s) via a variety of money multipliers and, finally, market interest rates would be determined through the equilibration of the demand and supply of money.

Of course, simple observation of the way that central banks and money markets actually behaved would reveal that this was the exact reversal of the truth. The process started with the Central Bank determining its official short-term interest rate, in pursuit of its current policy objectives. Then the demand for bank borrowing, at the chosen policy rate, was the main determinant of the growth of the monetary aggregates. Given M, the money multiplier worked effectively in reverse, to determine the amount of base money that the authorities had to make available to the banking system to sustain their initially chosen interest rate.

Faced with this divergence between reality and economic theorizing, the response of the profession was to ignore reality for pedagogic purposes; see any macroeconomics or 'money and banking' textbook until a few years ago. On the normative front, another reaction was to argue that Central Bank behaviour, in setting interest rates, was a suboptimal policy, and that Central Banks *should* adopt a policy of choosing, announcing and sticking to a policy of monetary targetry. Indeed it was argued, notably in the influential Sargent and Wallace (1975) article, that the Central Bank policy of setting interest rates was bound to lead to Wicksellian instability.

That argument was correct on its own terms, but assumed that the Central Bank would set its policy variable (either M or interest rates) exogenously, that is, without adjusting that variable endogenously in response to concurrent economic developments. That assumption was unrealistic, indeed somewhat silly. Central banks invariably set interest rates endogenously in response to perceived economic developments. At times they may have done so in a bad, or destabilizing, fashion because of political constraints, inappropriate objectives, misperceptions of reality or various human frailties. That said, the idea that central banks might try to 'fool' the public into working harder by creating 'surprise' inflation was never a realistic description of their activities. The papers by Kydland and Prescott (1977) and Barro and Gordon (1983a, 1983b) on this issue were academically extremely influential, and indeed contributed to the former authors' Nobel Prize in 2004, but were only tenuously related to the main causes of the inflation of the 1970s.

But the analysis of the way central banks can, and now generally do, set interest rates so as to achieve price stability, and as a necessary adjunct of that economic stability, has been worked out in practice through the adoption of inflation targetry, where Mervyn King has played a major role, and theoretically through the work of academics such as Bernanke, McCallum, Svensson, John Taylor and Woodford. The prior divorce between theory and practice has gone. This is a considerable and valuable step forward for the profession from its former state.

This reconciliation of theory and practice was marked for me by the publication of Michael Woodford's magisterial book on *Interest and Prices* (2003). But that is about as far as I go in applause for recent developments in macro. Let me now take aim at some of the other structural assumptions of modern macro, which mostly are evident in that same book. First, we believe, at least in a rather general sense, that if all prices and wages were infinitely flexible, the real economy would remain in equilibrium at all times, and money would be continuously neutral.

Consequently an understanding of the rationale and workings of wage and price stickiness would, one might have thought, be central to modern macroeconomies. Indeed there was an upsurge of interest in this topic, stimulated first by Clower and then by the work of Akerlof and Yellen in the mid-1980s, for example (1985a, 1985b), but I confess to seeing little real progress on this front since then, either in theory or, perhaps more important, in generally accepted empirical findings. Instead, what one sees much more often is that macro models are based on Calvo pricing mechanisms, whereby a particular (and constant) percentage of firms is allowed in each period to change prices, and the remaining firms are prevented from doing so – though why is never explained. Nobody believes this to be literally true; it is a mathematically convenient fiction, but it forms the pricing basis for much current macro work.

I might add, parenthetically, that quadratic utility functions are just such another convenient mathematical fiction. The likelihood that going from an inflation rate of, say, 100 per cent per annum to one of 103 per cent per annum, is likely to reduce utility by vastly more than going from 4 per cent to 5 per cent inflation is obvious nonsense, as Margaret Bray and I have recently argued (2003).

Be that as it may, many of the structural foundations, relating to price/wage stickiness in modern macro, rest on a convenient fiction, which has only a distant relationship with reality. Why such procedures are somehow regarded as professionally acceptable, whereas the assumption of adaptive expectations was not (especially when empirical studies generally show that purely backwards-looking expectations have a better forecasting record than purely forwards-looking ones), is beyond me.

Perhaps the greatest remaining gap between the work of academic money-macroeconomists and policy makers in central banks and Ministries of Finance relates to lags, specifically the lag before policy measures affect economic outcomes. In most of the formal models the policy change *immediately* affects current output, because not all prices and wages are allowed, by a deus ex machina, to adjust, and also affects current and expected future inflation, and usually, depending on the model, future output. Although the lag structure, engendered by price stickiness, can have a long tail, the usual implications are that the largest effects on both output and inflation are immediate.

This is not what policy makers observe from the data. The standard data-based rules of thumb are that, unless there is an immediate sharp shock to exchange rates, there is a short lag before output reacts at all, and then has a hump-shaped response, and an even longer lag before inflation responds. This latter delay of the inflation response behind the output response is especially problematical for the theoreticians. It can hardly be doubted that monetary policy initiatives, in the sense of interest rate changes, are front-page news, as indeed are continuous 'expert' commentaries on the likely future paths of both nominal interest rates and inflation. So any suggestion that those making the individual price/wage decisions are slow in learning about changes in current and future patterns of real interest rates is surely far-fetched; there are few islands where media reports of Alan Greenspan's latest words are not instantly relayed.[1] Yet if there is an observed change to the predicted future time path of real interest rates, then in theory those allowed to change prices/wages should now do so immediately. To summarize, current macro models find it extraordinarily hard to replicate the lag structure which is a key feature of the conjuncture for policy makers, and for their own forecasters/economists, especially the quite lengthy delay before inflation responds perceptibly to observed changes in monetary conditions. Is it unfair to claim that the reaction of most theoretical model builders is to ignore this discrepancy, and to continue with constructs where both the rationale for, and time profile of, the lag structures have little relationship with reality? To be blunt, I cannot quite see how theoreticians can square the apparent actual lag profiles with the present dominant paradigms about price-setting mechanisms, without substantial modification of their present theories.

The purest theoreticians of the Lucasian age get around the problem of modelling wage/price stickiness and lag profiles for the effects of monetary policy by assuming them away. In such real business cycle models money is neutral, prices are fully flexible and fluctuations come from real productivity shocks. Here we usually have representative agents, a representative consumer and firm, optimizing its utility over an indefinite time span and, normally, in a system of complete financial markets. Such an assumption of complete financial markets is, for example, a key element in Woodford's recent book which I have already mentioned. Why is this assumption central? It means that *all* eventualities can be foreseen and appropriately hedged at the correct insurance/option price.

If all eventualities can be appropriately foreseen, hedged and priced, then there are a number of consequentials. All information problems are effectively solved; rational expectations is a logical implication; there is no residual, unhedgeable risk, financial or otherwise; all agents can borrow/lend at the riskless rate (plus, in a world of heterogenous agents, an actuarially correct risk premium for the known risk of the agent defaulting, decamping or otherwise failing to meet the transversality condition: that is, that all debts are paid in full at the horizon). There could, moreover, never be any financial innovations since all the necessary instruments for transferring wealth among future states of nature would already exist.

This assumption, of complete financial markets, lends itself admirably to the construction of soluble models with 'rigorous' micro foundations of optimization within a general equilibrium system. The problem, of course, is that the assumption has no connection with the real world. Indeed, the favourite asset of such models, Arrow securities (which pay out one in the event of some given event and zero otherwise), only occur rarely (for example some insurance products, credit default swaps, and so on).

In particular, the complete financial markets assumption effectively means that all information problems relating to granting credit, expectation of repayment, and so on, have already been resolved. In such a system it is not clear why either money, or banks, or other financial intermediaries should exist. I have never been able to understand how the necessary information is collected and distributed to all participants in such a system in the first place.

An assumption of a system of complete financial markets, in effect, assumes away all Coaseian transactions costs, either because some Divine Auctioneer provides all the necessary information or because there is no time constraint, so we can all spend an infinite amount of time collecting information and establishing and pricing appropriate hedges.

Unfortunately for us there is no Divine Auctioneer, and the time constraint always binds. Besides the fact that this implies incomplete financial contracts, indeed incomplete contracts more generally, it also implies that I can use my scarce time to work, play, sleep, shop *or* to gain information and educate myself. Improving my knowledge of the world, and making my expectations more accurate, requires use of my scarce time. It is *not* rational for agents to have expectations that are consistent with the outcomes of the best (or even the currently used), model, let alone to have the best possible expectations. What is rational is to use up scarce time until the expected marginal addition to utility from spending more time in learning about aspects of the world equals the marginal opportunity cost in forgone use of time in other pursuits, as Stigler has argued. Applications to business schools rise during periods of downturn and lay-offs in financial markets.

On this basis there is nothing inherently irrational about backwards-looking adaptive expectations, or in relying on the views and forecasts of others (as a part-time sheep-farmer I am a proponent of rational herding). Yet the Lucas critique, of course, still holds. Faced with a shock, a regime change, one will have to reallocate one's scarce time, and that may well, indeed should, include a decision whether to allocate more time to learning about the new world. In calm conditions simple *rules of thumb* economize on scarce time; in disturbed conditions it pays to spend more time learning how best to navigate.

What this implies is that the expectations generating process will itself be time-variant and endogenous, and not constant, as most models assume. That said, there is a heavy initial cost to learning about complex issues, which can be recalled through memory at virtually zero cost, at least until Alzheimer's strikes. So expectation formation processes are likely to be subject to inertia, hysteresis and initial conditions. To summarize again, the way in which the rational expectations assumption is normally deployed assumes away Coaseian transactions costs and would itself be irrational in the real world of binding time constraints.

Once we dispense with complete financial markets, default (the failure of transversality conditions to hold) becomes a greater problem because it may, indeed usually is, impossible to hedge, or at least to do so completely, against it. That causes problems for representative agent models. Either the whole system collapses, or no agent does. If the solution chosen is to rule out all possibilities of default, then that is, I believe, equivalent to reverting to an implicit adoption of complete financial markets.

In any case the assumption that everyone, all consumers, all firms, is identical is again a convenient fiction and, for sure, far further from reality than adaptive expectations or the various other shortcomings in internal logical consistency of the earlier large forecasting macro models. It matters for several reasons. If your model contains a single representative consumer, you more or less have to assume that the consumer meets the transversality condition (that is, that in all conditions the consumer chooses a course of action so that her debts are ultimately repaid). That means that it is always *perfectly safe* to lend to the representative consumer, so that she can borrow or lend at the riskless rate. Consequently, the representative consumer is *never* financially constrained, and can always make a forwards-looking optimizing plan, subject to the transversality constraint.

But many of us (perhaps most of us, possibly all of us) choose courses of action which under some circumstances mean that we cannot, and do not expect to be able to, pay all our debts. Some of us, amongst them the criminal fraternity, only expect to pay our debts under unlikely circumstances; fraud is hardly unknown or uncommon. As Martin Shubik has argued (1973), default is a common chosen facet of optimizing behaviour.[2]

If we now assume the existence of incomplete financial markets and heterogeneous agents, then we start getting back into the real world of financial intermediaries, whose raison d'être is largely risk assessment, of risk premia, of financial constraints on behaviour (because of Stiglitz–Weiss type problems) and so on. In this world money, creditworthiness, confidence and collateral all play a major role. Some agents find that their optimizing plans are constrained, not by some ultimate transversality clause, but by immediate credit constraints; thus the young cannot anticipate future higher incomes to smooth their consumption over time; small firms cannot borrow enough from banks to finance all their perceived investment opportunities, and so on.

This is a much messier, but far more realistic, world than that represented by most macro models. The challenge is to meld, and to combine, theory and empirical realism. The Lucasian critique of the early large forecasting models was that they were developed by building up individual equations on an empirical, ad hoc, pragmatic basis; and that the resulting construction had little theoretical basis, and often had internal logical inconsistencies. My own riposte is that the resulting family of macro models, based on so-called 'rigorous' micro foundations, are in turn empirically absurd, with complete financial markets, no (credit) risk, no default, transversality conditions always met, representative agents, no necessity for financial intermediaries, hardly any of the attributes of the real world that fill the life and concerns of, for example, a Central Bank official.

Can theory and practice, in the money-macro field, be reconciled? My own view is that the best attempts to do so, and to give an explicit role for default, credit risk and money, are to be found in the work of Martin Shubik and his followers, amongst them Geanakoplos, Dubey and Polemarchakis. A basic problem is that models which embrace incomplete financial markets, default and heterogeneity are inherently complex and extremely hard to present lucidly and simply. Thus these real-life features, for example heterogeneity, money, default and incomplete markets make necessary the modelling of default laws, formal treatment of liquidity, regulatory policy, banks, and so on. Moreover, the importance of incomplete markets and heterogeneity (as well as institutions) is underlined by the fact that equilibria are constrained inefficient (Geanakoplos-Polemarchakis, 1986), that is, not achieving the second best. So, government, central bank and regulatory intervention can lead to efficiency gains. Partly in consequence of the inherent complexity of such models they have not made the impact, at least not yet, that I believe that they should.

One field where it is patently impossible to use the complete financial market, no default, representative agent type of model is in studying financial risk and contagion, which is one of the areas in which I have worked as a part-time consultant at the Bank of England. Instead one needs a model in which incomplete financial markets, default and heterogeneous agents, especially banks, are central to the process. In this respect I have been fortunate to find Dimitrios Tsomocos at the Bank. Fortunate for two reasons; first, my own mathematical, model-building skills are deficient; second, Dimitri is one of the best students and exponents of the Shubik school. Anyhow, using some of my suggestions about modelling heterogeneous banks and incomplete financial markets, he has developed a model for studying systemic financial stability issues. With the aid of Ton Sunirand, we have demonstrated that simplified versions can be numerically simulated; and our present, continuing exercise is to calibrate the model against the data: see Goodhart, Sunirand and Tsomocos (2003, 2004a, b).

One problematical deficiency in this field of trying to model and assess financial stability is that virtually all methods of monitoring such financial stability relate to *individual* banks, and other financial intermediaries, for example VARs, stress tests, solvency and capital requirements, liquidity ratios, and so on. What matters, from society's viewpoint, is systemic, not individual, stability. The two are obviously related; for example a system where most of the component members are weak is not likely to be systemically strong. Nevertheless, it does not take much ingenuity to construct examples where each individual bank appears to be initially strong, but the overall system is nevertheless fragile, for example because of various interconnections; or indeed vice versa, where the individual participants seem weak, but the overall system is well protected. This has been done ever since Henry Thornton (1802), if not before.

The Holy Grail in this field, which many of us are pursuing, is to be able to complement the known procedures for monitoring individual banks with new methods for assessing systemic strength. We are, I believe, moving forwards, but there is a long way to go.

THE ROLE OF GOVERNMENT

Let me turn, however, from modelling to another area where I believe that theory has become divorced from reality. One of the main subjects of topical interest over the last two decades has been the formation of the euro system. The main academic tool for assessing whether it was appropriate for countries to have a common currency has been optimal currency area theory, or OCA. This theory described several factors that would make a common currency appropriate, for example openness, wage/price flexibility, trading patterns, size; but it gave very little role to the interaction of government, and especially of governments' fiscal policies, with the domain of monetary policy. Yet, as Michael Mussa noted, the greatest economic regularity in this field, prior to the euro system, had been the association between country and currency; whereas the predictive power of OCA theory was almost nil (apart from correctly predicting that micro states, such as the Vatican, Andorra and Liechtenstein, would share the currency of their larger neighbours).

Now one might try to dismiss the currency/country link as an inessential symbol of sovereignty, like flags, or national anthems, or 'made in France' labels of origin; but in my view such dismissal would be wrong (also, see Issing, 1996). It is, perhaps, easiest to appreciate the necessity of some link between governments and their fiscal policies on the one hand and money on the other in the case of a fiat money system. Why do people accept such unbacked pieces of paper? The answer, of course, is because of the power of the government, and in particular of its power to tax and to specify what paper currencies it will accept in payment. Of course, such sovereignty can be shared, and the acceptability of the euro is completely assured by the agreement of all member states in the euro system to do so.

But there are additional key links between fiscal and monetary policies. Within a given monetary domain, one cannot use monetary policy to iron out asymmetric regional imbalances and shocks, but, when the monetary and fiscal domains overlap, one can use fiscal policy to stabilize and to redistribute, as far as political consent allows. Within the euro system the monetary system is federal; the main fiscal competences are national. Earlier in the 1990s I worked on a specialist group commissioned by the European Commission to try to bridge that gap. Our Report, 'Stable Money – Sound Finances' (1993) (also see 'The Economics of Community Public Finance, Reports and Studies' (1993), then was pigeonholed, dismissed by representatives of most member states, and largely ignored. Ever since, I have felt that the failure to deal with that separation of the domains of monetary and fiscal policies was a potential flaw in, the soft underbelly of, the euro system. The travails of the Stability and Growth pact, now coming to a head with the possible legal challenge by the Commission to the decisions of national Ministers of Finance, underline both the difficulties and the complexity of trying to run a system that divorces the locations of fiscal and monetary competencies.

It is not just in macro policy, stabilization issues, that this separation matters. In the field of financial stability, financial crises often require resolution through the use of taxpayers' money, frequently a lot of money, as multiple examples around the world attest. There are insufficient funds in the ECB for such a purpose, and none effectively available for such uses from the federal budget in Brussels. If a bail-out in a crisis is undertaken, it will have to come from national budgets and taxpayers in each separate nation state. He who pays the piper calls the tune. One can talk as long as one likes about the tidiness and efficiency of combining the monetary domain with the regulatory domain at the federal level, and of likely overspills between nations in any financial crisis. So long as the actual fiscal payments to resolve a crisis come out of national Treasuries, not from the federal budget, the corollary will be that regulatory and supervisory issues will be decided in conclaves in which national Treasuries take the lead, and the federal institutions become sidelined as observers.

The relationship and, in particular, the separation between a federal monetary system and national fiscal competence, to my mind, was *the* main problem facing the euro system. Yet it did not get, and still hardly receives, sufficient attention. It received no mention in the latest discussion on the European Constitution, perhaps because it was perceived as 'too difficult' to resolve. This failure to tackle what is *the* crucial issue, in my view, arose largely because economic theorists have consistently tended to ignore, or to underestimate, the essential links between government, fiscal policies and money. This goes right back to the theories of the evolution of money itself.

The dominant mainstream theory of the evolution of money is that this developed from indirect barter in a private sector trial and error process with the aim of reducing transactions costs in (market) exchange. It is often emphasized that, whereas governments may have played some subsidiary role in extending and enhancing monetary functions, for example in establishing mints for coinage, they were strictly inessential in its initial evolution.

This was one of the key messages of Carl Menger's seminal work in this field at the end of the 19th century, work that our President this year, Erich Streissler, has recently commented upon (see his chapter on 'Carl Menger's Article "Money": From Barter to Money', in Latzer and Schmitz (2002), *Carl Menger and the Evolution of Payments Systems*). It remains the dominant paradigm today, involving technically fancier papers, such as Kiyotaki and Wright, for example (1989, 1991, 1992), but they maintain the same basic intuition.

Although most economists take this same view about the evolution of money, most other social scientists working in this field, amongst them numismatists, archaeologists, anthropologists, and so on, and a minority of economists, do not. This latter group, of which I am a member, find the origins of money in the need to resolve social interrelationships, for example the bride price, restitution of personal injuries, settling feuds, and so on, rather than, or certainly as well as, market relationships.

I have written several papers on this theme recently (2003, 2004), and I do not want to go over the ground again at any length. Let me, however, give a brief quotation:

> [The standard mainstream, Mengerian] M-form theory finds it difficult to account for the role, or existence, of money within a general equilibrium model. Money in the

utility function, or cash-in-advance models, are proposed, without much conviction. This difficulty is not surprising given that such models also abstract from the existence and role of government. While it is, of course, the relationship between taxation and the demand for money that the [Cartalist, Keynesian] C-form theory emphasizes, it should also be remembered that it is the maintenance of law and order, the form and enforcement of contracts, and the whole infrastructure of regulation within society, that allows the epiphenomena of (organized) (private sector) markets to occur at all.

A disclaimer may, however, also be needed. The purpose of this [passage] was to argue, first, that money frequently played an initial means-of-payment role in inter-personal social and governmental roles *before* it played a major role as a medium-of-exchange in market transactions, and second that the relationship of the State, the governing body, to currency in all its roles has almost always been close and direct. But I do *not* claim that the private sector cannot, and has not, ever been able to develop monetary systems without the involvement of state authorities.

Let me just give you one more telling example. A common word for a monetary recompense is that it is pecuniary. The word 'pecuniary' derives from the Latin word *pecus* which means cow, or cattle. Cattle were commonly used in large deals in early Roman history before the introduction of coinage (see Burns, 1927), and are commonly used in societies studied by anthropologists for such socially related exchanges. But does a cow satisfy the standard characteristics required for market exchange? Is a cow standardized, durable, divisible? Could you go out shopping with a couple of cows in your purse? On all this, also consult the excellent paper by Hudson (2004).

Economics is a very new social science. Recently both the London School of Economics and the Faculty at Cambridge University celebrated their centenaries. Few statistical series go back before about 1870. Perhaps in consequence, economists focus mostly on current and near-future prospective events. For such purposes the underlying institutional framework of law and governance tends to be taken largely for granted, as a given. Yet the successful functioning of markets depends on that same legal and governance structure.

In the field in which I have been working recently, concerned with the prevention of financial crises, linkages between the infrastructure of markets and the maintenance of financial stability are clear and important. The development of globally accepted accounting standards, the use of standardized legal proforma for financial contracts, netting arrangements, the role of centralized counterparties, clearing and settlement systems, to name but a few examples, are crucial to the health and continuing development of financial markets and the financial system.

It is not possible to build a superstructure of (financial) markets, or of theories relating to the workings of such markets, unless the underlying infrastructural plumbing is sound. That plumbing, which relates to the organization, administration and resolution of disputes within such markets, is a social construct and relies on law and governance. It may often be boringly detailed, but it is essential. Our monetary and financial systems will not work without it.

Normally, this governance infrastructure, of which I suggest that the institution of money is itself a part, is taken largely for granted, as a constant in the background. Recently, however, there have been shocks that have underlined its importance. Foremost amongst these has been the collapse of communism. Trying to shift from a directly controlled command system to a market economy has been made much more difficult by the need to build up a governance system that extended beyond the passage of laws onto the record book, also to a general understanding and acceptance of the underlying governance principles by the wider population. It is particularly hard to do so in countries with no prior history of the rule of law, outside the state's will. Not that such principles are always followed in our own economies, as various scandals at home and abroad have testified.

In a series of justly celebrated papers (amongst them 1997, 1998), Shleifer and various colleagues have attributed the relative economic success of countries to their adoption of differing legal systems. I wonder whether their focus was perhaps too narrow, so that possibly the successful working of a particular legal system reflected a more broadly well-functioning governance system.

When I consider cross-country and regional differences in income and wealth, my own view is that governance is hugely important. If you could offer a benighted country, say in Africa or the Middle East, extra resources, for example access to oil, or extra capital, or extra foreign aid, or better governance, which would you think most important? With the exception of (applied, empirical) studies, such as those by Barro (1991, 1995), most of the formal models of growth omit any role for government and associated legal and governance structures. Indeed, almost all the studies examining the influence of government and governance on growth have been empirically based.

Once again, the simplifications which macro theory has employed seem to me to have excluded many of the key features of the real economy. But how could one best incorporate governance issues within a long-run growth model? Alas, an answer to that question is well beyond my own abilities or competence.

CONCLUSION

You all know that joke about the parade of armed forces in Moscow where the procession of weapons of increasing destruction, tanks, planes, rockets, was concluded with a truck carrying a few grey-suited men. But 'Who are these?' asked an onlooker. 'Economic theorists,' was the reply – 'But why?' 'You should see the devastation that they can achieve.'

As an epitaph for the economic desolation caused by command and control centralized systems, it is perhaps reasonable to allocate a great deal of blame to bad theory, as Keynes emphasized more widely. Moreover, I have recently been doing a review of the first volume of Allan Meltzer's monumental History of the Fed, in which, of course, the Great Depression of the 1930s takes central place. In this sad story, it seemed to me that reliance on prior theories, particularly on the Classical Dichotomy, whereby price/wage flexibility will soon allow the real economy to be equilibrated by real determinants, but also on the Real Bills Theory, in the face of overwhelming evidence to the contrary, played a major role in encouraging the Fed to remain passive.

Fortunately, no disasters on that scale are currently affecting the developed world, though conditions in parts of Africa still seem terrible enough. Even so, the divorce between much of modern macro theorizing and what I take to be empirical reality strikes me as being greater today than in earlier decades. Back in the 1960s, we tried to build up our models, equation by equation, on a largely pragmatic basis, to fit the empirical facts as we perceived them.

The criticisms of this earlier approach, its lack of theoretical micro foundations, its internal inconsistencies, its ill-considered treatment of expectations, were all fully justified. But has the Lucasian counterrevolution tossed out plausible empirical foundations, thrown out the baby along with the bath water? When I try to read much of modern macro, I generally find that the initial structural assumptions are chosen largely to facilitate the subsequent technical/mathematical analysis; the fact that their relationship with reality might be tenuous, or even non-existent, seems to be of little, or no, concern.

I have tried to give examples along the way, amongst them Calvo pricing, complete financial markets, no default, representative agents, rational expectations (as usually defined), and so on. This covers so much of the guts of modern macro that you may think that I am simply against all macro theory. Not so. There are a few theorists, notably Martin Shubik and his followers, who have tried to build up theory on the basis of real-world conditions, such as incomplete financial markets, default, credit and confidence, rather than try to cram down an overly simplified, but internally rigorous, theoretical system upon reluctant economic data.

Perhaps the greatest such gap in money/macro, between theory and reality, has been the general exclusion of the role of government, especially in setting the underlying infrastructure of governance and law, from our analysis. Again I have tried to give examples, relating to the evolution of money itself, to the centrality of the links between fiscal and monetary policies, including effects on the structure of financial regulation and its importance for the working of the euro system, and, indeed, to economic growth and welfare more widely.

The 1960s were a great decade of hope for macroeconomists, that we could steer the economy in a successful way. Those hopes were punctured by the bad decade of the 1970s, and the theoretical explanations of the inherent failings of the 1960-type macro models. In the last decade, or so, that hope about steering the economy, through the monetary policies of independent central banks, seems to me to have been seeping back, but, in my view, as much despite, rather than because of, mainstream macro theorizing.

NOTES

1. Information was more slowly diffused in the 19th century, yet most studies find that prices/wages were more flexible then than in the 20th century.
2. Also see Shubik and Wilson (1997) and Dubey, Geanakoplos and Shubik (2000).

REFERENCES

Akerlof, G.A. and J. Yellen (1985a), 'Can small deviations from rationality make significant differences to economic equilibria?', *American Economic Review*, **75** September).

Akerlof, G.A. and J. Yellen (1985b), 'A near rational model of the business cycle with wage and price inertia', *Quarterly Journal of Economics*, **100** (September), supplement.

Barro, R. (1991), 'Economic growth in a cross section of countries', *Quarterly Journal of Economics*, May.

Barro, R. and D.B. Gordon (1983a), 'Rules, discretion and reputation in a model of monetary policy', *Journal of Monetary Economics*, **12** (1) (July).

Barro, R. and D.B. Gordon (1983b), 'A positive theory of monetary policy in a natural rate model', *Journal of Political Economy*, **91** (4) (August).

Barro, R. and X. Sala-i-Martin (1995), *Economic Growth*, New York: McGraw-Hill.

Bray, M. and C.A.E. Goodhart (2002), 'You might as well be hung for a sheep as a lamb: the loss function of an agent', Financial Markets Group discussion paper no. 418, July.

Burns, A.R. (1927), *Money and Monetary Policy in Early Times*, New York: Alfred A. Knopf.

Commission of the Economic Communities (1993), 'Stable money – sound finances', report of an independent group of economists, *European Economy*, 53.

Dubey, P., J. Geanakoplos and M. Shubik (2000), 'Default in a general equilibrium model with incomplete markets', Cowles Foundation discussion paper no. 1247, Yale University.

European Commission Directorate-General for Economic and Financial Affairs (1993), 'Reports and studies on the economics of Community public finance', *European Economy*, 5.

Geanakoplos, J.D. and H.M. Polemarchakis (1986), 'Existence, regularity and constrained suboptimality of competitive allocations when the asset market is incomplete', in W. Heller and D. Starret (eds), *Essays in Honour of K. Arrow*, vol. III, Cambridge: Cambridge University Press.

Goodhart, C.A.E. (2003), 'The two concepts of money: implications for the analysis of optimal currency areas', in S.A. Bell and E.J. Nell (eds), *The State, the Market and the Euro*, Cheltenham, UK and Northampton, MA, USA: Edward Elgar.

Goodhart, C.A.E. (2004), 'Money, stability and growth', in C.A.E. Goodhart (ed.), *Financial Development and Economic Growth: Explaining the Links*, London: Palgrave Macmillan.

Goodhart, C.A.E., P. Sunirand and D.P. Tsomocos (2003), 'A model to analyse financial fragility', Oxford Financial Research Centre working paper no. 2003fe13.

Goodhart, C.A.E., P. Sunirand and D.P. Tsomocos (2004a), 'A model to analyse financial fragility: applications', Oxford Financial Research Centre working paper no. 2004fe05.

Goodhart, C.A.E., P. Sunirand and D.P. Tsomocos (2004b), 'A risk assessment for banks', Oxford Financial Research Centre working paper no. 2004fe11.

Hudson, M. (2004), 'The archaeology of money: Debt versus barter theories', in L. Randall Wray (ed.), *Credit and State Theories of Money: The Contributions of A. Mitchell Innes*, Cheltenham, UK and Northampton, MA, USA: Edward Elgar, pp. 99–127.

Issing, O. (1996), 'Europe: political union through common money', Institute of Economic Affairs, occasional paper, no. 98.

Kiyotaki, N. and R. Wright (1989), 'On money as a medium of exchange', *Journal of Political Economy*, **97**, 927–54.

Kiyotaki, N. and R. Wright (1991), 'A contribution to the pure theory of money', *Journal of Economic Theory*, **53**, 215–35.

Kiyotaki, N. and R. Wright (1992), 'Acceptability, means of payment, and media of exchange', *Federal Reserve Bank of Minneapolis Quarterly Review*, 2–10.

Kydland, F.E. and E.C. Prescott (1977), 'Rules rather than discretion: the inconsistency of optimal plans', *Journal of Political Economy*, **85** (3), June.

La Porta, R., F. López-de-Silanes, A. Shleifer and R.W. Vishny (1997), 'Legal determinants of external finance', *The Journal of Finance*, **52** (3), 1131–50.

La Porta, R., F. López-de-Silanes, A. Shleifer and R.W. Vishny (1998), 'Law and finance', *Journal of Political Economy*, **106** (6), 1113–55.

Latzer, M. and S.W. Schmitz (2002), *Carl Menger and the Evolution of Payments Systems*, Cheltenham, UK and Northampton, MA, USA: Edward Elgar.

Meltzer, A. (2003), *A History of the Federal Reserve: Volume 1: 1913–1951*, Chicago: University of Chicago Press.

Sargent, T. and N. Wallace (1975), '"Rational" expectations, the Optimal Monetary Instrument, and the Optimal Money Supply Rule', *Journal of Political Economy*, **83** (2) (April).

Shubik, M. (1973), 'Commodity money, oligopoly, credit and bankruptcy in a general equilibrium model', *Western Economic Journal*, **11**, 24–38.

Shubik, M. and C. Wilson (1997), 'The Optimal Bankruptcy Rule in a trading economy using fiat money', *Journal of Economics*, **37**, 337–54.

Stigler, G.J. (1987), *The Theory of Price*, 4th edn, London: Collier Macmillan.

Streissler, E. (2002), 'Carl Menger's article "Money" in the history of economic thought', in M. Latzer and S.W. Schmitz (eds), *Carl Menger and the Evolution of Payments Systems*, Cheltenham, UK and Northampton, MA, USA: Edward Elgar.

Thornton, H. (1802), *An Inquiry into the Nature and Effects of the Paper Credit of Great Britain*, reprinted 1962, New York: Kelley.

Woodford, M. (2003), *Interest and Prices*, Princeton, NJ: Princeton University Press.

3. System dynamics of interest rate effects on aggregate demand

Linwood Tauheed and L. Randall Wray

INTRODUCTION

'Perverse' Interest Rate Effects on Aggregate Demand?

Heterodox economics has always been sceptical of the Fed's ability to 'fine-tune' the economy, in spite of the long-running Monetarist claims about the efficacy of monetary policy (even if orthodox wisdom is used to disdain discretion). The canonization of Chairman Greenspan over the past decade and a half has eliminated most orthodox squeamishness about a discretionary Fed, while currently fashionable theory based on the 'new monetary consensus' has pushed monetary policy front and centre. As Galbraith argues, lack of empirical support for such beliefs has not dampened enthusiasm. Like Galbraith, the followers of Keynes have always insisted that 'Business firms borrow when they can make money and not because interest rates are low' (Galbraith, 2004, p. 45). Even orthodox estimates of the interest rate elasticity of investment are so low that the typical rate adjustments used by the Fed cannot have much effect.

Conventional belief can still point to interest rate effects on consumption, with two main channels. Consumer durables consumption, and increasingly even consumption of services and non-durables, rely on credit and, thus, might be interest-sensitive. Second, falling mortgage rates lead to refinancing, freeing disposable income for additional consumption. Ultimately, however, whether falling interest rates might stimulate consumption must depend on different marginal propensities to consume (MPCs) between creditors and debtors. In reality, many consumers are simultaneously debtors and creditors, making analysis difficult because a reduction of rates lowers both debt payments and interest income. If we can assume that these do not have asymmetric effects (a highly implausible assumption), we can focus only on net debtors and creditors. The conventional wisdom has always been that net creditors have lower MPCs than do net debtors, so we can assume that lower rates stimulate consumption by redistributing after-interest income to debtors. Still, the consumer lives in the same business climate as firms, and if the central bank lowers rates in recession, the beneficial impacts can be overwhelmed by employment and wage and profit income effects. Further, as society ages and net financial wealth becomes increasingly concentrated in the hands of the elderly whose consumption is largely financed out of interest income, it becomes less reasonable to assume a low MPC for net creditors. Perhaps the MPC of creditors is not much different from that of debtors, which makes the impact of rising rates on consumption all the more ambiguous. This does not mean that lowering rates in recession (or raising them in expansion) is bad policy, but it could account for the observation made by Galbraith and others before him that monetary policy is ineffectual.

Most conventional and even unconventional explorations of interest rate effects have focused on demand-side effects. It is also possible that raising interest rates can have a perverse impact on prices coming from the supply side. Interest is a business cost much like energy costs that will be passed along if competitive pressures permit. The impact on aggregate demand arising from this might be minimal or ambiguous, but it is conceivable that tight monetary policy might add to cost-push inflationary pressures while easy policy would reduce them. For monetary policy to work in the conventional manner on constraining inflation, interest rate effects on aggregate demand would have to dominate such supply-side impacts. This seems ambiguous at best, given the uncertain impacts of interest rates on demand.

What has been largely ignored is the impact that interest rate changes have on government spending, and hence on aggregate demand through the 'multiplier' channel. In a somewhat different context to the issue to be pursued here, some Post Keynesian authors have recognized that rising rates tend to increase the size of government budget deficits. Indeed, in the late 1980s, a number of countries with large budget deficits would have had balanced budgets if not for interest payments on outstanding debt – Italy was a prime example, with government interest payments amounting to more than 10 per cent of GDP (Brazil was another). It was recognized at the time by a few analysts that lowering rates was probably the only way to reduce the government's deficit, a path later successfully followed. However, conventional wisdom holds that high deficits cause high interest rates, hence government can quickly find itself in an 'unsustainable' situation (rising rates increase deficits that cause markets to raise rates even higher) that can be remedied only through 'austerity': raising taxes and cutting non-interest spending. In truth, for countries on a floating exchange rate, the overnight interbank lending rate (Fed funds rate in the US) is set by the Central Bank, and government 'borrowing' rates are determined relative to this by arbitragers mostly in anticipation of future overnight rate targets. The heterodox literature on rate setting by the Central Bank is large and the arguments need not be repeated here. What is important is to recognize the government's ability to reduce its deficit spending by lowering interest rates.

What we want to investigate is the nearly ignored possibility that lowering/ raising interest rates will lower/raise aggregate demand in a manner opposite to normal expectations. This would occur if lowering rates lowered government deficits by reducing interest payments, which are essentially the same as any other transfer payments from government to the private sector. Assume an economy in which private debt is small relative to GDP, and in which the interest elasticity of private investment (and other private spending) is small. By contrast, government debt is assumed to be large with holdings distributed across 'widows and orphans' with high spending propensities. Raising interest rates will have little direct effect on the private sector, which carries a low debt load and whose spending is not interest-sensitive, in any case. However, rising interest rates increase government interest payments: to the extent that the debt is short-term or at variable interest rates, the simulative impact on private sector incomes and spending is hastened.

This is, of course, the most favourable case. However, on not implausible assumptions about private and public debt ratios and interest rate elasticities, it is possible for the government interest payment channel to overcome the negative impact that rising rates have on private demand. We will proceed as follows. First, we will briefly introduce the methodology to be used, system dynamics modelling. We then set out the model and explain the variables and parameters. For the first part of our analysis, we will use historical US data to set most parameters. We will determine, given those parameters (debt ratios and interest elasticities), at what level of interest rates we can begin to obtain 'perverse' results – where further increases actually stimulate demand. For the final part of the analysis, we will determine values for government debt ratios at which 'perverse' results can be obtained, for different levels of interest rates. Throughout we will assume uniform MPCs, and so leave for further research the questions about distribution effects. Further, we will not include interest rate effects on consumer borrowing; this is equivalent to assuming that consumer borrowing is not interest-sensitive, or that any interest rate effects on net (private) debtors is exactly offset by effects on net (private) creditors. Finally, as we will briefly mention below, further research will be needed to explore implications arising from international debtor/creditor relations (Americans hold foreign liabilities, while foreigners hold American liabilities – both private and public – and, even if domestic MPCs are the same across debtors and creditors, the MPCs of foreigner creditors and debtors could be different).

System Dynamics Modelling

System Dynamics is a numerical method for creating dynamic models of systems. The origin of System Dynamics (SD) modelling is to be found in its development by MIT's Jay Wright Forrester in the 1950s, initially as a method for designing and understanding electronic feedback control systems known as 'servomechanisms'. Its later expansion from engineering into social applications came with Forrester's writing of *Industrial Dynamics* (Forrester, 1961) and later *Urban Dynamics* (Forrester, 1969) where SD was applied to city planning.[1] As SD modelling expanded its scope from engineering applications to business management to social systems, its underlying method remained consistent: 'the application of feedback control systems principles and techniques to managerial, organizational, and socioeconomic problems' (Roberts, 1978, 3).[2]

The use of SD allows a form of experimentation with the theoretical model under analysis, by allowing the observance of the effects of manipulation of relevant variables. This facility becomes most useful when dealing with complex models of social systems with many feedbacks loops that cannot be solved analytically by a closed system of equations (see Forrester, 1995).

In this study, interest rate effects on aggregate demand are observed in both 'static' and dynamic modes. A detailed discussion of SD is beyond the scope of this chapter. For additional information on SD modelling, particularly in a heterodox context, refer to (Radzicki, 1988, 1990).

METHOD

The Model

The model used in this study, represented in Figure 3.1, is the familiar Aggregate Demand/GDP model. The definition and description of model variables are in Table 3.1. Variables are set to 2000 National Income and Product Account (NIPA) values as listed in the Statistical Abstract of the United States (2001).

Model Structure

In the model (see Figure 3.1), there are three feedback loops to note.

1. The positive loop from GDP to NI (national income) to DI (disposable income) to C (consumption) to AD (aggregate demand) to dGDP (change of GDP) to GDP.
2. The positive loop from GDP to Dp (public debt) to DS (public debt service) to XP (transfer payments) to DI ... back to GDP.
3. The negative loop from dGDP to GDP back to dGDP.

The first two loops drive the increase/decrease in GDP, as producers, with some delay, increase/decrease aggregate supply in response to the perceived increase/decrease in aggregate demand (AD). The third loop prevents the

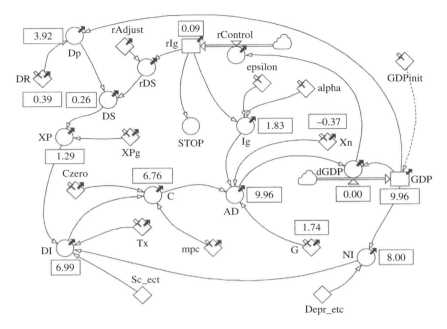

Figure 3.1   Aggregate demand/GDP model

positive loops from driving the system explosively and brings GDP into 'equilibrium' with aggregate demand, again with some delay, by decreasing the change in GDP (dGDP) as the AD–GDP gap decreases.

In addition, although not strictly loops, two feedback effects are the basic effects analysed in this study:

4. The positive debt service 'loop' from rDS (average interest rate on public debt) to DS … interfacing with loop #2 back to GDP.
5. The negative Investment 'loop' from rIg (average prime rate) to Ig (investment) to AD … back to GDP.

The Investment Function
A constant elasticity investment function is derived as follows:

1. $\varepsilon = (dI_g/dr) * (r/I_g) = \overline{\varepsilon}$
2. $(dI_g/I_g) = \overline{\varepsilon}dr/r$
3. $\ln(I_g) = \overline{\varepsilon}\ln(r) + c$
4. $I_g = e^c r^{\overline{\varepsilon}}$
5. $let \ldots \alpha = e^c$

Table 3.1 Equations for aggregate demand/GDP model (values in trillions)

Variable	Definition	Description
AD	$C + G + I_g + Xn$	aggregate demand
alpha (α)	1.0	coefficient of investment function
C	mpc * (DI) + Czero	consumption function
Czero	0.473540	estimated autonomous consumption given C and mpc
Depr_etc.	$-0.3706 + 0.3749 + 1.2571 +$ $0.7696 - 0.0279 - 4.042$	NI adjustments (depr, factor income, etc.)
dGDP	(AD – GDP)	change in GDP per quarter (in static model dGDP = 0)
DI	NI – Tx + XP – Sc_etc.	disposable income
Dp	DR * GDP	public debt
DR	(3.4101 + 0.5114)/9.9631	debt ratio (public + FRB debt)/ GDP
DS	MAX(Dp * rDS, .01 * Dp)	debt service (max of Dp*rDS or 1%*Dp)
epsilon (ε)	–0.25	interest rate elasticity of investment
G	1.7437	government spending
GDP	GDPinit	(set to GDPinit at start of simulation)
GDPinit	9.9631	GDP initial value for simulation
I_g	alpha * $rI_g^{epsilon}$	investment function
mpc	0.90	assumed marginal propensity to consume
NI	GDP – Depr_etc.	national income
rDS	rI_g – rAdjust	average debt service rate (rounded)
rI_g	0.09	average prime rate (rounded)
rAdjust	$0.09 - (0.2552/3.9215) =$ 0.024923	prime rate adjustment to debt service rate
rControl	IF((ABS(dGDP) < 0.01), 0.01,0)/Timestep	increases rI_g by 1% when simulation reaches temporary 'equilibrium'
Sc_etc.	0.01990	personal income adjustment from NI (includes corporate savings)
STOP	STOPIF(r > 0.2)	stops simulation when rI_g is > 20%
Tx	0.7056 + 0.286 + 1.2919	personal and corporate tax and social security contributions
Xn	–0.3707	net exports
XP	XPg + DS	transfer payments (includes federal debt service)
XPg	1.036	government transfer payments

6. $\therefore I_g = \alpha r^{\bar{\varepsilon}}$

A cursory review of the literature on interest rate elasticity found a fairly wide range of estimates, with most below –0.25, although a few were substantially larger. We also found that setting ε = –0.25, the investment function approximates the 2000 value for gross private domestic investment (Ig = 1,832.7) when α = 1 and rIg = 0.09 – (Ig = 1.8257). Hence we use –0.25 as the interest rate elasticity of investment for this analysis. The graph of the function for interest rates from 1 per cent to 20 per cent is shown in Figure 3.2.

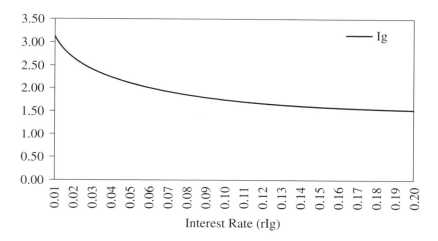

Figure 3.2   Constant elasticity investment function

The Debt Service Function and the Debt Ratio

Government debt service (DS) is a linear function of the prime rate (rIg) and public debt (Dp). In 2000 this debt was 3.9215 (3.4101 owed to the public and 0.5114 owed to the Fed). Payment on this debt equalled 0.2552. This corresponds to an effective average interest rate of 6.5077 per cent. This is, of course lower than the prime rate used in the investment function. The difference is used as an adjustment (rAdjust) to the prime rate for computing rDS, the debt service rate, and equals approximately 2.4923 per cent. This value is used throughout as the spread between rIg and the DS rate (rDS).[3]

The public debt (Dp) to GDP debt ratio (DR) is calculated from 2000 values (Dp=3.9215/GDP=9.9631) and equals 0.3936. This ratio is held constant for the first parts of this study.

Static Analysis

The model is initialized in 'equilibrium' at 2000 values with GDP = 9.9631 and other variables set accordingly. In order to obtain 'static' results from an essentially dynamic model, the linkage between AD and GDP is broken. This linkage is modelled by the flow 'dGDP' that functions to gradually increase or decrease the level of GDP if the gap between AD and GDP (AD–GDP) is positive or negative, respectively. To perform a 'static' analysis, dGDP is forced to zero (0). Thus GDP (as well as NI and Dp) will remain constant regardless of changes in AD (see Figure 3.5).

Dynamic Analysis

For the dynamic analysis, the model is also initialized in 'equilibrium' at 2000 values with GDP = 9.9631, other variables set accordingly. However, the linkage between AD and GDP is fully active since dGDP is set to AD–GDP. The functioning of a 'flow' variable such as dGDP in an SD model is that it does not respond to its value immediately, but over some adjustment time period. In this simulation, the dGDP adjustment time is one year, which is four times the simulation time step of one quarter. This causes a gradual increase or decrease in the level of GDP as the gap between AD and GDP (AD–GDP) is positive or negative, respectively.

RESULTS

Static Analysis

Under the control of the variable rControl, the value of rIg is increased from 9 per cent to 20 per cent and then stops. The results are shown in Table 3.2, Figure 3.3 and Figure 3.4.

As the value of rIg increases from 9 per cent to 20 per cent, Ig decreases while DS increases. Ig decreases in accordance with it functional form. Since there is no change in Dp, DS increases linearly as rDS (rIg – rAdjust) increases (see Figure 3.3 and Table 3.2).

AD changes value in response to the change in Ig (ΔIg) plus the change in DS (ΔDS), both resulting from the change in rIg alone. The total effect on ΔAD, with mpc = 0.9, is ΔIg + 0.9*ΔDS, but since ΔDS is constant all change in ΔAD is attributable to ΔIg. As can be seen in Figure 3.4 and Table 3.2 the combined effect on ΔAD is initially negative but becomes positive between an rIg of 12 per cent and 13 per cent (remember that this represents the investment function interest rate; the debt service function interest rate is lower by approximately

Table 3.2 Static mode interest rate effects on key variables

AD (s)	GDP	rIg	Ig	DS (s)	ΔIg	ΔDS	ΔAD=ΔIg+ 0.9*ΔDS	Dp
9.9631	9.9631	0.09	1.8257	0.2552	na	na	na	3.9215
9.9509	9.9631	0.10	1.7783	0.2944	−0.0475	0.0392	−0.0122	3.9215
9.9444	9.9631	0.11	1.7364	0.3336	−0.0419	0.0392	−0.0066	3.9215
9.9423	9.9631	0.12	1.6990	0.3728	−0.0374	0.0392	−0.0021	3.9215
9.9439	9.9631	0.13	1.6654	0.4121	−0.0337	0.0392	**0.0016**	3.9215
9.9486	9.9631	0.14	1.6348	0.4513	−0.0306	0.0392	0.0047	3.9215
9.9560	9.9631	0.15	1.6069	0.4905	−0.0280	0.0392	0.0073	3.9215
9.9656	**9.9631**	0.16	1.5811	0.5297	−0.0257	0.0392	0.0096	3.9215
9.9771	9.9631	0.17	1.5574	0.5689	−0.0238	0.0392	0.0115	3.9215
9.9903	9.9631	0.18	1.5353	0.6081	−0.0221	0.0392	0.0132	3.9215
10.0049	9.9631	0.19	1.5146	0.6474	−0.0206	0.0392	0.0147	3.9215
10.0209	9.9631	0.20	1.4953	0.6866	−0.0193	0.0392	0.0160	3.9215

Note: Bold type in columns AD(s) and GDP identifies the point of return to (near) initial values. Bold type in the ΔAD column identifies the point where ΔAD changes from negative (AD declining) to positive.

2.4923 per cent). The effect on AD can be seen in Figure 3.5 as the slope of the AD curve becomes positive at this point.

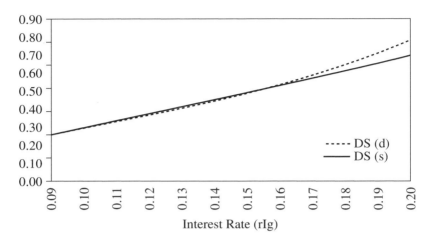

Figure 3.3   Static (S) v. dynamic (D) mode debt service function

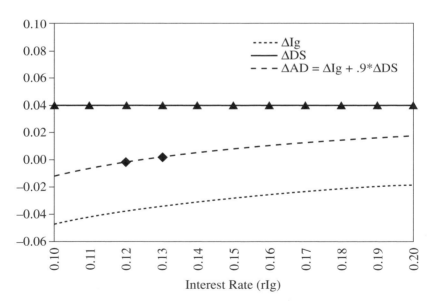

Figure 3.4   Static mode interest rate effects on investment and debt service and their combined effect on aggregate demand

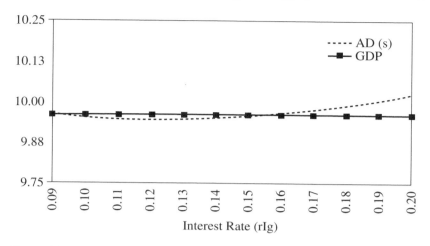

Figure 3.5   Static mode interest rate effects on aggregate demand and GDP

Dynamic Analysis

As in the 'static' case, under the control of the variable rControl the value of rIg is increased from 9 per cent to 20 per cent and then stops. The results are shown in Table 3.3, Figure 3.6, and Figure 3.7. The results are those of the relevant variables at the time step in which the simulation reaches a temporary 'equilibrium' and before rIg is increased by 1 per cent.[4]

As the value of rIg increases from 9 per cent to 20 per cent, Ig decreases while DS increases. Again, this results in a decrease in Ig in accordance with its functional form, and an increase in DS. However, since Dp increases/decreases as GDP increases/decreases the DS function no longer yields linear results with respect to rIg (see Figure 3.3 and Table 3.3).

The AD to GDP interface is fully active through dGDP, and AD now changes value not only in response to the change in Ig (ΔIg), which as in the 'static' mode depends only on the change in rIg, but also in response to the change in DS (ΔDS) which varies as both Dp and rIg vary.[5] The total effect on AD from ΔIg and ΔDS is as before, ΔIg + 0.9*ΔDS. However, there is also an effect on DI (and therefore C and therefore AD) through NI that is an effect of the change in GDP. GDP changes non-linearly in the direction of AD, as seen in Figure 3.7. Thus the total effect on AD is the sum of all changes in GDP, Ig and DS as the simulation moves from 'equilibrium' to 'equilibrium' and equals $\Sigma(\Delta$Ig + 0.9*(Δ_GDP + ΔDS)) (see the note for Table 3.3).

As can be seen in Figure 3.6 (right axis) the combined effect on ΔAD is initially negative but becomes positive between an rIg of 13 per cent and 14 per

Table 3.3 Dynamic mode interest rate effects on key variable

Qtrs	AD (d)	GDP	rIg	ΣΔ_GDP	DS (d)	ΣΔIg	ΣΔDS	ΔAD=Σ(ΔIg+0.9*(Δ_GDP+ΔDS))
0	9.9631	9.9631	0.09	0.00000	0.2552	0.0000	0.0000	0.0000
12	9.9226	9.9325	0.10	-0.03055	0.2935	-0.0475	0.0383	-0.0405
42	9.8261	9.8359	0.11	-0.09661	0.3294	-0.0419	0.0359	-0.0965
55	9.7900	9.8000	0.12	-0.03596	0.3667	**-0.0374**	**0.0374**	-0.0361
56	9.7887	9.7975	0.13	-0.00250	0.4052	-0.0337	0.0385	-0.0013
57	9.7908	9.7953	0.14	-0.00220	0.4437	-0.0306	0.0385	**0.0021**
58	**9.7964**	**9.7942**	0.15	-0.00113	0.4822	-0.0280	0.0385	0.0057
68	9.8287	9.8187	0.16	**0.02457**	0.5220	-0.0257	0.0399	0.0323
130	10.0567	10.0468	0.17	0.22808	0.5737	-0.0238	0.0517	0.2280
206	10.3549	10.3450	0.18	0.29818	0.6314	-0.0221	0.0577	0.2982
299	10.7420	10.7321	0.19	0.38715	0.6973	-0.0206	0.0659	0.3871
409	11.2329	11.2229	0.20	0.49073	0.7734	-0.0193	0.0761	0.4908

Note: Δ_GDP is the **actual** change in GDP per time step rather than the AD/GDP gap (dGDP=AD–GDP) which is roughly four times Δ_GDP per time step. Bold type in columns ΣΔIg and ΣΔDS identifies the point where the cumulative negative effect on ΔIg (because of increases in rIg) equals the cumulative positive effect on ΔDS. Bold type in the ΔAD column identifies the point where ΔAD changes from negative (AD declining) to positive. Bold type in the ΣΔ_GDP column identifies the point where ΣΔ_GDP changes from negative (GDP declining) to positive.

cent. This is later than in the 'static' case and will be explained below. The effect on AD can be seen in Figure 3.7 as the slope of the AD curve becomes positive

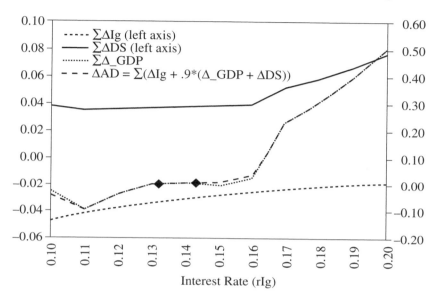

Figure 3.6   Dynamic mode interest rate effects on investment, debt service and GDP and their combined effect on aggregate demand

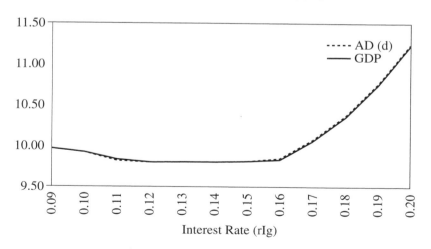

Figure 3.7   Dynamic mode interest rate effects on aggregate demand and GDP

at this point with AD overtaking GDP between an rIg of 14 per cent and 15 per cent.

The slope of GDP increases dramatically around an rIg of 16 per cent (Δ_GDP becomes positive between an rIg of 15 per cent and 16 per cent, Table 3.3) causing accelerated feedback effects through DS by way of Dp, and AD by way of DI (Figure 3.6).

Static v. Dynamic Comparison

As seen in Figure 3.8, the feedback effects of GDP on AD causes dynamic AD initially to drop below static AD, but eventually to overcome static AD at an rIg between 16 per cent and 17 per cent. The rates of change are dramatically different before an rIg of 12 per cent and after an rIg of 16 per cent.

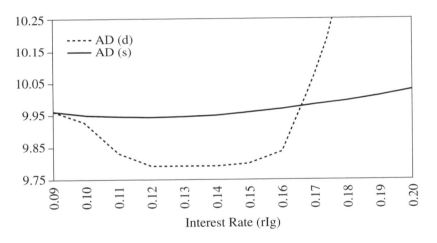

Figure 3.8   Comparison of static v. dynamic aggregate demand

This outcome depends on the functional form of the investment function (see Figure 3.2). Before an rIg of 12 per cent the negative change in Ig (ΔIg) dominates the positive change in DS (ΔDS) becoming approximately equal at an rIg of 12 per cent. After an rIg of 16 per cent the combined positive effects of ΔDS and Δ_GDP dominate the increasing smaller negative ΔIg effect.[6]

The shift to positive ΔAD occurs later for the dynamic case than for the static case (between 13 per cent–14 per cent rather than between 12 per cent–13 per cent; see Figure 3.9) because of the 'inertia' caused by the lower GDP level which takes longer for dGDP (AD-GDP) to overcome.

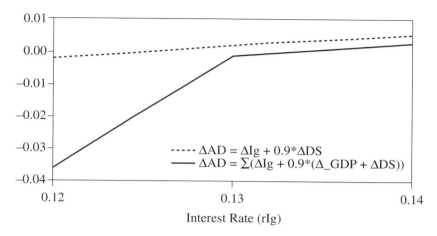

Figure 3.9   Static v. dynamic change in aggregate demand by interest rate

Static Model with Variable Debt Ratio

In this section we make the government's debt ratio variable to find the 'knife edge' or 'tipping point' at which an increase of the interest rate will actually stimulate the economy. We derive the debt ratio (DR) where the interest rate change effect on AD from a change in Ig and change in DS equals zero, that is $\Delta Ig\ (r) + \Delta DS(r) = \Delta AD(r) = 0$.

Let:
1. $I_g = \alpha r^{\bar{\varepsilon}}$,
2. $let\ldots\alpha = 1$,
3. $\Delta I_g = (r + \Delta r)^{\bar{\varepsilon}} - r^{\bar{\varepsilon}}$,
4. $DS = mpc * GDP * DR * r$,
5. $\Delta DS = mpc * GDP * DR * [(r + \Delta r) - r] = mpc * GDP * DR * \Delta r$,
6. $let\ldots\Delta I_g + \Delta DS = \Delta AD = 0$,
7. $-[(r + \Delta r)^{\bar{\varepsilon}} - r^{\bar{\varepsilon}}] = mpc * GDP * DR * \Delta r$,
8. $\therefore DR = \dfrac{-[(r + \Delta r)^{\bar{\varepsilon}} - r^{\bar{\varepsilon}}]}{mpc * GDP * \Delta r}$.

We obtain the following results for DR with mpc = 0.9, $\varepsilon = -0.25$, $\Delta r = 0.01$ and various values for GDP, for investment interest rates from 3 per cent to 20 per cent. For the change in prime rate the change in the debt service interest rate is the same:

$$[(r + \Delta r) - r] = \Delta r = [(r - rAdjust) + \Delta r] - (r - rAdjust).$$

Table 3.4 *'Equilibrium' debt ratios for various GDP/interest rate combinations*

Investment Interest Rate r	Investment Ig=r^e	−Change in Investment −dlg = −[((r+Δr)^e)−r^e]	'Equilibrium' Debt Ratio at GDP1 DR1 = −dlg/(mpc*GDP1*Δr)	'Equilibrium' Debt Ratio at GDP2 DR2 = −dgl/(mpc*GDP2*Δr)	'Equilibrium' Debt Ratio at GDP3 DR3 = −dlg/(mpc*GDP3*Δr)
0.03	2.4028	0.1667	3.7191	1.8596	0.9298
0.04	2.2361	0.1213	2.7061	1.3531	0.6765
0.05	2.1147	0.0942	2.1017	1.0508	0.5254
0.06	2.0205	0.0764	1.7037	0.8519	0.4259
0.07	1.9441	0.0638	1.4237	0.7118	0.3559
0.08	1.8803	0.0546	1.2169	0.6085	0.3042
0.09	1.8257	0.0475	1.0586	0.5293	0.2647
0.10	1.7783	0.0419	0.9339	0.4670	0.2335
0.11	1.7364	0.0374	0.8334	0.4167	0.2083
0.12	1.6990	0.0337	0.7508	0.3754	0.1877
0.13	1.6654	0.0306	0.6819	0.3409	0.1705
0.14	1.6348	0.0280	0.6235	0.3118	0.1559
0.15	1.6069	0.0257	0.5736	0.2868	0.1434
0.16	1.5811	0.0238	0.5305	0.2652	0.1326
0.17	1.5574	0.0221	0.4928	0.2464	0.1232
0.18	1.5353	0.0206	0.4597	0.2299	0.1149
0.19	1.5146	0.0193	0.4305	0.2152	0.1076
0.20	1.4953	0.0181	0.4044	0.2022	0.1011

As can be seen in Table 3.4 and Figure 3.10 below, for plausible 'real world' prime rates in the range of 10 per cent to 12 per cent, and for a 'real world' GDP of just under $10 trillion, government debt ratios well under 50 per cent of GDP are sufficient to obtain perverse monetary policy results.

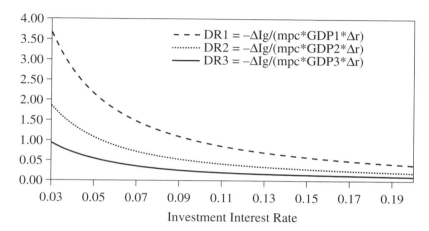

Figure 3.10   *'Equilibrium' debt ratios for various GDP/interest rate combinations*

Static Model with Variable Level of Public Debt

It is also useful to find the level of outstanding government debt at which the debt service impact of raising interest rates overwhelms the negative impact on aggregate demand resulting from effects of interest rates on investment. We might call this the 'equilibrium' public debt. Here we derive public debt where interest rate change effect on AD from change in Ig and change in DS equals zero, that is $dI_g(r) + dDS(r) = dAD(r) = 0$.

1. $I_g = \alpha r^{\bar{\varepsilon}}$,
2. $let \ldots \alpha = 1$,
3. $dI_g = \bar{\varepsilon} * r^{\bar{\varepsilon}-1} dr$,
4. $DS = mpc * Dp * (r - rAdjust)$,
5. $dDS = mpc * Dp * dr$,
6. $let \ldots dI_g + dDS = dAD = 0$,
7. $-[\bar{\varepsilon} * r^{\bar{\varepsilon}-1}] = mpc * Dp$,
8. $\therefore Dp = \dfrac{-[\bar{\varepsilon} * r^{\bar{\varepsilon}-1}]}{mpc}$.

Results for 'equilibrium' public debt (Dp) for mpc = 0.9, ε = –0.25, and investment interest rates of 3 per cent to 20 per cent are shown in Table 3.5 and Figure 3.11. With an interest rate of 10 per cent, if the public debt is $4.94 trillion (or about 50 per cent of GDP), interest rate hikes can stimulate aggregate demand.

Table 3.5 'Equilibrium' Public Debt

Investment Interest Rate	Change in Investment	'Equilibrium' Public Debt
r	$-dlg = -\varepsilon * r^{\wedge}(\varepsilon - 1)$	$Dp = -dlg/mpc$
0.03	20.0234	22.2483
0.04	13.9754	15.5282
0.05	10.5737	11.7486
0.06	8.4188	9.3542
0.07	6.9433	7.7148
0.08	5.8759	6.5288
0.09	5.0715	5.6350
0.10	4.4457	4.9397
0.11	3.9464	4.3849
0.12	3.5397	3.9330
0.13	3.2027	3.5585
0.14	2.9193	3.2437
0.15	2.6781	2.9757
0.16	2.4705	2.7450
0.17	2.2902	2.5447
0.18	2.1323	2.3692
0.19	1.9930	2.2144
0.20	1.8692	2.0769

Admittedly, this is a simple model that includes only one negative effect: the interest rate elasticity of investment. If other private spending is also interest rate-sensitive, and if the usual assumption that net debtors have higher spending propensities holds, then higher debt ratios will be required to obtain perverse results. However, note that Italy had a government debt ratio above 100 per cent and interest rates on government debt above 10 per cent in the late 1980s. Turkey flirts with interest rates of 28 per cent and government deficits above 25 per cent of GDP, perhaps sufficiently high for the lowering of rates actually to cool the economy. Finally, Japan has the highest deficits and debt ratio in the developed world, with high net private saving ratios and substantial private sector financial

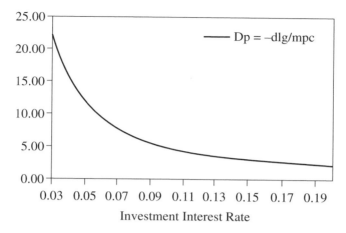

Figure 3.11 *'Equilibrium' public debt by interest rate*

wealth, all in the context of zero interest rates. It is entirely possible that raising rates in Japan would actually stimulate the economy by increasing private sector interest income.

CONCLUSIONS

This exercise has demonstrated that under not-too-implausible conditions, raising interest rates could actually stimulate aggregate demand through debt service payments made by the government on its outstanding debt. This is more likely if private sector indebtedness is small, if private spending is not interest rate-elastic, if interest rates are high, and if government debt is large (above 50 per cent) relative to GDP. In addition, the reset period of the government's debt affects the rapidity with which interest rate changes are transmitted to spending. Our analysis used fairly simple models and hence represents a first attempt at modelling these impacts.

In future work we need to take account of the distribution of ownership of the public debt – domestically and internationally. Foreign holdings of sovereign debt presumably would diminish the debt service effects we have explored; further, institutional ownership of the debt probably reduces the spending propensities of received government interest payments. Most government debt is not directly held by 'widows and orphans', but rather is held indirectly through financial institutions, pension funds, and so on. The 'pass through' effects of increased government interest payments on household income and thus on spending are not immediately clear in the case of institutionalized holdings.

Still, it is plausible that part of the reason for empirical evidence not supporting the conventional wisdom about monetary policy can be attributed to the debt service effects analysed here.

NOTES

1. The term 'System Dynamics' pertains to the practice of Industrial Dynamics applied to social systems modelling.
2. It should be noted that the application of feedback theory to problems of understanding organizational behaviour had been previously explored by Simon (1957) and to cybernetic models of human behaviour by Wiener (1948). See Richardson (1991) for additional examples.
3. To avoid negative DS rates, in the model the DS rate floor is set at 1 per cent. In this study, since rIg never goes below 9 per cent, rDS never goes below 6.5077 per cent.
4. The data points generated from the simulation are variably spaced in time (see figure and Table 3.3 variable 'Qtrs'). Each data point represents the 'equilibrium' level of AD/GDP immediately before the next change in rIg. As can be seen this occurs at irregular intervals becoming smaller from Quarter #0 (start of simulated time) to Quarter #55, and longer after Quarter #58. This has the effect of distorting the slope of the variables relative to the changes in interest rate. This should be kept in mind when interpreting the results temporally.

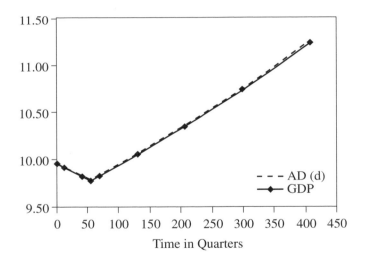

Figure 3.12   Dynamic aggregate demand/GDP by time in quarters

5. The total change on ΔDS as Dp and rI_g vary is the sum of the partial changes in both Dp and rDS, that is $dDS = rDS*\partial DP + \partial rDS*Dp$.
6. In this model $I_g(r)$ is independent of GDP and AD. A refinement might be to make I_g dependent on expected or perceived AD, shifting $I_g(r)$ as a function of dGDP.

REFERENCES

Forrester, J.W. (1961), *Industrial Dynamics*, Cambridge, MA: MIT Press.

Forrester, J.W. (1969), *Urban Dynamics*, Cambridge, MA: MIT Press.

Forrester, J.W. (1995), *Counterintuitive Behavior of Social Systems*; accessed 27 May 2003, at http://sysdyn.clexchange.org/sdep/Roadmaps/RM1/D-4468-2.pdf.

Galbraith, J.K. (2004), *The Economics of Innocent Fraud : Truth for our Time*, Boston: Houghton Mifflin.

Radzicki, M.J. (1988), 'Institutional dynamics: an extension of the institutionalist approach to socioeconomic analysis', *Journal of Economic Issues*, **22**(3), 633.

Radzicki, M.J. (1990), 'Institutional dynamics, deterministic chaos and self-organizing systems', *Journal of Economic Issues*, **24**(1), 57.

Richardson, G.P. (1991), *Feedback Thought in Social Science and Systems Theory*, Philadelphia: University of Pennsylvania Press.

Roberts, E.B. (ed.) (1978), *Managerial Applications of System Dynamics*, Cambridge: MIT Press.

Simon, H.A. (1957), *Models of Man: Social and Rational; Mathematical Essays on Rational Human Behavior in a Social Setting*, New York: Wiley.

United States Bureau of the Census (2001), *Statistical Abstract of the United States*, 121st edn, Washington, DC.

Wiener, N. (1948), *Cybernetics*, New York: J. Wiley.

4. Credibility versus confidence in monetary policy

Edwin le Heron and Emmanuel Carre

Since World War II, three monetary policy regimes have succeeded one another: the Keynesian regime until the mid-1970s, the monetarist regime until 1982; finally a New Consensus gradually forced itself upon central banking. Inside this New Consensus 'inflation targeting' became the prominent regime during the 1990s. This evolution was often explained through the debate rules versus discretion. This would thus give, first, *discretion* with Keynesianism, then *rules* with monetarism and the 'New' Classical Economy (NCE) and finally constrained discretion with the 'New' Keynesians.

We shall develop the opposition of credibility versus confidence as a more relevant and enlightening way to understand this evolution. In particular, for the last 25 years, a period in the course of which expectations became an important channel in the explanation of inflation and in the implementation of the monetary policy, we have been moving from a credibility strategy to a confidence strategy.

By a strategy of credibility, we mean a Central Bank that adopts a model of behaviour and then follows it. It says what it does and does what it says. With monetarism and the NCE, the model of behaviour issues from the common knowledge of natural laws of economy. To respect these laws, the real model imposes a rule of behaviour to be followed by economic agents and the Central Bank. Then credibility is connected to respect for 'truth' (the natural laws). The simplified chain of the credibility strategy is R-C-C: Rule–Commitment–Credibility. The monetary policy simply is an economic and technical problem. Credibility appears as the evolution from the NCE to propound an alternative to the quantity theory of money. The objective is also to preserve the image of a quite powerful Central Bank able to control inflation alone and perfectly. If uncertainty is studied, rational expectations make it possible to avoid the defects of coordination between economic agents and the Central Bank, which undertakes to respect a rule of monetary policy.

With confidence, natural laws and the underlying real model no longer exist. Knowledge is the result of an interaction between the Central Bank and the agents, which implies a high level of communication. There is confidence when there is a mutual understanding between the Central Bank and the economic agents. This common understanding should be understood on two levels: in the first place, each takes the other into account and, secondly, the strategy and the conventions of the Central Bank correspond to those of the other economic agents.

Therefore, it is possible to have credibility without confidence. The Central Bank should not only account for, but also take into account the economic model, which the agents hold at the moment. The simplified chain of the confidence strategy is C-C-C: Communication–Common Understanding–Confidence. The strategy of confidence is a return to Keynes's philosophy, which does not mean to Keynesianism: the monetary policy is above all a political problem and not the simple respecting of an economic rule. The accountability of a Central Bank, particularly if it is independent, is the cornerstone of the strategy of confidence. A single or predetermined equilibrium does not exist and strong uncertainty makes the management of expectations necessary. Good coordination between the Central Bank and economic agents is therefore essential. This implies a high level of communication and a definition of the objectives of monetary policy accepted by all.

We shall point out five conflicts between a credibility strategy and a confidence strategy: credibility versus confidence, independence versus governance, responsibility versus accountability, common knowledge versus common understanding, transparency versus openness.

In the debate on credibility versus confidence, inflation targeting (IT) carries an ambiguity. IT is often the end of the credibility strategy: the target replacing the rule. But sometimes, IT is the beginning of the confidence strategy: the target as a focal point, that is, part of a communication strategy. The absence of a specific theoretical model explains the numerous definitions and the varied practices of IT. The opposition credibility versus confidence can clear up the evolutions and the contradictions inside the New Consensus. The virulent debates within the Fed, notably between Greenspan, Kohn, Gramlich (opposing IT) and Bernanke, Mishkin, Goodfriend, Svensson (favourable to IT), can be explained by this opposition.

We shall be interested only in the countries that mostly pursue domestic stability and not those worried mostly with the exchange rates. We shall analyse first the history of credibility, and second the framework of confidence, before finally clarifying the ambiguous status of IT.

THE CREDIBILITY FRAMEWORK

A Survey of the Credibility Framework

At the beginning of the 1970s, Milton Friedman proposed an alternative policy framework to Keynesianism, in which inflation was only a monetary phenomenon. Monetarism believes that a long-term equilibrium exists. A rule is deduced from this presumption. An unconditional rule has to ensure the conditions of this long-term equilibrium, notably through the quantitative relation. Money is neutral in the long term and must be neutralized in the short term. Monetarism supposes that market forces are able to come to equilibrium naturally, over the long run. It frames the 'true model' of the economy.

The credibility framework is a synthesis of monetarism and the NCE, especially with the rational expectations hypothesis. The credibility literature usually starts with the model of Kydland and Prescott (1977)[1]. Its main contribution is the introduction of a game-theory approach; that is, to consider monetary policy as endogenous: 'Economic planning is not a game against nature but, rather, a game against rational economic agents' (ibid., p. 473). The credibility framework wanted to go beyond the lack of a convincing demonstration of the monetarist argument for rules. Time inconsistency is presented as a new argument in favour of rules over discretion. Under the rational expectations hypothesis, discretion leads to an average inflation bias, which is related to the augmented Phillips curve and to the natural rate of unemployment. The solution to this problem is that policy makers abandon the optimal control theory (OCT), and adopt 'policies such as constant growth in the money supply' (ibid., p. 487). In a context of high inflation, these authors defined price stability as zero per cent, to establish the condition of long-term equilibrium. Central Bank credibility relies on its ability to respect a rule. Thus policy makers would stop pursuing an impossible inflation/growth trade-off and so eliminate the inflation bias. Then, the credibility literature will generate a set of solutions to this inflation bias. The scheme of the credibility literature is Natural model–Rule–Announcement–Commitment–Enforcement.

Barro and Gordon (1983a, 1983b) really started the credibility framework. Problems arise from the lack of credibility of Kydland and Prescott's solution to time inconsistency. The solution is to find a commitment technology that makes the announced rule credible to the public. Barro and Gordon introduced reputation in monetary policy as a solution to the inflation bias. They developed a game theory approach (1983a). Concluding on the impossibility of an enforced commitment (rules), they advocate a reputational equilibrium. Repeated games between agents and Central Bank should make it possible to reveal the 'type' (Backus and Drifill, 1985) of Central Bank, and the construction of its reputation. In a second paper Barro and Gordon (1983b), preserve the 'naturalist' theoretical framework. A zero per cent inflation rate is now rejected, because the authority has too many temptations to lie. The conclusion is that a formal anchor to a rule is less important than institutional anchorage of expectations (institutional set-up).

The next contribution is the strategic delegation (Rogoff, 1985). Like Barro and Gordon, Rogoff puts the emphasis on institutional arrangements, moving from rules to the *independence* principle. Full independence is presented as the optimal enforcement that makes credible the commitment to price stability. Already, Nordhaus (1975) and Hibbs (1977) had underlined the necessity of isolating the monetary policy from government elections. It was necessary to avoid the political business cycles dependent on opportunist behaviour. For Rogoff (p. 1177), a rigid rule is impractical for three reasons:

- a cost in terms of unemployment exists in case of unexpected disturbances,
- it is 'difficult to alter after it becomes outmoded',
- uncertainty over the ever-changing structures of the economy 'complicates the problem of designing a permanent monetary rule'.

He tries to reduce the inflation bias under discretion. Rogoff's proposition consists in the delegation of the monetary policy to a conservative central banker. Nevertheless, Rogoff is concerned by the credibility/flexibility dilemma of the rule. He focuses on flexible targeting, adding that it is not optimal to constrain the central bank 'to hit their target exactly' (ibid., p. 1186). Contrary to previous authors, he defends a hierarchical mandate, not a unique mandate. Rogoff's solution suffers from democratic problems:

- a central banker has different preferences from those of the general public,
- monetary policy needs public support since it operates in the long run.

Lohmann (1992) accepts the conservative central banker. Following Rogoff, she insists on the credibility–flexibility dilemma, especially in the presence of large shocks. Her solution is a commitment to an override procedure. The government is allowed to take control of monetary policy in the case of a large shock. The knowledge of this institutional arrangement invites the conservative central banker to respond more actively to shocks. This institutional design gives support to the idea that credibility comes from democratic insurance, but also from performance of the Central Bank.

The weaker was the case for the natural model of the economy and its rule, the more credibility emphasized the optimal institutional design (Persson and Tabellini, 1993). Generally associated with the New Zealand Central Bank,

Walsh's model represents a new stage in the credibility framework. The possibility that the central bank lies is understood in a different conceptual framework: information asymmetry. Consequently, in a principal–agent model, the author presents an optimal incentive contract. Walsh develops the hypothesis submitted by Barro and Gordon (1983b, p. 607): commitments are 'long term contracts with the public'. Contracts have replaced rules. A contract is seen as the best institutional design for credibility; an institution is considered as an incentive structure. The contract eliminates any inflationary bias and 'credibility and flexibility are simultaneously achieved' (Walsh, 1995, p. 153). Walsh criticizes the reputational equilibrium. Information is imperfect, unobservable and unverifiable. He also points out a limitation of Rogoff's solution. He argues that preferences are not favourable to improvements in terms of the institutional design of central banking.

Svensson (1997) has definitely abandoned a perfect and naturalist model of the economy with its rules. He remains in the delegation perspective with a contract and inflation targeting. His proposal is a criticism of the previous models. Because of enduring unemployment, Rogoff's solution produces a restriction of output bias. For the same reason, Walsh's solution encounters both practical and political difficulty and becomes a third best equilibrium. Finally, Svensson defends a mix of 'weight-conservative and inflation-target-conservative targets'. That's why Svensson pinpoints the central question of accountability of the Central Bank. This is aimed at reducing the stabilization bias.

Woodford (2003) is the last major proponent of the credibility school. He develops a rule-based, policy-making strategy with history-dependent variables. He looks for 'optimal interest rate feedback rules by a commitment to inertial behaviour' or to predictable responses to shocks. His new Wicksellian model is based on three equations: an expectational IS curve, an inflation adjustment equation, and a specification of monetary policy, that is, an objective function for nominal interest rate. In the credibility literature, the current debate is targeting rules (monetary and inflation targeting of Svensson) versus instrument rules (McCallum, Woodford, Taylor). His proposal of interest rate inertia (optimal rule) uses the Wicksell natural rate of interest. So he gives a Wicksellian theoretical basis for the rule.

To summarise, a Central Bank is judged 'credible' when economic agents think that the central bank will continue to follow the same rule, making its reaction function stable, despite the necessary adjustment to temporary economic conditions (Le Heron, 2003, p. 12). As summarized by Blinder (2000, p. 1422): 'A central bank is credible if people believe it will do what it says'. The credibility apparatus can be reduced to RCC: Rule-Commitment-Credibility.

The natural model of the economy. The fundamental assumption of monetarism and the NCE framework is the existence of a single long-term natural equilibrium (with exogenous and neutral money). The Central Bank knows this 'true' model of the economy and its credibility comes from the respect for this.

Rule and commitment. The rule is founded on the belief in a natural equilibrium model. A fixed rule can be interpreted as a commitment to respect the 'true' model of the economy. As agents are representative and hold rational expectations, everyone knows the same model. They can observe whether the central bank is respecting it. That is why there must be an automatic and unconditional commitment to the rule. Monetary policy is, therefore, a technical and economic problem.

There is a vertical and hierarchical relationship between the Central Bank and economic agents, because there is no interaction (see Figure 4.1). They refer to the same model, which is common knowledge. There is no communication: the common knowledge is sufficient for expectations coordination and anchorage. It builds expectations; it is a benchmark for policy makers and agents. Full independence is the enforcement of the natural price stability-oriented and long-term oriented strategy, and its related culture of stability and neutrality of money.

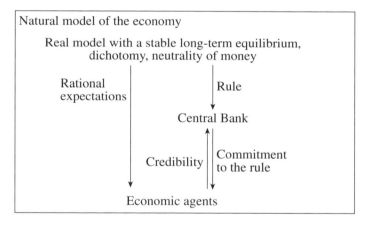

Figure 4.1   The credibility strategy in the NCE

Credibility Framework: Critical Appraisals

New historical period. According to Goodhart (1991, pp. 275–7), the macroeconomic conditions that generated a consensus around monetarism disappeared after 1982. The demand for money was increasing and unstable. The velocity of money became unpredictable. The main target of money supply could no longer be calculated. As a Bank of Canada manager remarked in 1982: 'We did not abandon M1, it was M1 that abandoned us.' This was the end of the perfect automatic transmission mechanism, via M3. New channels of transmission appearing in the literature made monetary policy more complex: a bank lending channel and a balance sheet channel were proposed. Furthermore, reaction lags of 18–24 months became a commonplace in monetary policy discussion. The implications of delays, according to central banking theory, are that monetary policy has a long-term horizon and forecasting is fundamental. Exogenous money (vertical curve) and monetary targeting should therefore be abandoned.

In the 1980s, credibility and independence first had to be built with respect to the financial market. Inflation remained the leading economic objective. Once established, a low and steady inflation would favour creditors (or 'rentiers'). The real interest rates would be higher and inflation expectations would decrease. But the long-term equilibrium was not being established. As growth was slowing and inflation falling, the imperative for employment grew. The new topic became whether the central banks should respond to shocks, that is, adopt a 'stabilization' policy. With the credibility strategy, the danger was a deflationary bias.

While the automatic monetary targeting rule disappeared, the underlying theoretical scheme of credibility faced criticism obliging it to evolve. Thus it moved from automatic rule to strategy.

Time inconsistency and the inflation bias. According to McCallum, even without any absolute commitment there is no reason to think that the Central Bank will act in a discretionary way that produces an inflation bias. McCallum (1995) believes that there is no credibility problem and there is no necessary trade-off between flexibility and commitment. Blinder (1997, p. 13) goes further and claims that time inconsistency does not exist: 'Let me begin with a non confession: during my brief career as a central banker, I never experienced this temptation. Nor do I believe my colleagues did. I firmly believe that this theoretical problem is a non problem in the real world'[2]. He shows that the credibility scheme is considered outdated in order to build credibility in practice by both central bankers and academics.

No natural model. Discrepancies between 'natural' assumptions of the economy and reality are easily identified. The case of the NAIRU does not appear to be a robust hypothesis. These strong theoretical weaknesses[3] necessitate the modification of monetary policy rule design. To follow a fixed rule could be problematic. A fixed rule, such as the Taylor rule, cannot be an ex ante rule, but only an ex post rule corresponding to the central bank convention. This rule only works under standard economic conditions. A monetary policy has to work especially when the economic situation is out of the ordinary. So this kind of rule is useless for implementing monetary policy.

Rational expectations. Another pillar of the credibility strategy was also confronted with theoretical criticisms. Even for the orthodox economists, it was established that RE was leading to multiple points of equilibrium[4]. This coordination failure requires something more than market forces alone. Stabilization policy is needed since there is no automatic long-term equilibrium.

From rule to institutional design. The credibility literature always alluded to an institutional theme, but in every case eluded it. In the credibility framework, a monetary institution is an incentive structure that tries to fill the incompleteness of the economy. As institutions are social structures, this raises the question of legitimacy. However, incentive contracts poorly mimic institutional design. Logically, time inconsistency would lead to full independence. Nevertheless, the credibility framework does not defend a free mandate for the Central Bank. Independence is usually limited, since government is the principle of the delegation. This is one of the contradictions of the credibility approach: defending the idea that the inflation bias comes from the political vulnerability of the Central Bank, while not recommending total insulation from political pressure and short-sightedness. Goodhart and Vinals (1994) insist on the political difficulty for a Central Bank to pursue preferences significantly different from the society (price stability rather than growth).

To sum up, the credibility literature appears to be an elegant way to solve the problem in the purely orthodox theory, but it is not really relevant to reality. For, in the day-to-day practice of central bankers, the time-inconsistency problem is a marginal issue. Credibility faced growing criticism in the literature. It appeared that the credibility literature had failed. By the end of the 1990s, commitment, delegation, incentive contracts, and probably most of the credibility literature, were no longer the basis of a monetary policy strategy. A New Consensus on monetary policy appeared in the 1990s.

THE 3Cs OF CONFIDENCE STRATEGY: COMMUNICATION, COMMON UNDERSTANDING AND CONFIDENCE

In the confidence strategy, the debate is not about the inflation bias of the opportunistic Central Bank. We can have confidence in central banks, they just do it right (McCallum, 1995). The real issue of today is organized around three major problematical issues, uncertainty, anticipations and democracy. They are analysed in a new programme that could briefly be presented as the 3Cs framework: communication, common understanding and confidence.

The Confidence Paradigm: New Theoretical Departures

Monetary policy under uncertainty. The confidence paradigm is founded upon the New Keynesian counterrevolution in which the 'true' model does not exist. This leads to a great shift in the nature of the economic environment in which the Central Bank operates. 'Uncertainty is not just an important feature of the monetary policy landscape, it is the defining characteristic of that landscape' (Greenspan, 2003, p. 1).

In this literature, coordination is simply natural. Monetary authorities are supposed to regulate the economy, that is, to try to coordinate agents and to exercise an influence over their expectations. If the 'natural' single long-term equilibrium is rejected, there is no longer a theoretical or natural anchor for expectations. In order to avoid coordination failures, monetary institutions have to propose a focal point (Schelling, 1960). A focal principle is one which, followed by everyone, involves the determination of a unique strategy. But, since there is no 'true' model, it could only be a procedural anchorage for expectations. To be accepted, this focal point has to undergo a social process of legitimacy[5] and 'Schelling' salience'[6]. Central banks and agents interact, forming an interactional learning process (see Figure 4.2).

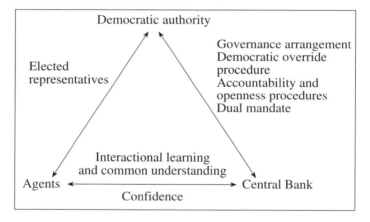

Figure 4.2   The confidence strategy in New Keynesian economics

Expectations formation process and interactional learning. Rejecting rational expectations, New Keynesians developed different conceptual tools in order to understand expectations formation: self-fulfilling prophecies, bootstraps, animal spirits, sunspots and beliefs. Most of these concepts came from the General Theory of Keynes, but only the Post Keynesians developed them before in a macroeconomic framework. By 'uncertainty', we mean a non-probabilistic or radical uncertainty, notably because it includes the expectations of private agents, who base their decision on unstable conventions. With radical uncertainty, we cannot implement optimal rules or contracts.

Because of imperfections and uncertainty, central banks and agents are in constant interaction. We leave aside rational expectations for learning and comprehension. Monetary policy is seen as a coordination process. This coordination approach to monetary policy differs from the non-cooperative conception defended by the credibility framework.

With the New Keynesians, explanation of inflation goes over from money to expectations. Money is no longer neutral. There is no natural rate of inflation. In accordance with Greenspan (1996), the confidence paradigm considers inflation is an expectation phenomenon: price stability is 'when economic agents no longer take account of the prospective change in the general price level in their economic decision-making … By price stability, however, I do not refer to a single number as measured by a particular price index' (Greenspan, 2001, p. 2).

Governance rather than independence. Full independence produced a 'democratic deficit' that was eliminated in the governance arrangement. Governance organizes the relation, not the separation between elected representatives and central banks. In a 'checks and balances' arrangement, governance balances the subservience of monetary policy to elected representatives on the one hand, and independence limited to instruments on the other. Governance counterbalances independence and accountability.

In a democracy, the Central Bank should be accountable first to elected representatives. It differs from full independence that claims to be directly responsible with the transparency to the general public, via transparency. In the credibility regime, central bankers are neither elected people nor government agents. The general public has no power over them. On the contrary, there is an effective accountability in governance. In a democracy, legitimacy is earned by the limitation of powers. Governance is the reminder that the Central Bank is a creature of Congress (Fed.), not of central bankers (ECB). It exists to serve the public, not the credibility of the Central Bank.

Communication and Monetary Policy Efficiency: Openness versus Transparency

Openness. In monetarist central banking, the Central Bank is not supposed to 'talk'. In this 'mystic' approach, central bank efficiency rests on secrecy and on 'constructive ambiguity': 'never explain, never excuse'. In the credibility approach, the 'true' model of the economy with rational expectations needs full transparency. Ambiguity has not totally disappeared in modern central banking, but openness is nowadays considered a requisite for monetary policy efficiency. However, openness is not full transparency. Reviewing the Fed literature, we can see that communication is considered a key aspect of its policy framework. It is linked to democratic and effectiveness considerations: 'openness is more than just useful in shaping better economic performance. Openness is an obligation of a central bank in a free and democratic society' (Greenspan, 2001, p. 3). More generally, central bankers admit that communication is the 'hidden pillar' of monetary policy strategy.

Openness better suits central banks' practice than transparency. Central banks cannot be fully transparent. With openness, central banks just open a window, for complete transparency could be counterproductive. The Fed shows this evolution towards more openness. Before, 'Fedspeak' corresponded to the enigmatic and esoteric art of the Fed. This mystique culture of central banking disappears in the confidence paradigm, which claims that 'explaining more, is understanding better'. Nowadays, 'Fedspeak' (Bernanke, 2004) means clear and extensive communication of the Fed's action.

Credibility. With credibility, transparency is a metaphor for the revelation of the 'truth'. Avoiding time inconsistency and building the Central Bank's reputation make it necessary to be transparent. Transparency is a substitute for accountability as soon as you claim to be directly responsible to the general public. There is no coordination problem among agents for they have common knowledge; they all know the 'right' model of the economy. In practice, transparency is rule-based, a rule that derives from the 'right model'. The 'right' action is not open to discussion.

Inflation targeting. This policy acknowledges that there is no 'true' model of the economy and that it is impossible to propose a rule-based monetary policy. The Central Bank has to explain what it is doing by giving the rationale for its policy framework and its decisions. Transparency is aimed at convincing the public that Central Bank action is the 'right' policy. Because of uncertainty, there are unforeseen contingencies that generate shifts in short-run tactics. These changes should be explained in order to keep inflation expectations anchored. Transparency passes through a communications strategy. Blinder et al. (2001, p. 2) defends the idea that 'the essential message that any central bank ought to convey to the public is its policy regime'. That is what Bernanke et al. (1999) suggest when they claim to 'educate the public' or to 'teach' the public. There is no longer common knowledge, but rather an *adaptive learning*. Behind the policy framework there is no rule but an underlying Friedman/Lucas model producing forecasts. Transparency is predictability via the publication of model-dependent forecasts.

The confidence paradigm. This believes there is no natural 'right' action. The 'right' action is open to discussion, that is why we talk about openness. Monetary policy becomes a *deliberative process* (Ferguson, 2002, p. 4), or an interactional learning[7] process between the Central Bank and the agents.

Yet communication remains a crucial issue since the Central Bank does not control inflation perfectly. Talk does matter after all. The Central Bank is not an all-powerful institution, but a statue with feet of clay. Indeed, the Central

Bank needs the support of the public to be efficient. Communication is a channel of monetary policy transmission. Communications do not reveal all information because agents do not need to know, they need to understand. Openness is meant to build a common understanding between the Central Bank and the agents.

Explanations facilitate the construction of common understanding. Communications should contain relevant information, that is be able to make the Central Bank understandable for the public. Comprehensive explanation rests on three characteristics: extensive, clear and forward-looking information.

Common Understanding

Common understanding is defined as 'how much the strategy is interpreted and understood in the same way by the central bank and the public' (Winkler, 2002, p. 413). In this respect, common understanding differs radically from common knowledge of the credibility strategy. This last conceptual tool suggests awareness: public statements of Central Bank action automatically lead to coordination and a unique equilibrium. Indeed, they realize the same inference since they all have the same 'true' model in their mind, and rational expectations.

In common understanding, the common inference of Central Bank action comes from understanding (interpretation), not from knowledge (induction). Common understanding highlights that announcement relevance and agents' interpretation should not be neglected in monetary policy. Common understanding is a mutual comprehension of the economic environment. The Central Bank needs to convince the public of the relevancy of its decision from democratic and economic points of view.

A Central Bank practising openness in a democratic society could be called a communicational[8] Central Bank, that is to say one that tries to build a consensus of the public on its monetary policy decisions. The common understanding creates the confidence link between the Central Bank and the agents.

The Confidence Strategy

The confidence link: a characterization

Confidence is different from reputation for it is not a question of anticipation (game), but a question of comprehension (communication). That is why prisoners cannot talk in the prisoner dilemma in game theory approach. On the contrary, central banks 'talk'. Rather than a zero-one variable (credibility), or an asset (reputation), confidence could be considered as a continuous though changing link between the Central Bank and agents. We speak about 'confidence' 'when the convention and the strategy of the central bank are in accordance with those of the other participants (actors in financial markets, political power, firms ...). Therefore, it is possible to have credibility without confidence and confidence may be limited' (Le Heron, 2003, p. 14).

When viewed as a link between the Central Bank and the public, confidence can offer different states, a mix of verticality (social norm) and horizontality (endogenous). The conceptual tool of focal point summarizes such a configuration.

Vertical confidence raises the question of monetary sovereignty and Central Bank legitimacy leads to the question of governance. The Central Bank's statutes, mandate and actions should be consistent with the principles, procedures and performances of democracy. The key point is that the Central Bank needs legitimacy to propose a focal point. It actually produces a common standard (norm) for coordination. This leads to the conclusion that governance is a more complete concept than independence to interpret the confidence strategy. In the credibility framework, independence is aimed at ensuring a formal commitment to a technical rule. Governance relies on a democratic commitment to the dual democratic mandate.

In an uncertain economic environment the key problem is that agents and their expectations are heterogeneous. Specifically, it leads to a special emphasis on the belief-formation process and beyond on the coordination-formation process. Coordination can also be produced by focalization (endogenous), creating an autonomous collective belief (self-fulfilling prophecies). In this case the confidence strategy is horizontal. For example, the Central Bank must sometimes follow the market convention. During a crisis, a new convention forces itself upon the central bank.

> There are also times when markets become particularly nervous and volatile because of economic shocks or concerns about policies, and central bank actions have to be directed to coping with disorderliness in markets ... In such circumstances, the Bank's immediate task was to calm markets by helping them to find new trading ranges with which they were comfortable. (Thiessen, Governor of the Bank of Canada, 1995, p. 9)

For the financial markets opinion, it is rather a question of convention than a question of legitimacy. In this complex interaction between the Central Bank and markets, it is sometimes difficult to know who decides.

> Together these two types of signals create a kind of biofeedback or grading system in which the markets first recommend or predict what the central banker should or will do, and then reward them for doing it. While I never show a single case of central bankers succumbing to the temptation that so worried Kydland and Prescott, I often witnessed central bankers sorely tempted to deliver the policy that markets expected or demanded. (Blinder, 1997, p. 15)

Investigating this theoretical field, some authors describe beliefs coordination as 'a signal-extraction problem' (Andolfatto and Gomme, 2003, p. 4). A good illustration of these findings could be the famous signals of Greenspan to markets. In uncertainty, we can figure out expectation formation in terms of beliefs inference.

The confidence approach to accountability: effective democratic accountability

Confidence introduces a political revival in central banking. It represents a breakdown of the consensus on independence in the 1980s that leads to the fascinating independence of the ECB. There is no trade-off between independence and accountability. If inflation targeting does not draw implications from this re-examination of independence, the confidence strategy starts from the evidence that the Central Bank is embedded in a larger democratic system. It pursues the idea that accountability is a quid pro quo for independence. Independence is balanced by democratic accountability; we talk about 'governance'. The confidence scheme is GOA: Governance–Accountability–Openness.

Accountability is not a purely technical question, but a democratic issue. It is connected to openness because accountability means that the Central Bank is accountable for its actions to democratic authorities, and has to take into account its democratic mandate in its day-to-day functions. The Humphrey–Hawkins procedure of the Fed. is a good example of this confidence conception of accountability. As Greenspan (2001, p. 1) emphasizes, central bankers 'are accountable both to the Congress from which we derive our monetary policy mission and, beyond, to the American people'. Ultimately, accountability highlights that there is no clear evidence on the benefits of total independence. It is a tough question for members of the Fed., as Meyer (2000, p. 4) says: 'there is no consistent evidence of a relationship between central bank independence and real economic activity nor consistent evidence that central bank independence lowers the cost of reducing inflation or increases the effectiveness of stabilisation policy'.

A Central Bank is actually an independent institution with unelected officials. Central banks earn legitimacy not by the ballot box, but by procedures of accountability. As Ferguson (2002, p. 2) points out: 'Such democratic accountability is even more important for central bankers, because the voting populace does not directly elect them'. Democratic accountability reveals a mutual dependency between agents and central banks (the confidence link).

The economic and democratic cases for a dual democratic mandate

In an ever-changing economy, risks can be either of deflation, of inflation or of the lack of growth. With uncertainty, the Central Bank has to face multiple risks. The central banks have to identify and regulate firstly the most imminent risks: that is, the balance of risks. The question is not 'why and how price stability?', but 'why only price stability?' The democratic mandate of the Central Bank should be multiple goals; and in practice the bank should publish a monetary policy report, not just an inflation report (Meyer, 2003, p. 1). A monetary policy report makes clear the multiple goals and the current balance of risks.

In addition to the reduction of the asymmetry of goals, a dual mandate would also facilitate the coordination of fiscal and monetary policies by reducing the coordination failures. A dual mandate signifies the reduction of monetary policy predominance over fiscal policy; that is, the predominance of the price stability objective over the economic stabilization objective. The confidence strategy imposes the combination of monetary policy with other policies, that is, a policy mix.

INFLATION TARGETING: FROM CREDIBILITY TO CONFIDENCE

More than 20 central banks adopted inflation targeting after 1990, so this system constitutes the mainstream within the New Consensus. But three of the major central banks in the world have not adopted IT: the Fed, the ECB and the Bank of Japan. This illustrates that IT is not the 'one best way' to achieve desired macroeconomic performance. Nevertheless Bernanke et al. (1999, p. 6) advocate that 'inflation targeting has had important benefits for the countries that have used it'. As far as the works of Ball and Sheridan (2003) show, those countries having adopted IT did not obtain better results than the others did. In the credibility versus confidence debate, IT holds an ambiguous place. IT is often the end of a credibility strategy: the target replacing the rule. But, sometimes, IT is the beginning of a confidence strategy: the target as a focal point in a 'communication' policy.

Why should Inflation Targeting not be a Credibility Strategy?

IT is largely embedded in the New Keynesian theoretical approach, that is, in the New Consensus Macroeconomics (Arestis and Sawyer, 2003; Le Heron, 2003). However, the synthesis Friedman–Lucas model remains the theoretical background of IT: long-term neutrality of money, Nairu and so on. While IT should be new bankers (confidence) in old clothes (independence), it is more often old bankers (credibility) in new clothes (inflation targeting).

Inflation matters. Dichotomy between real and monetary facts is not assumed, so *inflation matters*. Money is endogenous.[9] Agents are hierarchical and heterogeneous. The cause of inflation is no longer excess money but the expectations of inflation. These expectations of inflation are linked to a 'steady growth of nominal GDP in excess of the growth of natural or potential real output' (Gordon, 1997). Nominal anchorage tends to be the main issue. The short-term non-neutrality of money, the indeterminacy of expectations and the uncertainty in the economy force the Central Bank to regulate the economy, that is, to anchor expectations.

Procedural price stability. The Central Bank has to make price stability a convention. The monetary policy must not appear arbitrary. Inflation is less an exogenous than an endogenous variable (Bernanke and Mishkin, 1997, p. 109). With IT, the announced target is presented as the definition of price stability. That is why this announced target 'provides a nominal anchorage for policy and the economy'. However, there is no evidence of the existence of a 'natural' definition of price stability. This indeterminacy finds a democratic solution. The inflation target is usually defined by a negotiation process between the Central Bank and the government which is embedded in an institutional process.[10] Part of the indeterminacy is also taken into account by revision procedures for the inflation target, range target or medium-term horizon. We should note that IT supposes instrument independence, not goal independence.

From monetary targeting to inflation targeting. In monetary targeting, inflation is indirectly controlled via an intermediate target of monetary aggregate (M3), which is the main instrument. In IT, the Central Bank targets inflation directly, and the short-term interest rate is the main instrument. Inflation forecasts could be regarded as intermediate targets. Expectations are the key channel of transmission from the official short-term interest rate to the long-term market rate (Biefang-Frisancho Mariscal and Howells, 2002). But the main goal remains price stability.

A hierarchical mandate. Monetary targeting focuses only on monetary elements. When IT responds to shocks, it takes care of growth. There is no longer a unique mandate for price stability, but a hierarchical mandate with price stability taking primacy over growth. Growth is measured by the output gap. This approach is purely orthodox with a Nairu formula. Price stability is considered the best contribution to economic growth. Only 'flexible-IT' (Svensson, 1999) is in practice an 'implicit dual mandate' (Meyer, 2003, p. 4).

Uncertainty. This is a key element of IT, contrary to the credibility strategy. There is no common knowledge, but an 'adaptive learning in imperfect knowledge' (Orphanides and Williams, 2003, p. 1). Contrary to monetary targeting, IT is supposed to take shocks into account. Even when switching to discretion, the credibility versus flexibility dilemma generated by the rule remains. Furthermore, it signifies we are no longer searching for the solution to the inflation bias, but rather for the solution to the restriction of output bias. IT has no inflation bias incentive because of the commitment to the inflation target that constitutes a credible constraint. Moreover, discretion calls for a temporal shift: with IT, the monetary policy horizon moves from the short-run (rule) to the medium–long run.

A 'policy framework, not a rule' (Bernanke, 2003, p. 6). The end of the strict rule is a major break with the credibility framework. Differing from a short-term rule, the inflation target has to be achieved in the medium term. Thus, for regulation needs, the inflation target should be above zero per cent.[11] For the New Keynesians, there are numerous reasons: the possible existence of a long-term Phillips curve, nominal rigidities, the Boskin effect, the risk of a liquidity trap and the danger of deflationary adjustments. There is no theoretical basis either to defend a rule or to define price stability. The ultimate objective is to anchor expectations of inflation. The inflation target is both the objective and the instrument to anchor expectations. The target can be rule-like (credibility) or a focal point in a communications strategy (confidence). IT does not need a theoretical model to establish a rule because a policy framework with an inflation target can obtain the result directly.

Constrained discretion. Short-run flexibility, but medium-run discipline (required by the unpredictable states of the economy), is summarized by Bernanke[12] as 'constrained discretion'. It suggests that the dichotomy between rules and discretion is an outdated question. 'By imposing a conceptual structure, and its inherent discipline on the central bank, but without eliminating all flexibility, inflation targeting combines some of the advantages traditionally ascribed to rules with those ascribed to discretion' (Bernanke et al., 1999, p. 6). IT labelled 'constrained discretion' means we are first in discretion.

IT rests upon two pillars: a policy framework and a communications strategy (Bernanke, 2003). The target is only a part of the strategy; it is embedded in a more general policy framework that is composed of accountability and transparency procedures.

Why is Inflation Targeting only a 'Soft Confidence' Strategy?

The new consensus in monetary policy is still influenced by the credibility strategy (hysteresis phenomenon). This is one of the reasons why IT is only one step inside the confidence paradigm. We call it a 'soft confidence' strategy.

Inflation targeting: some critical appraisals

IT is less flexible than the dual mandate to respond to unforeseen shocks and to seek full employment. Special emphasis is put on the rigidity problems generated by the analytical credibility–IT scheme: the price stability quantification–announcement–commitment–enforcement. Firstly, it requires an exact quantification of price stability, which is impossible. Secondly, an explicit target is presented as a solution to the complex question of anchoring expectations. But IT represents a will to convince expectations rather than to anchor expectations. Inflation forecasts are the cornerstone of the decision-making process. This is a misconception of monetary policy since inflation forecasts are only one indicator among others. Expectations on income distribution are more significant and good inflation forecasts are very difficult in conditions of uncertainty due to unpredictable shocks. Thirdly, as price stability is the overriding goal, IT does not allow enough flexibility to pursue both price stability and economic stabilization.

There is a democratic dilemma. For the long-run price stability mandate, IT asserts it is necessary to insulate the Central Bank from the democratic authority. But the Central Bank is goal-dependent, democratically accountable, and economic agents are more interested in steady growth and full employment. IT defenders advocate a democratic mandate on price stability to solve this dilemma. It suggests price stability is the best goal in order to achieve growth. This hierarchical mandate for price stability to maximize growth is a fallacy for four reasons:

1. Practical reason: inflation target offers no practical guidance for the central bank. It does not indicate how to achieve this mission in practice.
2. Theoretical reason: there is no consensus on the numerical definition of price stability. You need long-term neutrality of money to justify this hierarchical mandate (Nairu, output gap).
3. Policy reason: in an uncertain environment, price stability is not automatically the right objective to pursue to stabilize the economy. Moreover, you cannot achieve price stability without focusing on growth.
4. Political reason: in an ever-changing economy and because of the heterogeneity of agents, public preferences shift regularly. So there is no reason to fix preferences on price stability definitely, which leads to an anti-democratic arrangement. Indeed, in a democratic society, Central Bank preferences cannot long differ from those of the public, because the bank is inefficient without public support.

This looks very much like the 'weight conservative central banker' as described by Rogoff. This primacy of price stability is possible as soon as there is no trade-off between growth and inflation; that is, no Phillips curve. In this new macroeconomic consensus, price stability is judged the best contribution to growth. Fiscal policy is considered ineffective.

IT develops an unclear theory of transparency IT promotes both ambiguity and transparency for central banking practice. IT is in contradiction because its theoretical definition of the 'right' action is targeting only inflation, while in practice its action focuses also on growth. In IT, transparency is identified as 'say what you do, but don't do what you say'.

IT gives too much priority to communication IT follows the folk wisdom of central banking: 'do what they do, but only talk about inflation' (Faust and Henderson, 2003, p. 23). Openness is not a goal per se. It is aimed at enhancing action. Communication cannot be a substitute for action. To sum up, 'actions speak louder than words, but actions and words likely speak louder than actions alone' (Thornton, 2002, pp. 11–12).

Inflation targeting is a targeting rule. Because the credibility issue (surprise inflation) is still discussed in IT, the commitment solution is the 'institutional commitment to price stability'. The latter makes it possible to monitor the Central Bank. The target could be viewed as a solution to the time-inconsistency problem by reducing political pressure and creating an appropriate incentive structure, a technology of commitment to price stability, a nominal anchor for expectations and a benchmark for Central Bank performance measurement. IT is then in the credibility framework.

'*There is no evidence that inflation targeting improves performance*' (Ball and Sheridan, 2003). Kohn (2003, p. 16) is more provocative: 'gains from putting numbers on "price stability" are likely to be limited'.

From credibility to 'soft confidence': diversity of IT

Leaving the rule and the predominance of the strict commitment to the target, there is room for the economic stabilization objective, that is, for a dual mandate (Table 4.1). According to Greenspan, we can distinguish two periods of inflation targeting. IT includes a growth objective in the recent period. That is to say it evolves toward the confidence paradigm:

> The emergence of inflation targeting in recent years is an interesting development in this regard. As practised, it emphasises forecasts, but within a more rule-like structure that skews monetary policy toward inflation containment as the primary goal. ... Inflation targeting often originated as a fairly simple structure concentrating solely on inflation outcomes, but it has evolved into more discretionary forms requiring complex judgements for implementation. Indeed, this evolution has gone so far that the actual practice of monetary policy by inflation-targeting central banks now closely resembles the practice of those central banks, such as the European Central Bank, the Bank of Japan, and the Federal Reserve, that have not chosen to adopt that paradigm. (Greenspan, 2004, p. 8)

Meyer (2001, p. 5) is more direct: 'Such an evolution has brought many inflation targeting regimes closer in practice to a dual mandate regime.' IT represents a breakdown in the monetary policy regime, but also in terms of a theoretical background for monetary policy. By adopting this New Consensus, we abandon the credibility framework to embrace a 'soft confidence' paradigm.

To understand the last 25 years of monetary policy, credibility versus confidence is a better opposition than the outdated perspective rules versus discretion (Table 4.2). Five oppositions between the credibility and the confidence strategies were revealing: credibility versus confidence, independence versus governance, responsibility versus accountability, common knowledge versus common understanding, transparency versus openness.

Table 4.1 *Inflation targeting, from credibility to 'soft confidence'*

Evolutions of inflation targeting	Incentive structures	Enforcement mechanism	Democratic mandate	Theoretical foundations	Limits to IT
Inflation targeting rule credibility	Rule	Pre-commitment or commitment to the rule	Unique mandate	Rule *vs.* discretion Inflation bias Reputation	Credibility *vs.* flexibility Uncertainty Multiple rules
Strict IT Credibility	Rule-like Instrument independence Contract	Commitment to price stability	Unique mandate	Conservatism and delegation Contract Nairu	Credibility *vs.* flexibility Uncertainty Credibility *vs.* legitimacy (democratic accountability)
Flexible IT 'soft confidence'	Policy framework and communication strategy	An inflation-control target aims at the *expected inflation* Target range Accountability for achieving the target	Hierarchical mandate (some weight on stabilizing the output gap)	Uncertainty Unforeseen contingencies Constrained discretion Anchoring expectations Core inflation Nairu	Credibility dilemma Control of inflation in a stochastic environment Commitment *vs.* credibility Reaction lags Definition of price stability
Forecasting IT 'soft confidence'	Institutional and constitutional arrangements Accountability and openness Override procedures	Institutional commitment to price stability Commitment to the inflation target at a specified horizon	Implicit dual mandate	Uncertainty Anchoring expectations Short-term deviations (tactic) but long-term achievement of the target (strategy) Core inflation	Transmission channels of monetary policy Credibility of Central Bank forecasts Inflation expectations formation process Quantification of price stability Forecasting *vs.* volatility Credibility *vs.* confidence

Table 4.2 Credibility strategy versus confidence strategy

Credibility strategy	Confidence strategy	
	'Soft confidence': inflation targeting	'Hard confidence'
Foundation	*Foundation*	*Foundation*
1) 'True', natural model of the economy: long-term equilibrium	1) Indeterminacy, imperfect knowledge of the 'true' model of the economy	1) No 'true' model of the economy
2) Probabilistic uncertainty	2) Non-probabilistic uncertainty	2) Radical uncertainty
3) Asymmetric and private information	3) Imperfect, incomplete information	3) Imperfect, incomplete information
4) Monetary policy is a technical issue	4) Monetary policy is both a technical and a democratic question	4) Central banks are embedded in a democratic society
5) All-powerful Central Bank	5) Central Bank is a statue with feet of clay	5) CB is a statue with feet of clay
6) Expectations anchorage	6) Expectations management	6) Acceptance (or not)
Analysis	*Analysis*	*Analysis*
1) Friedman/Lucas doctrine	1) Friedman/Lucas doctrine	1) No underlying doctrine
2) Exogenous money theory	2) Endogenous money theory	2) Endogenous money theory
3) Neutrality of money, dichotomy	3) Neutrality of money at long run	3) Non-neutrality of money
4) Quantitative theory of money	4) Expectations theory of the term structure.	4) Expectations theory of the term structure
5) Game theory	5) Game theory	5) Deliberative process; language, interpretation abilities
6) Fooling game	6) Coordination game	6) Confidence game
7) Rational expectations	7) Expectations inference process	7) Self-fulfilling expectations
8) Rational expectations	8) Adaptive learning process	8) Interactional learning process
9) Time-inconsistency, inflation bias, surprise inflation	9) Time inconsistency	9) Deflation bias
10) Unique equilibrium	10) Multiple equilibria, indeterminacy	10) Learning
11) Natural price stability	11) Procedural price stability	11) Procedural and expectational price stability

Policy

1) Unique mandate
2) Full independence
3) Technical approach
4) Monetary targeting
5) Transparency
6) Rule, target as a rule
7) Commitment, binding agreement
8) Rule-based anchorage, reputation
9) Common knowledge
10) Common knowledge ('true' model)
11) Automatic monetary transmission mechanism
12) No responsibility

Theories

1) Monetarism
2) New Classical Economics with rational expectations

Policy

1) Unique or hierarchical mandate
2) Instrument independence
3) Framework and strategic approach
4) Inflation targeting
5) Politically optimal level of ambiguity, limited transparency
6) Targeting rule, target as a framework
7) Commitment, contract, policy frame
8) Communications (target) and policy framework anchorage
9) Imperfect knowledge
10) Signal
11) Expectations and communication channels of transmission
12) Operational responsibility

Theories

1) New Classical Economics
2) New Keynesian Economics

Policy

1) Dual mandate
2) Governance
3) Democratic and strategic approach
4) Balance of risks
5) Openness
6) No quantified targets
7) Institutional democratic framework
8) Action, institutions and communication anchorage
9) Common understanding
10) Signal extraction problem; focal point, salience
11) Multiple channels of transmission
12) Democratic accountability

Theories

1) New Keynesian Economics

The mainstream is the credibility literature, which goes from Kydland and Prescott to Woodford. This literature is based on the synthesis between monetarism and the NCE, in which a 'true' model of the economy exists: stable long-run equilibrium, dichotomy, neutrality of money. With rational expectations, everybody knows this true model; it is common knowledge. The model imposes a rule on the Central Bank, which takes a commitment to respect it and credibility follows at once. As the true model is common knowledge, complete transparency is possible and required for credibility. To avoid the inflation bias of governmental policies, the independence of the Central Bank becomes obviously imperative. As money is neutral in the long run, there is no problem of democracy. The monetary policy is only a technical problem, of respect for the rule. A Central Bank assumes responsibility only for the respect for the true economic model. Monetary targeting and the Taylor rule are part of the credibility literature.

In the 1990s, a new consensus appeared, notably with inflation targeting. IT suffers from the hysteresis effect. IT often comes at the end of a credibility strategy, the target replacing the rule and then credibility implies only honesty. But sometimes it is the beginning of the confidence strategy: the target as a focal point, that is, part of a communication strategy. Even though more than 20 countries chose different kinds of IT (New Zealand, Canada, GB), the ECB stays with a credibility strategy and the Fed. prefers a confidence strategy.

In a confidence strategy, the debate is not the inflation bias of the opportunistic Central Bank. We can be confident in central banks, they just 'do it right'. A confidence strategy highlights the importance of uncertainty, expectations and democracy in monetary policy. With uncertainty and with the New Keynesian framework, there is no rule since there is no underlying 'true' model of the economy. The 'right' monetary policy decision is open to discussion and needs a common understanding. A rule-based transparency is infeasible so we talk about 'openness'. This acknowledges that the Central Bank is not an all-powerful institution controlling inflation perfectly, but a statue with feet of clay that needs the confidence of the general public in order to anchor expectations. A Central Bank is not the sole pilot of a money-dropping helicopter, but rather the Keynes conductor of an orchestra (Dalziel, 1998, p. 212). Inflation is no longer a monetary phenomenon but an expectation phenomenon.

The confidence strategy puts a special emphasis on democracy. Independence is limited and has to be balanced by democratic accountability to elected representatives. So we prefer governance to independence. This means the revival of politics in central banking. It just reminds us that the Central Bank is a creature of the democratic authorities, and not a creature of central bankers. The bank must respect its mandate and this mandate must respect the general public's ideas. The Central Bank is embedded in a democratic order. It has the obligation to regulate the economy, which requires flexibility. Keynes (1924, p. 88) makes the point striking when he declares: 'Economists set themselves too easy, too useless a task if in tempestuous seasons they can only tell us that when the storm is long past the ocean is flat again.'

NOTES

1. Following Forder (2000, p. 2), we consider that time inconsistency is prior to and separate from the credibility framework. But the credibility framework emerges by shedding light on the lack of credibility of the solution to time inconsistency proposed by Kydland and Prescott.
2. In accordance with Blinder, Meyer (2000, p. 3), says: 'I have never found the literature on time inconsistency particularly relevant to central banks.'
3. Meyer, Swanson and Wieland (2001, p. 226).
4. On this particular subject, we can read Orléan (2002, pp. 722–6), Bryant (1983). As regards reputation literature, recent researches draw attention to the theoretical and practical weaknesses of this mechanism in monetary policy. In particular, Persson and Tabellini (1999, pp. 1412–15) consider 'as in the theory of repeated games, there is a multiple-equilibrium problem, which strikes with particular force against a positive model of monetary policy'.
5. According to Orléan (1996, p. 25), 'A social institution is legitimated when normative principles which appear in the construction of community representation benefit from a unanimous consensus.'
6. Schelling (1960). Referring to Mehta et al. (1994), Orléan (2002, p. 729), defines a 'Schelling' salience' as 'la possibilité de deferminer un équilibre particulier, dominant, capable de degager une large majorité'.
7. For the evolution from indeterminacy to learning, see McCallum (2003, p. 30): 'learnability, not indeterminacy, should be viewed as the relevant issue for policy-oriented theoretical analysis of monetary policy'. For learning literature, see Evans and Honkapojha (1999, 2001).
8. This is related to the communicational theory of Habermas (1987).
9. This point of view is defended in Taylor (1999, p. 661), Svensson (1999, p. 611), Aglietta (2003, p. 7), Fontana and Palacio-Vera (2002, pp. 548, 557, 564) or Dalziel (2002, p. 522).
10. A good example is the PTA (Policy Target Agreement), organized by the Reserve Bank of New Zealand reform in 1989.
11. Developing this thesis, see Akerlof, Dickens and Perry (1996), Bernanke and Mishkin (1997, p. 110), Mishkin (1999, p. 592), Aglietta and Orléan (2002, p. 234), Gali (2002, p. 5).
12. Bernanke (2003, p. 2): 'Constrained discretion attempts to strike a balance between the inflexibility of strict policy rules and the potential lack of discipline and structure inherent in unfitted policymaker decision'. The term 'discretion optimization', proposed by Svensson and Woodford (2003, p. 2), could alternatively be used to describe IT.

REFERENCES

Aglietta, M. (2003), 'Inflation targeting and financial stability', paper presented at the workshop, 'Globalisation and Diversity of Capitalism: New Concepts for a Post-Liberal Era', LSE, London, June.

Aglietta, M. and A. Orléan (2002), *La Monnaie entre violence et confiance*, Paris: Odile Jacob.

Akerlof, G., W. Dickens and G. Perry (1996), 'The macroeconomics of low inflation', *Brookings Papers on Economic Activity*, **1**, 1–76.

Akerlof, G., W. Dickens and G. Perry (2000), 'Near-rational wage and price setting and the long-run Phillips curve', *Brookings Papers on Economic Activity*, **1**, 1–59.

Andolfatto, D. and P. Gomme (2003), 'Monetary policy regime and beliefs', *International Economic Review*, **44**(1), 1–30.

Arestis, P. and M. Sawyer (2003), 'Inflation targeting: a critical appraisal', The Levy Economics Institute working papers series, no. 388.

Backus, D. and J. Drifill (1985), 'Inflation and reputation', *American Economic Review*, **75**(3), 530–38.

Ball, L. and N. Sheridan (2003), 'Does inflation targeting matter?', NBER working papers series no. 9577, March.

Barro, R. and D. Gordon (1983a), 'Rules, discretion and reputation in a model of monetary policy', *Journal of Monetary Economics*, **12**(1), 101–21.

Barro, R. and D. Gordon (1983b), 'A positive theory of monetary policy in a natural rate model', *Journal of Political Economy*, **91**(4), 589–610.

Bernanke, B. (2003), 'Constrained discretion and monetary policy', remarks by Governor Bernanke before the money marketers of New York University, 3 February.

Bernanke, B. (2004), 'Fedspeak', remarks by Governor Bernanke at the meetings of the American Economic Association, San Diego, 3 January.

Bernanke, B. and F. Mishkin (1997), 'Inflation targeting: a new framework for monetary policy', *Journal of Economic Perspectives*, **11**(2), 97–116.

Bernanke, B., T. Laubach, F. Mishkin and A. Posen (1999), *Inflation Targeting: Lessons from the International Experience*, Princeton, NJ: Princeton University Press.

Biefang-Frisancho Mariscal, I. and P. Howells (2002), 'Central banks and market interest rates', *Journal of Post Keynesian Economics*, **24**(4), 569–85.

Blinder, A. (1997), 'What central bankers could learn from academics and vice versa', *Journal of Economic Perspectives*, **11**(2), 3–19.

Blinder, A. (2000), 'Central bank credibility: why do we care? How do we build it?', *American Economic Review*, **90**(5), 1421–31.

Blinder, A., C. Goodhart, P. Hildebrandt, D. Lipton and C. Wyplosz (2001), 'How do central banks talk?', Geneva Reports on the World Economy no. 3, CEPR.

Bryant, J. (1983), 'A simple rational-expectations Keynes-type model', *Quarterly Journal of Economics*, **98**, 525–8.

Dalziel, P. (1998), 'New Zealand experience with an independent central bank since 1989', in P. Arestis and M. Sawyer (eds), *The Political Economy of Central Banking*, Cheltenham, UK and Lyme, USA: Edward Elgar, pp. 199–216.

Dalziel, P. (2002), 'The triumph of Keynes: what now for monetary policy research?', *Journal of Post Keynesian Economics*, **24**(4), 511–27.

Evans, G. and S. Honkapohja (1999), 'Learning dynamics', in J. Taylor and M. Woodford (eds), *Handbook of Macroeconomics*, vol. 1A, Amsterdam: North-Holland, pp. 449–542.

Evans, G. and S. Honkapohja (2001), *Learning and Expectations in Macroeconomics*, Princeton, NJ: Princeton University Press.

Faust, J. and D. Henderson (2003), 'Is inflation targeting best-practised monetary policy?', paper prepared for the Federal Reserve Bank of Saint Louis 28th annual economic policy conference, 'Inflation Targeting: Prospects and Problems', 15 January.

Ferguson, R. (2002), 'Why central banks should talk', remarks by Federal Reserve Board Vice Chairman R. Ferguson, 8 January.

Fontana, G. and A. Palacio-Vera (2002), 'Monetary policy rules: what are we learning?', *Journal of Post Keynesian Economics*, **24**(4), 547–68.

Forder, J. (2000), 'Could reputation-bias be a bigger problem than inflation-bias?', Oxford University discussion paper series no. 22.

Gali, J. (2002), 'Monetary policy in the early years of EMU', Universitat Pompeu Fabra, mimeo, March.

Goodhart, C. (1991), 'The conduct of monetary policy', in C.J. Green and D.T. Llewellyn (eds), *Surveys in Monetary Economics*, Oxford: Blackwell, pp. 263–323.

Goodhart, C. and J. Vinals (1994), 'Strategy and tactics of monetary policy: example from Europe and the antipodes', in J.C. Fuhrer (ed.), *Goals, Guidelines and Constraints facing Monetary Policymakers*, Federal Reserve Bank of Boston Conference Series, no. 38.

Gordon, R.J. (1997), 'The time-varying NAIRU and its implications for economic policy', *Journal of Economic Perspectives*, **11**(1), 11–32.

Greenspan, A. (1996), 'Opening remarks', in *Achieving Price Stability*, Jackson Hole conference, Federal Reserve Bank of Kansas City, pp. 1–5.

Greenspan, A. (2001), 'Transparency in monetary policy', remarks by Federal Reserve Board Chairman A. Greenspan, 11 October.

Greenspan, A. (2003), 'Monetary policy under uncertainty', remarks by Federal Reserve Board Chairman A. Greenspan at a symposium sponsored by the Federal Reserve Bank of Kansas City, 29 August.

Greenspan, A. (2004), 'Risk and uncertainty in monetary policy', remarks by Federal Reserve Board Chairman A. Greenspan at the meetings of the American Economic Association, San Diego, 3 January.

Habermas, J. (1987), *Théorie de l'Agir Communicationnel*, vol. 2, Paris: Fayard.

Hibbs, D. (1977), 'Political parties and macroeconomic policy', *American Political Science Review*, 71.

Keynes, J.M. (1924), *A Tract on Monetary Reform*, London: Macmillan.

Kohn, D. (2003), 'Comments on M. Goodfriend's inflation targeting in the United States?', remarks by Federal Reserve Board Governor D. Kohn, 25 January.

Kohn, D. and P. Sack (2003), 'Central bank talk: does it matter and why?', Board of Governors of the Federal Reserve System, 23 May.

Kydland, F. and E. Prescott (1977), 'Rules rather than discretion: the inconsistency of optimal plan', *Journal of Political Economy*, **85**(3), 473–92.

Le Heron, E. (2003), 'A new consensus on monetary policy?', *Brazilian Journal of Political Economy*, **23**(4), 3–27.

Lohmann, S. (1992), 'Optimal commitment in monetary policy: credibility versus flexibility', *American Economic Review*, **82**(1), 286–99.

McCallum, B.T. (1995), 'Two fallacies concerning central bank independence', *American Economic Review*, **85**(2), 207–11.

McCallum, B.T. (2003), 'Multiple solutions indeterminacies in monetary policy analysis', mimeo, 3 March.

Mehta, J., C. Starmer and R. Sugden (1994), 'The nature of salience: an experimental investigation of pure co-ordination games', *American Economic Review*, **84**(2), 658–73.

Meyer, L. (2000), 'The politics of monetary policy: balancing independence and accountability', remarks by Federal Reserve Board Governor L. Meyer, 24 October.

Meyer, L. (2001), 'Inflation targets and inflation targeting', remarks by Federal Reserve Board Governor L. Meyer, 17 July.

Meyer, L. (2003), 'Practical problems and obstacles to inflation targeting', paper presented at the Federal Reserve Bank of Saint Louis 28th annual economic policy conference, 'Inflation Targeting: Prospects and Problems', 16–17 October.

Meyer, L., E. Swanson and W. Wieland (2001), 'NAIRU uncertainty and non-linear policy rules', *American Economic Review*, **91**(2), 226–31.

Mishkin, F. (1999), 'International experiences with different monetary policy regimes', *Journal of Monetary Economics*, **43**(1), 579–605.

Nordhaus, W. (1975), 'The political business cycle', *Review of Economic Studies*, **42**(1), 169–90.

Orléan, A. (1996), 'Réflexions sur la notion de légitimité monétaire, l'apport de G. Simmel', in J.M. Baldner and L. Gillard (eds), *Simmel et les Normes Sociales*, Collection Logiques Sociales, Paris: L'Harmattan, pp. 19–34.

Orléan, A. (2002), 'Le tournant cognitif en économie', *Revue d'Economie Politique*, **112**(5), 717–38.

Orphanides, A. and J.C. Williams (2003), 'Imperfect knowledge, inflation expectations, and monetary policy', paper presented at NBER's conference on 'Inflation Targeting', 23–5 January.

Persson, T. and G. Tabellini (1993), 'Designing institutions for monetary stability', *Carnegie Rochester Conference Series on Public Policy*, **39**, 53–84.

Persson, T. and G. Tabellini (1999), 'Political economics and macroeconomic policy', in J. Taylor and M. Woodford (eds), *Handbook of Macroeconomics*, vol. 1C, Amsterdam: North-Holland, pp. 1397–482.

Rogoff, K. (1985), 'The optimal degree of commitment to an intermediate monetary target', *The Quarterly Journal of Economics*, **100**(4), 1169–90.

Schelling, T. (1960), *The Strategy of Conflict*, Oxford: Oxford University Press.

Svensson, L.E.O. (1997), 'Optimal inflation targets, conservative central banks and linear inflation contracts', *American Economic Review*, **87**(1), 98–114.

Svensson, L.E.O. (1999), 'Inflation targeting as a monetary policy rule', *Journal of Monetary Economics*, **43**(3), 607–54.

Svensson, L.E.O. and M. Woodford (2003), 'Implementing optimal policy through inflation-forecast targeting', paper presented at NBER's conference on 'Inflation Targeting', 23–5 January.

Taylor, J.B. (1999), 'The robustness and efficiency of monetary policy rules as guidelines for interest setting by the European Central Bank', *Journal of Monetary Economics*, **43**(3), 655–79.

Thiessen, G. (1995), 'Uncertainty and the transmission of monetary policy in Canada', The Hermes-Glendon Lecture, delivered at York University, Glendon College, Toronto, March.

Thornton, D. (2002), 'Monetary policy transparency: transparent about what?', paper prepared for the conference 'Monetary Policy Transparency' held at the Bank of England, 10 May.

Walsh, C. (1995), 'Optimal contracts for central bankers', *American Economic Review*, **85**(1), 150–67.

Winkler, B. (2002), 'Which kind of transparency? On the need for effective communication in monetary policy-making', *Ifo Studien*, **48**(3), 401–28.

Woodford, M. (2003), *Interest and Prices: Foundations of a Theory of Monetary Policy*, Princeton, NJ: Princeton University Press.

5. Understanding the link among uncertainty, instability and institutions, and the need for stabilization policies: towards a synthesis between Post Keynesian and Institutional Economics

Slim Thabet[1]

INTRODUCTION

'Institutions do matter', 'the determinants of institutions are susceptible to analysis by the tools of economic theory':[2] such phrases frequently recur in economic literature over the last few decades and many international meetings in our discipline have a session on this topic. Recent crises in banking sectors and in financial markets have led economists to pay more attention to the role played by the institutions in the stabilization of the economic system. As one can see, the consideration of institutions is at the heart of many works. Even mainstream economics seems to rediscover notions and concepts such as institutions, conventions, beliefs, rules, coordination and cooperation as well as trust. The birth, in the 1970s, of a New Institutional School that was awarded two Nobel Prizes (in 1992 for Ronald Coase and in 1994 for Douglass North) is a good illustration.

Two strands of institutional political economy can be distinguished. The first 'style of thought' is the Historical Institutionalism, also called Original Institutionalism, founded on the work of Thorstein Veblen, John Rodger Commons and Wesley Mitchell in the early years of the 20th century. Since the 1970s, work in this tradition has undergone a revival after a relative decline.

In parallel with the 'return of [Original] Institutional Economics' (Hodgson, 1994), the last 20 years have seen the emergence of a New Institutional Economics, which is an amalgamation of Coase's transactions cost theory, new theories of the firm, Public Choice, Austrian and other variants of mainstream thought that have attempted to render mainstream economics more realistic by endogenizing institutions. But, in this debate, a voice seems to be missing. In spite of their great interest in institutions, the Post Keynesians do not take part in these discussions. Do Post Keynesians have nothing to say on this topic? We are not of this opinion.

The aim of this chapter is to show that the Post Keynesians have much to say about this field even if their theory of institutions still remains underdeveloped and should attract more attention in the near future. So if Post Keynesian economists want to reinforce their theory of institutions, we call for building bridges between Post Keynesianism and Institutionalism. From now on, the terms 'Institutional Economics', 'Institutionalism' and 'Institutionalist(s)' will refer to the tradition of thought emanating from Veblen, Commons, Mitchell and their contemporary followers such as Samuels and Hodgson, and not the so-called 'New Institutional Economics' represented by Douglass North and Oliver Williamson. We will draw out the links between 'Institutionalism' thus defined and Post Keynesianism.

The chapter is divided into three sections. First of all, we will expose the concepts of time, the decision making process and uncertainty developed by the Post Keynesians. The second part explores the Post Keynesian theory of institutions that is directly related to their conception of uncertainty and its weakness. We will finally stress the important dialogue that Post Keynesians and Institutionalists could start around the concept of uncertainty and its crucial link with the question of instability, institutions and the need for stabilization policies.

TIME, DECISION MAKING AND FUNDAMENTAL UNCERTAINTY

Here we will refer to uncertainty in its radical sense following the path initiated by John Maynard Keynes. Keynes presented his ideas on uncertainty in his 1921 *Treatise on Probability* and gave some other important remarks on this topic in *The General Theory* and in his famous 1937 article, *The General Theory of Employment*. Let us consider how Keynes defines it:

> By 'uncertain' knowledge, let me explain, I do not mean merely to distinguish what is known for certain from what is only probable. The game of roulette is not subject, in this sense, to uncertainty ... Or ... the expectation of life is only slightly uncertain. Even the weather is only moderately uncertain. The sense in which I am using the term is that in which the prospect of a European war is uncertain, or the price of copper and the rate of interest twenty years hence ... About these matters there is no scientific basis on which to form any calculable probability whatever. *We simply do not know.* (Keynes, 1973b, XIV, pp. 113–14, emphasis added)

Uncertainty is possibly the most important element in Keynes's *General Theory*. As H. Minsky noted, 'Keynes without uncertainty is something like Hamlet without the Prince' (Minsky, 1975, p. 57). G.L.S. Shackle offered the same opinion when he declared that 'uncertainty is the very bedrock of Keynes's theory of employment' (Shackle, 1967, p. 112). Keynes insisted on the notion of uncertainty because he was convinced that it is a crucial element of our environment.

Uncertainty refers to a situation in which knowledge concerning the future effects of our current actions does not and cannot exist. As Jan Kregel pointed out, 'what must be known to decide today will be known only when the effects of those decisions take place' (Kregel, 1980, p. 37). In other words, there can be important differences between our ex ante decisions and ex post results. Moreover, the decision maker finds himself in a situation in which all future events and the distribution of probability associated with them cannot be listed. One can precisely say that this lack of knowledge is not due to the limitation of an agent's computational abilities, 'we simply do not know' (Keynes, 1973b, XIV, p. 114) because the future cannot be anticipated, it is yet to be created.

Taking its cue from Keynes, the acceptance of uncertainty is one of the major features of Post Keynesian Economics and it is one of the crucial differences with mainstream economics represented by the General Equilibrium Analysis. As Robert Lucas notes, 'in case of uncertainty, economic reasoning will be of no value' (1981, p. 224).

The main figure within the Post Keynesian tradition who relies most on the importance of uncertainty is probably Paul Davidson. Following G.L.S. Shackle's works, Davidson, in a series of articles and books, has rejected the general applicability of the *ergodic hypothesis* in the understanding of economic processes. Borrowing from the statistical concept of modern stochastic process theory, Davidson has proposed a technical distinction between ergodic and non-ergodic processes. (Davidson, 1982–3, 1988, 1991, 1994). In his *Reality and Economic Theory* (1996), he broadened his approach by delineating between immutable and transmutable reality models, as in Table 5.1.

An ergodic process is one for which time averages coincide with space averages. What happens at points in time for different initial states is supposed to coincide with what happens over time for a given initial state (Rosser, 2001, p. 90). In this approach, 'the future is merely the statistical reflection of the past. Economic activities are timeless and immutable' (Davidson, 1996, p. 90). As Davidson has shown, the ergodic hypothesis is implicitly or explicitly assumed in immutable reality models, even if he recognizes two variants of this conception (see Table 5.1A).

Post Keynesian economists strongly reject this conception and suggest replacing it with a different one in which the economic and social environment is seen as transmutable, marked by creativity and structural changes (Table 5.1B). The

Table 5.1   Concept of external economic reality

A. Immutable reality
    Type 1: in both the short run and the long run, the future is known or at least knowable. Examples are:
    a. Classical perfect certainty models.
    b. Actuarial certainty equivalents, such as rational expectations models.
    c. New Classical models.
    d. Some New Keynesian theories.
    Type 2: in the short run, the future is not completely known owing to some limitation in human information processing and computing power. Examples are:
    a. Bounded rationality theory.
    b. Knight's theory of uncertainty.
    c. Savage's expected utility theory.
    d. Some Austrian theories.
    e. Some New Keynesian models (for example, coordination failure).
    f. Chaos, sunspot, and bubble theories.
B. Transmutable or creative reality: some aspects of the economic future will be created by human action today and/or in the future. Examples of theories using this postulate are:
    a. Keynes's General Theory and Post Keynesian monetary theory.
    b. Post-1974 writings of Sir John Hicks.
    c. G.L.S. Shackle's crucial experiment analysis.
    d. Old Institutionalist theory.

---

human condition is perceived as non-ergodic, therefore the gathering of past data market signals will be of no value 'to defeat the forces of time' (Keynes, 1972a, VII, p. 157). The condition for existence of such non-ergodic and non-deterministic processes is the presence of crucial decisions. In this conception, any important decision is unique and non-repeatable:

> The human individual process is an intimate two-way relation between what the human being sees taking place and what he imagines as able to take place on condition of his acting in some specific way. By his choice of action he can delimit the imagined possibilities. What takes place may reflect some part of what he supposed himself to be making possible, and suggest fresh possibilities. (Shackle, 1989, p. 48)

In other words, the very act of performing the experiment destroys automatically and forever the circumstances in which the choice is made (Shackle, 1955, p. 6; Davidson, 1982–3, p. 192). Thus every new moment in time leads to the appearance of an entirely new situation and a totally different future, which the individual's imagination permanently creates. Thus historical time is a succession of heterogeneous moments. As Davidson said, 'when agents make crucial decisions, they necessarily destroy any ergodic stochastic processes that may have existed at the point of time of decision' (Davidson, 1982–3, p. 192). In such a world, a probabilistic forecast has little to tell us. However, it is indeed a non-ergodic world that Post Keynesian economics gives an account of. It remains to be seen what the action of the agents can become in such a universe.

The questions now become, where do we go from here? How are individuals likely to behave in such an environment? Post Keynesian economists insist on uncertainty as a central feature of capitalist economies in which 'a myriad of independent agents make decisions whose impacts are aggregated into outcomes that emerge over a range of tomorrows' (Minsky, 1996, p. 360). So, is a world of fundamental uncertainty inherently chaotic? The study of history demonstrates that modern economies are not chaotic and they move through time with a certain degree of order and stability that is disrupted only by structural and discontinuous changes. As Keynes said, one 'must not confuse uncertainty with instability' (Keynes, 1973b, XIV, p. 137). Following Coddington (1982, p. 482), we can argue that it is not the fact of uncertainty that matters but rather how individuals are supposed to respond to it.

UNCERTAINTY AND THE ROLE OF INSTITUTIONS

Keynes argues that 'many of the greatest economic evils of our time are the fruit of risk, uncertainty and ignorance' (Keynes, 1972b, IX, p. 221). Nevertheless 'it is an outstanding characteristic of the economic system in which we live [to be] not very unstable' (Keynes, 1972a, VII, p. 249) because the capitalist system provides 'certain [institutional] factors which somewhat mitigate in practice the effects of our ignorance' (p. 163). Keynes and the Post Keynesians develop a conception in which order and stability are possible in the capitalist system in spite of the radical uncertainty that individuals face. Here the link between the concept of uncertainty and institutions becomes of crucial importance. As Davidson has stated:

> The economic system is potentially very unstable. Recognising the mercurial possibility of the economic system, man has, over time, devised certain institutions and rules of the games, which, as long as they are operational, avoid such catastrophes by providing a foundation for a conventionality of belief in the stability of the system and hence in the quasi-stability of the state of expectations. (Davidson, 1978, p. 385)

Post Keynesians, in situating uncertainty at the heart of their analysis, gave us a theory where agents' economic behaviours, fundamentally affected by the environment of a non-ergodic world, escape from neoclassical individual rationality. Precisely, the non-ergdocity implies that an agent should be able to proceed to different choices at different moments of time when the problem which he is submitted to remains rigorously the same. In a non-ergodic world, the errors of expectations constitute the rule and not the exception. This is why the environment of the firms' decisions must be able to restrict the number of risks. The environment identifies itself with monetary institutions which characterize modern production economies.

It is intrinsic to Post Keynesian thought to stress the importance of institutions for economic activities. Post Keynesians are institution builders because institutions and policy 'can contain the thrust of instability' (Minsky, 1986, p. 10). Mainstream economists, in stressing the central role of the market, clearly neglect the necessary institutions of which actual markets are necessarily composed, such as the conventions that serve as guidelines to market behaviour, the establishment and reinforcement of institutional arrangements which reduce uncertainty and foster confidence, and the monetary and financial institutions that finance investment. The Post Keynesian approach insists on the influence of institutions which mould individual and group decision making. So let us list the major institutions that help agents to face uncertainty and reduce it. We shall begin with money.

Money

We generally consider money as that universally accepted medium which enters into most exchange in a monetized system. 'Money is as money does' means that money is generally defined by its primary functions: medium of exchange, unit of account, means of payment and store of wealth. For Post Keynesian economics, 'money matters': a crucial implication of uncertainty is that money is non-neutral in both the short run and the long run.

In accordance with Keynes's *Treatise on Money* (1971, V–VI), money – here we refer to its role as a unit of account – appears as an abstract unit of calculation accepted by all the agents. Thus money provides for a common language that permits a precise and identical evaluation for each and every individual.

As we have seen above, money is closely linked to uncertainty. Rather than emphasizing money as a medium of exchange as Neoclassical economists do, Post Keynesians insist on the role of money in discharging contractual obligations. Only money possesses the property of being the means of contractual settlement. Agents hold money in an uncertain environment in which a liquid position is desirable. By definition, liquidity is the ability to meet contractual obligations as they come due. It follows that the holding of money involves the possession of the ultimate liquidity.

In its role as a store of wealth, money also provides the possibility for agents to postpone decisions when uncertainty is high. As discussed in Keynes (1973b, XIV, p. 116), money is a 'time machine' that allows the transfer of purchasing power from the present to the future.

Forward Contracts

Money is associated with legal contracts (Minsky, 1975; Davidson, 1978). Money-denominated contracts are the principal method used by individuals to organize the process of production. An example of an important contract is the money-wage contract. It is the cornerstone of an entrepreneurial system where money is used because it is a fundamental determinant of the stabilization of the price level and, therefore, of expectations. It follows that stickiness of wages and prices is the result of voluntary choice made by the agents.

Fixed money contracts represent a rational method used by agents to reduce disquiet about the future because they reduce uncertainty about future values of nominal variables. One may add that the existence of contracts has to be associated with the existence of another institution, the state, which is supposed to enforce contracts.

Banking System

Other institutions, such as the banking system, are fundamental to prevent the system from collapsing. Commercial banks permit investment to be financed by endogenously creating both the resources for firms to purchase the inputs of production and the entrepreneur's capacity to generate monetary profits. Another important institution within the banking system is the Central Bank. In its role as a market maker, the Central Bank, through its influence on prices and interests, reduces uncertainty by stabilizing expectations, reducing volatility and preventing panic. Post Keynesians argue that the bank's interventions – here we refer to the fundamental role the Central Bank plays as a lender of last resort – must be able to prevent or, if necessary, contain and offset financial disruption (Minsky, 1986; Davidson, 1990).

There is an institutional context, that limits the true uncertainty which the agents are subject to. Nevertheless, one has to admit that the description of this context is not enough to understand the positive content of the decision-making process which is peculiar to a non-ergodic world. Post Keynesians attach importance to institutions that lend stability to economies. But one has to recognize that the concept of institutions does not appear so clearly in Post Keynesian theories. Their theory of institutions does not form the subject of any explicit statement. In this chapter our task has been to reconstruct it. Institutions typically seem to be exogenous. There is little reflection on how they emerge and how they evolve. Their theory of institutions remains on the whole weak and relatively underdeveloped. It is a curious fact that neither *A Guide to Post Keynesian Economics* (Eichner, 1979) nor *A New Guide to Post Keynesian Economics* (Holt and Pressman, 2001) has a chapter on institutions despite the fact that this topic was central to the concerns of John Maynard Keynes.

In this sense, Post Keynesian theorists remain behind what we could develop starting from Keynes's institutions. In both the texts preceding and following the *General Theory*, as well as in chapters of the *General Theory*, John Maynard Keynes indeed continually highlights the importance of considering institutions in order to understand the working of a monetary economy of production. Institutions should attract greater attention in the near future. This is precisely what the editors of *A New Guide to Post Keynesian Economics* call for in the last chapter, 'A look ahead':

> there are several key Post Keynesian ideas that need to drive this future research – *the importance of fundamental uncertainty, the importance of institutions and historical time* ... Post Keynesian Economics can play a more influential role in the twenty-first century. (Holt and Pressman, 2001, p. 129, emphasis added)

So if Post Keynesian economists want to reinforce their theory of institutions, we think that substantial gains are to be expected from interacting with Institutionalism.

TOWARD A CONNECTION BETWEEN POST KEYNESIANISM AND INSTITUTIONALISM[3]

Keynes was also very close to one of the founding fathers of Institutionalism. He once wrote Commons a letter, in which the former confessed:

> Many thanks for sending me your article in the 'An[n]nalist'. I an entirely in sympathy with it. Indeed, a good deal of your analysis runs on very closely similar lines to some material which I already have in my manuscript for a forthcoming book [that is, the *Treatise on Money*] ... [Moreover,] I quite agree with your practical proposals ... I should very much like to have some conversations with you on this and others matters. Judging from limited evidence and at a great distance, there seems to me no other economist with whose general way of thinking I feel myself in such a genuine accord.[4]

However, he was much less clear about the details of this agreement. In return, Commons paid tribute to Keynes's enterprise of edification of a monetary theory of production at odds with the neoclassical and classical monetary economics (Commons, 1937).

Certainly the key of this agreement can be found in Keynes's famous lecture '*Am I a Liberal?*' (1925). In this text, he cited the work of 'an eminent American economist, Professor Commons, who has been one of the first to recognize the nature of the economic transition amidst the early stages of which we are living' (Keynes, 1972b, IX, p. 303). Keynes drew on Commons's non-Marxist conceptualization of the economic process circumscribed by the existence of 'three epochs, three economic orders, upon the third of which we are entering' (p. 304). The first, the era of scarcity, referred to pre-capitalist modes of governance and coercion, including communitarian, feudal and medieval power structures. Then came the period of abundance, prior to World War I, and dominated by capital accumulation and technical progress, economic efficiency and individual liberty, in which the stimulus of competition guaranteed economic and social progress under the leadership of the business class: '[In] the nineteenth century this epoch culminated gloriously in the victories of laissez-faire and historic liberalism' (p. 304). The third age of stabilization is characterized by a general transition towards an organized form of capitalism, in which societal or governmental controls will replace laissez-faire 'in the interests of *social justice and social stability*' (p. 305, emphasis added). The central feature of organized capitalism was the increasing prominence of institutions whose characteristic feature was a commitment to 'the public good' rather than individual gain. Keynes and Commons converged on a conception in which order, stabilization and the security of expectations is possible through the creation of additional institutions that can reduce uncertainty.

Institutionalists such as G. Means, R. Tugwell and R.T. Ely, who reacted very favourably to Keynes's *General Theory* and perceived very quickly the affinity between Keynes and institutionalist research took an active part in F.D. Roosevelt's *New Deal* policies.[5] The goal of the *New Deal* policies was to restructure capitalism by creating institutions that contained uncertainty. This connection could have been very fruitful considering the similarities of the schools. So, very soon, A. Gruchy called for a synthesis of the ideas between both the streams, underlining the importance of such a connection:

> In spite of all the differences in their interests and opinions, the economic studies of Keynes and Institutionalists have contributed much to a synthesis of the economics of the individual firm, to studies of the flow of national income, and to investigate into the nature of the economic order. Such synthesis seems to be, and may very well turn out to be, the major contribution of this century. (Gruchy, 1950, pp. 125–6)

Unfortunately, the Neoclassical Synthesis broke the beginnings of a connection between Keynes and Institutionalism, eclipsing and relegating to a second level both the schools and directing research towards formalizable and quantifiable models.

Institutionalists, and especially Commons, adopt a methodological position which questions the primacy granted to abstract reasoning. Rather, primacy is granted to a methodology including principles of pragmatism. It thus follows that a multidisciplinary and evolutionist theory is established, to the detriment of a formal conception, and the corollary of this is the impossibility of systematization and axiomatization. The position Keynes adopted lies within the same perspective. He liked to remind us that economics is essentially a social science rather than a natural one. It is thus with no hesitation that Keynes firmly and harshly attacked J. Tinbergen's first econometric works. Econometrics seems unable to take into account fundamental dimensions such as 'political, social and psychological factors' (Keynes, 1973b, XIV, p. 309). This is probably one of the most essential reasons why Keynes never tried to model his theory in spite of a great experience in the field of statistics and mathematics. This appears clearly in a letter of 16 July 1938 that he wrote to Harrod: 'In Economics … to convert a model into a quantitative formula is to destroy its usefulness as an instrument of thought' (1973b, XIV, p. 299).

In the end it is the conjunction between the advent of a very particular interpretation of Keynes's works and the powerful tendency of formalization and modelling which eclipses Institutionalism and scuttles the possible connections between Keynes and Institutionalism. The meeting between the two trends gave rise to the Neoclassical Synthesis of Samuelson, Hicks and Hansen. This 'missed link' between Keynes and Institutionalism (Thabet, 2003) suggests that an interesting synthesis, or at least shared research agenda, may be developed between Post Keynesian and Institutional Economics.

Post Keynesianism and Institutionalism: Compatibility and Complementarity

Post Keynesians have close affinity with institutionalists. Primarily, what unites the two schools is their rejection of Neoclassical economics as being of any use to understanding the problems of the real world in which we live. Post Keynesians and institutionalists see economies as operating in historical time, moving from an irrevocable past to an unpredictable future, where expectations have important effects on economic and social outcomes. Institutions provide patterns that serve as guidelines for individual and group behaviour.

One can identify an institutionalist tradition on which Post Keynesian Economics draws (Arestis, 1996). Some prominent authors straddled the two schools: the works of Gardiner Means, described by his biographers as 'Institutionalist and Post Keynesian' (Samuels and Medema, 1990), Alfred Eichner, one of the disciples of the latter and the author of *Toward a New Economics: Essays in Post-Keynesian and Institutionalist Theory*, Dudley Dillard (1948), who was among the first to interpret Keynes's *General Theory* as a monetary theory of production in which money is the central institution of the capitalist system,[6] John Kenneth Galbraith, an early patron and financial supporter of the *Journal of Post Keynesian Economics*, who has meticulously analysed the institutions of post-war capitalism, and John Cornwall, who frequently makes reference to the role of institutions and to Institutionalism, could equally be described as Post Keynesians and institutionalists. But whenever one discusses the link between Post Keynesian and Institutional Economics, one name will always be mentioned – Hyman Minsky. Minsky represents probably one of the most important links between Post Keynesian and Institutional schools of thought, even if he did not want to be labelled 'Post Keynesian' (Papadimitriou and Wray, 1998). According to those two authors, Minsky wanted to distance himself from a tendency in Post Keynesianism to push institutions into the background in order to develop 'general theories'. Such theories remain too general and unhelpful. For Minsky, institutions must be brought into the analysis at the beginning because theory must be appropriate to the specific stage of development of the economy under analysis. He claimed that useful theory must be 'institution-specific' (Minsky, 1992).

This is precisely the way to promote a fruitful dialogue in which both traditions can greatly benefit. It is possible to identify several areas in which gains from mutual borrowing could be very substantial. Here we will focus on the link between uncertainty, the question of agency and institutions. There are great gains from trade to be had between the institutionalist theory of institutions and the Post Keynesian conception of uncertainty and transmutable processes.

Institutionalists had almost no explicit theory of uncertainty. A potential contribution that Post Keynesian Economics can make to Institutionalism is the extension and clarification of their concept of uncertainty. The Post Keynesians still remain weak on the question of institutions. As Tony Lawson has argued, 'the analytical consequences of accepting the fact of uncertainty, remain, on the whole, unexplored' (Lawson, 1985, p. 909). Robert Dixon (1986) has noted too the failure in Shackle's work to draw out the full implication of uncertainty and expectations. Accordingly, an important contribution that Institutionalism can offer to Post Keynesianism is the extension and clarification of their underdeveloped theory of institutions, as regards not only formal institutions but also informal institutions.

Keynes wrote to Townshend in 1938:

> Generally speaking, in making a decision we have before us a large number of alternatives, none of which is demonstrably more 'rational' than the others, in the sense that we can arrange in order of merit the sum aggregate of the benefits obtainable from the complete consequences of each ... We fall back, therefore, and necessarily so, on motives of another kind, which are not 'rational' in the sense of being concerned with the evaluation of consequences, but are decided by *habit, interest, preference, desire, will* etc. (Keynes, 1979, XXIX, p. 294, emphasis added)

Keynes claimed his analysis could be deemed institutional. He always stressed the role of institutions in the stabilization of the economic system. As James Crotty notes, 'The General Theory is historically contingent and institutionally specific' (Crotty, 1990, p. 762). Joan Robinson has noted that Keynes was 'concerned with actual contemporary problems and put [his] arguments in terms of the structure and behaviour of the economy in which [he was] living, while the neoclassic enunciated what purported to be universal laws, based on human nature – greed, impatience and so forth' (Robinson, 1980, p. 53). This remark clearly reflects Institutionalist thought. One may note that there is no consensus on a common definition of institution (Maki, 1993: p. 13). Some authors[7] define it as patterns of behaviour or thought, habits, rules or a set of social norms. Sometimes they are considered as organizations derived from the market when transaction costs become too important.[8] Nevertheless, in our opinion, the broad definition proposed by Commons seems to be appropriate and includes all the dimensions described above. Commons defines 'institution' as a 'collective action in restraint, liberation and expansion of individual action' (Commons [1934] 1990, p. 73). He makes a distinction between formal and informal institutions, as we can see in Figure 5.1.

One can identify three types of influence that institutions have on economic behaviour (Dequech, 2002). The first may be called the restrictive function of institutions. They exert a powerful and a controlling influence on individual

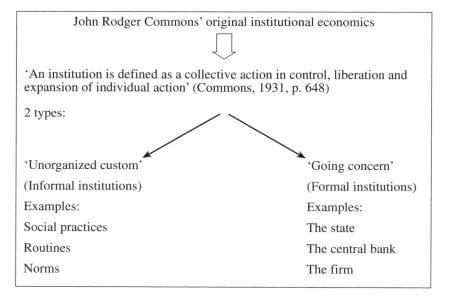

Figure 5.1   Formal and informal institutions

choice: 'Institutions transcend individuals. They enforce constraints on actions and events because they orient, constrain and direct the behaviour of individuals' (Carvalho, 1983–4, p. 271).

Nevertheless, institutions are not to be considered simply as constraints, as in Neoclassical Economics. Commons clearly regarded institutions as a liberating as well as constraining force (Commons [1934] 1990, p. 73). The second influence refers to the informational–cognitive function of institutions. They provide information about the possible actions of other agents and influence the very perception that individuals have of reality:

> One of the roles that institutions play is to create knowledge and information for the individual decision maker. In particular, institutions provide social knowledge which may be needed for interaction with other individual decision makers. (Boland, 1979, p. 963)

One may add that institutions have an influence on people's behaviour, while agents can act on institutions, as in Figure 5.2.

One has to keep in mind that, despite their influence on individual behaviour, agents retain an important freedom of action. The last function may be called the teleological function of institutions. As Dequech (2002) noted, institutions can influence the ends that people pursue. Institutions may constrain and inform but also guide and direct the behaviour of human actors. Thus institutions play the role of an anchor for decision making.

After describing the influence of institutions on the behaviour of the agents, we can take a further step. Institutionalism can provide the microfoundations

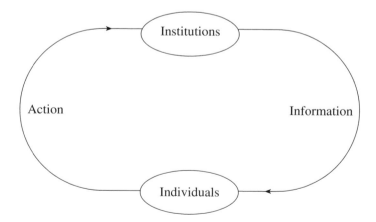

Figure 5.2   The institutionalist action-information loop (Hodgson, 1998, p. 176)

for Keynesian macroeconomics. As emphasized by Geoffrey Hodgson (1993), it is from a theory based upon institutions that a pertinent macroeconomics can be developed, as this makes it possible to explain the coexistence of individual variety and systemic stability. In this light, Institutionalism can help us to perfect and complete Post Keynesian Economics. It is in that way that a fruitful research programme can be built.

CONCLUDING REMARKS: THE NEED FOR STABILIZATION POLICIES

We live in a complex, messy and uncertain world dominated by unstable financial markets. Unlike Neoclassical economists, Post Keynesians and Institutionalists together give us an appropriate picture of the economic and social reality. The question arises, then, what policies do we need to stabilize capitalist economies?

An important area directly related to the question of uncertainty and institutions in which both our schools can engage in a major dialogue is the necessity of stabilization policies to improve economic and social outcomes. The state has a crucial role to play by creating institutional structures that provide for stability in a world of uncertainty (Larson, 2002). Post Keynesians and Institutionalists are both advocates of regulation and reform and strongly reject laissez-faire policies. It is not surprising that one of the earliest and most radical critiques of 'shock therapies' imposed on East European countries was jointly developed by Post Keynesians and Institutionalists (Kregel *et al.*, 1992). There are several mechanisms by which the state can fulfil several institutional functions. Through correct macroeconomic policies, the state has a crucial role to play by developing institutional 'ceilings and floors' that can constrain instability. The state can also create a favourable environment through the establishment and enforcement of laws and regulations that provide stability and security to the firms, households and workers.

In addition, a programme of spending policies can also create a favourable environment for private business investment. Keynes argued that 'the main task should be to prevent large fluctuations by a stable long-term programme' (Keynes, 1980, XXVII, p. 322). Bateman (1994, p. 115) notes that Keynes 'offered his proposals for stable monetary policies and the socialization of public investment with the intention that they would both help to create more stable expectations among private investors'. Similarly Smithin (1989, pp. 219–20) notes that Keynes's proposals for the social control of investment would not only add to private investment but 'also encourage more private investment itself (crowding in rather than crowding out) by promoting a more stable environment and lowering uncertainty'. Finally, let us quote Hyman Minsky, the best illustration of a possible and necessary synthesis between Post Keynesianism and Institutionalism:

> Public tolerance for uncertainty is limited. The New Deal restructuring of capitalism created institutions that contained uncertainty. The evolution of the economy has decreased the effectiveness of the New Deal reforms, and money manager capitalism has radically increased uncertainty. The creation of new economic institutions that constrain the impact of uncertainty is necessary. (Minsky, 1996, p. 359)

Throughout this chapter we have attempted to show the compatibility between Post Keynesian and institutionalist thought. The idea is that both research programmes, after decades of relative mutual ignorance, should start a major dialogue, taking advantage of many possible connections between both schools. The objective is to lead to discussions, which would lead up to enrichments and to bridges. The purpose of this chapter consists in advocating the construction of bridges between Post Keynesian and institutionalist thought. The importance of these bridges must be considered from the perspective of the deep isolation both these schools faced from the mainstream but also in line with the parallel development of both new orthodoxies, the New Keynesian Economics and the New Institutionalist School of thought, which claim to be the heiresses to the Keynesian Revolution and Original Institutionalism. This is the price to pay for the survival of heterodox economics which are currently isolated and dismissed from the official forums and policy-making institutions.

NOTES

1. The author would like to thank Ali Bouhaili and Nabil Nafa for their helpful comments on an earlier draft of this chapter. The comments of other participants at the Eighth International Post Keynesian workshop, Kansas City, June 2004, are also much appreciated. The usual disclaimer applies. Financial support from the CRIISEA is also gratefully acknowledged.
2. Matthews (1986, p. 903); see also Williamson (2000, p. 595).
3. The case for a fruitful dialogue between Post Keynesian and Institutional Economics has gained ground in recent years and is most persuasively argued in Brazelton (1981), who represents an early attempt to link both these schools. See also Keller (1983), Hogdson (1989) and Dunn (2000).
4. Letter to Professor Commons, 26 April 1927. John R. Commons Papers (1982), microfilm, reel 4, p. 448.
5. See Barber (1994) and Stoneman (1972).
6. See also Dillard (1980, 1987).
7. Thorstein Veblen ([1919] 1990, p. 239) defined institutions as 'settled habits of thought common to the generality of men'. Walton Hamilton (1932, p. 84) described an institution as 'a way of thought or action of some prevalence and permanence, which is embedded in the habits of a group or the customs of a people'. Andrew Schotter (1981, p. 11) notes that an institution is 'a regularity in social behavior that is agreed to by all members of society, specifies behavior in specific recurrent situations, and is either self-policed or policed by some external authority'. Douglass North (1990, p. 3) writes: 'Institutions are the rules of the game in society or, more

formally, are the humanly devised constraints that shape human interaction. In consequence they structure incentives in human exchange, whether political, social, or economic.'
8.   This is the New Institutional Economics position.

REFERENCES

Arestis, P. (1996), 'Post-Keynesian Economics: towards coherence', *Cambridge Journal of Economics*, **20** (1), 111–35.

Barber, W.J. (1994), 'The divergent fates of two strands of institutionalist doctrine during the New Deal years', *History of Political Economy*, **26** (4), 569–87.

Bateman, B. (1994), 'Rethinking the Keynesian Revolution', in J. Davis (ed.), *The State of Interpretation of Keynes*, Boston: Kluwer, pp. 103–21.

Boland, L. (1979), 'Knowledge and the role of institutions in economic theory', *Journal of Economic Issues*, **13** (4), 957–72.

Brazelton, R.W. (1981), 'Post Keynesian economics. An institutional compatibility?', *Journal of Economic Issues*, **15** (2) (June), 531–42.

Carvalho, F. (1983–4), 'On the concept of time in Shacklean and Sraffian economics', *Journal of Post Keynesian Economics*, **6** (2), 265–80.

Coddington, A. (1982), 'Deficient foresight: a troublesome theme in Keynesian economics', *American Economic Review*, **72** (June), 480–87.

Commons, J.R. (1931), 'Institutional economics', *American Economic Review*, **21** (December), 648–57.

Commons, J.R. [1934], *Institutional Economics. Its Place in Political Economy*, New York: Macmillan; reprinted with a new introduction by M. Rutherford, New Brunswick, NJ: Transaction Books, 1990.

Commons, J.R. (1937), 'Capacity to produce, capacity to consume, capacity to pay debts', *American Economic Review*, **27**, December, 680–97.

Commons, J.R. (1982), *John R. Commons Papers*, microfilm edn, State Historical Society of Wisconsin.

Crotty, J. (1990), 'Keynes on the stages of development of capitalist economy: the institutional foundation of Keynes's methodology', *Journal of Economic Issues*, **24** (3) (September), 761–80.

Davidson, P. (1978), *Money and the Real World*, London: Macmillan.

Davidson, P. (1982–3), 'Rational expectations: a fallacious foundation for studying crucial decision-making processes', *Journal of Post Keynesian Economics*, **5** (2), 182–98.

Davidson, P. (1988), 'A technical definition of uncertainty and the long-run non-neutrality of money', *Cambridge Journal of Economics*, **12** (3), 329–37.

Davidson, P. (1990), 'Shackle and Keynes vs. Rational Expectations Theory on the role of time, liquidity, and financial markets', in S.F. Frowen (ed.), *Unknowledge and Choice in Economics*, London: Macmillan, pp. 64–80.

Davidson, P. (1991), 'Is Probability Theory relevant for uncertainty? A post Keynesian perspective', *Journal of Economic Perspectives*, **5** (1), 129–43.

Davidson, P. (1994), *Post Keynesian Macroeconomic Theory*, Aldershot, UK and Brookfield, US: Edward Elgar.

Davidson, P. (1996), 'Reality and economic theory', *Journal of Post Keynesian Economics*, **18** (4), 479–508.

Dequech, D. (2002), 'The demarcation between the 'old' and the 'new' Institutional economics: recent complications', *Journal of Economic Issues*, **36** (2), 565–72.

Dillard, D. (1948), *The Economics of John Maynard Keynes*, New York: Prentice-Hall.
Dillard, D. (1980), 'A monetary theory of production: Keynes and the Institutionalists', *Journal of Economic Issues*, **14** (2), 255–73.
Dillard, D. (1987), 'The evolutionary economics of a monetary economy. Remarks upon receipt of the Veblen–Commons Award', *Journal of Economic Issues*, **21** (2), 575–85.
Dixon, R. (1986), 'Uncertainty, unobstructedness and power', *Journal of Post Keynesian Economics*, **8** (4), 585–90.
Dunn, S.P. (2000), 'Wither Post Keynesianism?', *Journal of Post Keynesian Economics*, **22** (3), 343–64.
Eichner, A.S. (ed.) (1979), *A Guide to Post Keynesian Economics*, London: Routledge.
Gruchy, A.G. (1950), 'Keynes and the Institutionalists: important contrasts' in L.C. Christenson (ed.), *Economic Theory in Review*, Bloomington, IN: University Press, pp. 106–26.
Hamilton, W.H. (1932), 'Institutions' in E.R. Seligman and A. Johnson (eds), *Encyclopaedia of the Social Sciences*, vol. 8, New York: Macmillan, pp. 84–9.
Hodgson, G. (1993), *Economics and Evolution. Bringing Life Back into Economics*, Michigan: University of Michigan Press.
Hodgson, G.M. (1989), 'Post Keynesianism and Institutionalism: the missing link', in J. Pheby (ed.), *New Directions in Post-Keynesian Economics*, Aldershot, UK and Brookfield, US: Edward Elgar, pp. 94–123.
Hodgson, G.M. (1994), 'The Return of Institutional Economics', in N.J. Smelser and R. Swedberg (eds), *The Handbook of Economic Sociology*, New York: Princeton University Press, pp. 58–76.
Hodgson, G.M. (1998), 'The approach of Institutional Economics', *Journal of Economic Literature*, **36** (1), 166–92.
Holt, R. and S. Pressman (eds) (2001), *A New Guide to Post Keynesian Economics*, London: Routledge.
Keller, R.H. (1983), 'Keynesian and Institutional Economics: compatibility and complementarity?', *Journal of Economic Issues*, **17** (4) (December), 1087–95.
Keynes, J.M. (1971), *The Collected Writings of John Maynard Keynes, Vols V–VI: A Treatise on Money*, D. Moggridge (ed.), Royal Economic Society, London: Macmillan.
Keynes, J.M. (1972a), *The Collected Writings of John Maynard Keynes, Vol. VII: The General Theory of Employment, Interest and Money*, D. Moggridge (ed.), Royal Economic Society, London: Macmillan.
Keynes, J.M. (1972b), *The Collected Writings of John Maynard Keynes, Vol. IX: Essays in Persuasion*, D. Moggridge (ed.), Royal Economic Society, London: Macmillan.
Keynes, J.M. (1973a), *The Collected Writings of John Maynard Keynes, Vol. VIII: A Treatise on Probability*, D. Moggridge (ed.), Royal Economic Society, London: Macmillan.
Keynes, J.M. (1973b), *The Collected Writings of John Maynard Keynes, Vol. XIV: Part II Defence and Development*, D. Moggridge (ed.), Royal Economic Society, London: Macmillan.
Keynes, J.M. (1979), *The Collected Writings of John Maynard Keynes, Vol. XXIX: The General Theory: A Supplement*, D. Moggridge (ed.), Royal Economic Society, London: Macmillan.
Keynes, J.M. (1980), *The Collected Writings of John Maynard Keynes, Vol. XXVII: Activities 1940–1946. Shaping the Post-War World Employment and Commodities*, D. Moggridge (ed.), Royal Economic Society, London: Macmillan.

Kregel, J. (1980), 'Markets and institutions as features of a capitalistic production system', *Journal of Post Keynesian Economics*, **3** (1), 32–48.

Kregel, J., E. Matzner and G. Grabher (eds) (1992), *The Market Shock: An Agenda for the Economic and Social Reconstruction of Central and Eastern Europe*, Vienna: Austrian Academy of Sciences/Research Unit for Socio-Economics.

Larson, S. (2002), *Uncertainty, Macroeconomic Stability and the Welfare State*, Aldershot: Ashgate.

Lawson, T. (1985), 'Uncertainty and economic analysis', *Economic Journal*, **95** (December), 909–27.

Lucas, R. (1981), *Studies in Business Cycle Theory*, Cambridge, MA: MIT Press.

Maki, U. (1993), 'Economics with institutions: agenda for methodological inquiry', in U. Maki, B. Gustafson and C. Knudsen (eds), *Rationality, Institutions and Economic Methodology*, New York: Routledge, pp. 5–42.

Matthews, R.C.O. (1986), 'The economics of institutions and the sources of growth', *Economic Journal*, **96** (December), 903–18.

Minsky, H. (1975), *John Maynard Keynes*, New York: Columbia University Press.

Minsky, H. (1986), *Stabilizing an Unstable Economy*, New Haven, CT: Yale University Press.

Minsky, H. (1992), 'Profits, deficits and instability: a policy discussion', in D. Papadimitriou (ed.), *Profits, Deficits and Instability*, New York: St Martin's Press.

Minsky, H.P. (1996), 'Uncertainty and the institutional structure of capitalist economies', *Journal of Economic Issues*, **30** (2), 357–68.

North, D. (1990), *Institutions, Institutional Change and Economic Performance*, Cambridge, Cambridge University Press.

Papadimitriou, D. and R.L. Wray (1998), 'The economic contribution of Hyman Minsky: varieties of capitalism and institutional reform', *Review of Political Economy*, **10** (2), 199–225.

Robinson, J. (1980), *Collected Economic Papers*, vol 5, Cambridge: MIT Press.

Rosser, J.B. (2001), 'Alternative Keynesian and Post Keynesian perspectives on uncertainty and expectations', *Journal of Post Keynesian Economics*, **23** (4), 545–66.

Samuels, W.J. and S.G. Medema (1990), *Gardiner C. Means: Institutionalist and Post Keynesian*, Armonk, NY: Sharpe.

Schotter, A. (1981), *The Economic Theory of Social Institutions*, Cambridge: Cambridge University Press.

Shackle, G.L.S. (1955), *Uncertainty in Economics and Other Reflections*, Cambridge: Cambridge University Press.

Shackle, G.L.S. (1967), *The Years of High Theory*, Cambridge: Cambridge University Press.

Shackle, G.L.S. (1989), 'What did the General Theory do?', in J. Pheby (ed.), *New Directions in Post-Keynesian Economics*, Aldershot, UK and Brookfield, US: Edward Elgar, pp. 48–58.

Smithin, J. (1989), 'The composition of government expenditures and the effectiveness of fiscal policy' in J. Pheby (ed.), *New Directions in Post-Keynesian Economics*, Aldershot, UK and Brookfield, US: Edward Elgar, pp. 209–27.

Stoneman, W. (1972), *A History of the Economic Analysis of The Great Depression*, New York: Garland.

Thabet, S. (2003), 'Keynes and Institutionalism: the missed link', presentation to the 5th Annual Conference of the Association for Heterodox Economics, Nottingham, Nottingham Trent University, 8–9 July.

Veblen, T.B. [1919], *The Place of Science in Modern Civilization and Other Essays*, New York: Huebsch; reprinted with a new introduction by W.J. Samuels, New Brunswick, NJ: Transaction Books, 1990.

Williamson, O.E. (2000), 'The New Institutional Economics: taking stock, looking ahead', *Journal of Economic Literature*, **38** (4), 595–613.

6. Saving, asset-price inflation and debt-induced deflation

Michael Hudson

The National Income and Product Accounts (NIPA) measure the circular flow between production, consumption and new investment. Employers earn profits which they invest in capital goods, and they pay their employees who spend their income to buy the goods they produce (Figure 6.1).

Production and consumption represent only part of the economy. Governments levy taxes and user fees, which they spend and sometimes run budget surpluses (the government's way of saving) that drain income from the economy's flow of spending. But, more often, governments inject spending power by running deficits (financed by running into debt). The NIPA measure these fiscal removals or injections of revenue by taxing and spending (Figure 6.2).

A half-century ago, economists anticipated that rising incomes and living standards would lead to higher savings. The most influential view of the economic future was that of John Maynard Keynes. Addressing the problems of

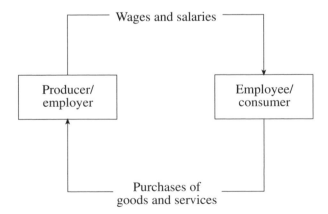

Figure 6.1   Economy no. 1 – production/consumption (the 'real economy' without FIRE and government)

104

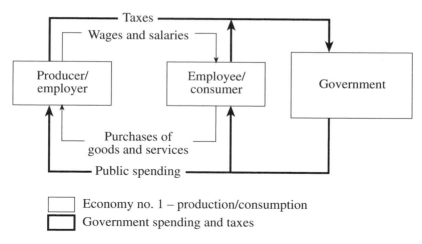

Figure 6.2   Economy no. 1 with government (the 'real economy' with government and without FIRE)

the Great Depression in 1936, his *General Theory of Employment, Interest and Money* warned that people would save relatively more as their incomes rose. Spending on consumer goods would tail off, slowing the growth of markets, new investment and employment.

This view of the saving function – the propensity to save out of wages and profits – saw saving break the chain of payments simply by not being spent. The modern dynamics of saving, and the debts in which savings are invested, are more complex. Most savings are lent out. Nearly all new investment in capital goods and buildings comes from retained business earnings, not from savings that pass through financial intermediaries. Under these conditions, higher personal saving rates are reflected in higher indebtedness.

Since World War II, in fact, each new business upswing has started with a higher set of debt ratios. A rising proportion of savings find their counterpart more in other people's debts rather than being used to finance new direct investment. The net savings rate has fallen, even though debt ratios and gross savings have increased.

To understand these dynamics it is necessary to view economies as composed of two distinct systems. The largest system is that of land, monopoly rights and financial claims that yield *rentier* returns in the form of interest, other financial fees, rents and monopoly gains (which can be viewed as either economic rents or super-profits). These returns far overshadow the profits earned on investing in capital goods and employing labour to produce goods and provide actual services. This reflects the fact that the value of *rentier* property and financial securities far exceeds that of physical capital in the form of factories and machinery, buildings or research and development.

Keynes was not careful to analyse how the savings functions associated with financial securities and *rentier* claims – and the property rights backing them as collateral – differed from personal savings functions. Some help, however, is provided by the NIPA, which break out the distinct flow of property and financial income that accrues to the FIRE sector, an acronym for Finance, Insurance and Real Estate.

To fill out the picture from the investor's vantage point, especially that of FIRE, it is necessary to recognize the increasingly important role played by capital gains rather than current earnings. The economy's wealthiest layers take their 'total returns' primarily in the form of capital gains, not profit, interest or rental income.

No regular measures of capital gains are published, but they can be estimated on the basis of the Federal Reserve Board's balance-sheet data published in Table Z of its annual Flow-of-Funds statistics on financial assets (stocks, bonds and bank deposits and loans) and tangible assets (land, buildings and capital goods). These statistics show that capital gains and the returns to property and finance (rent, interest and capital gains) far overshadow profits.

This distinction between the property and financial sectors and the rest of the economy is not immediately apparent, however. NIPA statistics follow modern 'value-free' economics in conflating all forms of current income (excluding capital gains) into the single category of 'earnings'. Interest, rent, insurance and financial fees are treated as payments for current services, not claims by property, credit or monopoly power that find no counterpart in direct outlays.

These forms of revenue are not inherently necessary expenses of production, but are best viewed as being institutional in character. Returns to finance and property may be viewed as transfer payments rather than as actual costs entailed by producing goods and services. This contrast makes the savings and debt functions of these *rentier* sectors differ from those associated with the wages and profits paid to labour and tangible capital investment (Figure 6.3).

MONETARY CONSIDERATIONS

Industry and agriculture, transport and power, and similar production and consumption expenditures account for less than 0.1 per cent of the economy's flow of payments. The vast majority of transactions passing through the New York Clearing House and Fedwire are for stocks, bonds, packaged bank loans, options, derivatives and foreign-currency transactions. The entire stock-market value of many high-flying companies now changes hands in a single day, and the average holding time for currency trades has shrunk to just a few minutes.

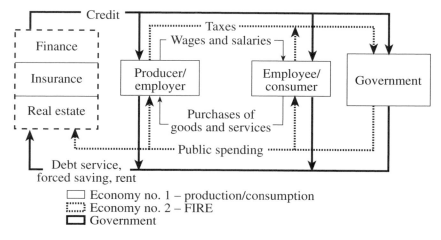

Figure 6.3   Interaction of economy no. 1, economy no. 2 and government

The value of these financial transactions each day exceeds that of the entire annual US national income. It therefore seems absurd to relate the money supply only to consumer and wholesale prices, excluding asset prices.

TODAY'S ANOMALIES THAT NEED TO BE EXPLAINED

Today's world requires more variables to be analysed. The (net) savings rate has moved in the opposite direction from what Keynes had anticipated. The NIPA report a zero savings rate for the economy at large. If the recycled dollar holdings of foreign central banks are excluded, the domestic US savings rate is a negative 2 per cent. *A time series of the US propensity to save since 1945 shows a steady decline in (net) S/Y* (see Figure 6.4).

Despite a falling savings rate, however, the economy never has been flusher with savings and credit. The growth of savings, wealth and net worth is less and less the result of new direct investment in tangible capital formation, rather the product of rising asset prices for real estate, stocks and bonds. *In balance-sheet terms, gross savings are soaring while net savings are zero or negative.*

This growth in net worth occurs despite the fact that most new saving is offset on the liabilities side of the balance sheet by growth in debt. The rise of net worth is the result of savings being lent to borrowers who bid up asset prices by using new loans and credit to buy property and securities, that is, wealth and financial claims on wealth.

These features of today's economy appear to be an anomaly as compared to the formulae that Keynes traced out in 1936. Today's economy is best seen as

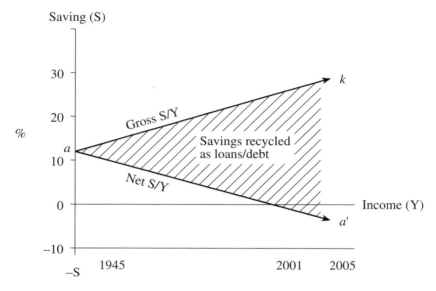

Notes:
S/Y = Saving (S) as percentage of income (Y)
ak = Keynes's expected rise in saving
aa' = Actual net domestic US saving (from NIPA)
−S = Net debt (dis-saving)
* = As reported in the National Income and Product Accounts (NIPA)

Figure 6.4   Actual saving* vs. Keynes's expected saving

a financial bubble, just the opposite of the deflationary Great Depression described by Keynes. Credit – and hence, debt – is being created to inflate the
bubble rather than to finance direct capital formation. In this respect the banking
and financial systems have become dysfunctional.

Monetary expansion and prices in the commodity and asset markets move
asymmetrically. Today's asset-price inflation goes hand in hand with commodity-price stagnation and a deflation of labour's spending power. Upon closer
examination this inverse relationship is not an anomaly, but the phenomenon
shows that the savings problem has become more serious than Keynes feared,
for reasons that he had little reason to discuss 70 years ago.

For one thing, the volume of savings compounds by being recycled into the
creation of new interest-bearing debt as savers or financial institutions use
their accrual of income, dividends and capital gains to buy more securities,
make more loans or buy property, rather than spend this revenue on current
output. The growing debt overhead, and the savings that form the balance-
sheet counterpart to this debt, bears interest charges that divert income to debt

service rather than being available for spending on consumption and direct investment.

THE FIRE SECTOR IN RELATION TO THE REST OF THE ECONOMY

The institutions that distinguish one national economy from another are the property and financial institutions that steer saving and investment, and the public tax policies that shape markets. These policies determine the character of the FIRE sector. The largest and defining features of any economy are those of the property and financial sector, whose rent, interest, monopoly revenue and 'capital' gains (most of which are real-estate gains) rise relative to overall national income.

Instead of examining these contrasting financial and fiscal policies, most economics texts concentrate on the abstract technological production and consumption dimension of economic life. It is as if the property and financial dimension – tangible wealth and financial claims on property and income – lie somewhere on the far side of the moon, invisible to earth or at least wrapped in a cloak of invisibility.

When Keynes viewed individuals as saving a portion of the income they earned, he defined (S) as a function of income (Y) multiplied by the marginal propensity to save (*mps*, or simply *s*), so that S = sY. Keynes thus derived the savings function s = S/Y for economies as a whole. This formula does not acknowledge that financial institutions tend to save all their income. Furthermore, over time a rising proportion of this inflow of interest, dividends and rent is ploughed back into new loans rather than invested in tangible capital formation.

Keynes recognized that wealthy individuals save a higher portion of their income as they earn more. He feared that, as economies grew richer over time, the propensity to save would rise. But he did not describe corporate financial institutions as having a distinct propensity of their own to save all their interest and dividend receipts.

Today we can see that the problem with saving is not simply that it is 'nonspending'. A rising proportion of savings are lent out or invested in loans and securities, dividend-yielding stocks and rent-yielding properties, to become interest-bearing debts owed by the economy at large. These savings expand of their own accord as their interest receipts are recycled into new loans and other income-yielding assets, growing in an exponentially rising curve. This exponentially rising curve is that of compound interest, so that $S_t = S_{t-1}^{(1+i)}$, where i represents the rate of interest. Meanwhile, the growth of debt grows *pari passu*, as Keynes would have put it.

Thus it is helpful to distinguish between the propensity to save (1) by labour and industrial firms out of income earned by producing goods and services, and (2) by the FIRE sector out of debt service and rental charges. Drawing this distinction requires that the economy itself be viewed as a combination of two separate parts, by separating the FIRE sector from the rest of the economy. I refer to these two sectors as (1) the production and consumption economy comprising fixed capital and labour, and (2) the economically larger property and financial sector receiving *rentier* income (defined to include financial 'service' fees).

Although net saving does not increase in such cases, the volume of loanable funds expands. These funds are built up as interest, dividends and rents accrue to owners of securities and property. To the extent that these revenues accrue to large financial institutions – insurance companies, pension and mutual funds – the propensity to save such returns is nearly 100 per cent. To be sure, bankers pay interest to their depositors while insurance and pension funds pay their policy holders. However, most of these interest and dividend accruals are left in accounts to accumulate. The result is an exponentially rising curve of savings at compound interest.

The idea of a propensity to consume is appropriate only for consumer income, not that of the financial, insurance and real estate (FIRE) sectors. Consumers, especially retirees, do indeed consume some part of their *rentier* income, but this is not true of institutional investors. Keynes recognized that the wealthiest income brackets have a high propensity to save, while less affluent brackets have a lower propensity. Today, the wealthiest 10 per cent of the population holds most of the savings in every economy. The bottom 90 per cent tend to be net debtors rather than net savers in today's highly financialized economies of North America and Europe.

 Additional saving is created when banks create credit. Most finds its counterpart in the new debts that borrowers owe, so that the *net* saving rate is not affected. Keynes concerned himself almost entirely with net saving, not gross savings and their counterpart debt.

When Keynes defined saving as equal to investment, he did not emphasize the distinction between direct investment in tangible capital goods and loans that became the debts of the economy's non-financial sectors. Failure to draw this distinction led to an ambiguity between gross or net saving. National income accounts define saving net of the growth in debt, so that no increase in net saving occurs when savings are lent out.

This condition has become more and more the case for the US economy in recent decades. Today's propensity to save is less than zero as the economy is running into debt faster than it is building up new savings. Keynes did not address this possibility, and indeed it was not a pressing concern back in 1936 when he wrote his *General Theory*.

Modern national income accounts also combine the wages and profits that labour and industry earn with the interest and rent that finance and property receive. The basic idea is that providing land, the radio spectrum, subsoil minerals and even monopoly goods supplies a 'service' alongside the goods and services produced by labour and capital goods. But it is equally possible to view finance and property, not as 'factors of production' producing services that earn interest, financial fees and rent, but as receiving transfer payments or what Henry George called 'value from obligation'. This distinction enables the classical distinction between 'earned' and 'unearned' income to be preserved in a way that I believe Keynes would have appreciated in view of his call for 'euthanasia of the *rentier*'.

Nearly all new fixed capital formation is financed out of retained business earnings, not out of bank borrowing. Banks finance sales, foreign trade, consumer debt and the purchase of property already in place, but hardly ever have they taken the risk of financing new direct investment. Their time horizon is short-term, not long-term.

This chapter proposes a model to integrate the analysis of asset-price inflation with debt deflation and Say's Law. Viewing savings and debt in their institutional context, it relates the behaviour of banks and institutional investors to the dynamics of asset-price inflation and debt deflation. A central theme is that *most lending and credit creation are directed into the capital markets via borrowers who buy property or financial securities*. As the economy's assets are loaded down with debt and its interest charges, this credit growth extracts interest payments that divert revenue away from current demand for goods and services. That is why asset-price inflation usually involves debt deflation. The deflationary effect may be mitigated by lowering interest rates, as occurred in the United States during 1994–2004. The debt/savings overhead can rise without extracting a higher flow of interest payments as interest rates approach their nadir (about 1 per cent today).

Keynes viewed saving as causing insufficient market demand to provide full employment. The long-term threat seemed to be that, as economies grew richer, people would save more, disrupting the circular flow of spending between producers and their employees as consumers. What was not emphasized was that, as savings were recycled into loans, economies would polarize between creditors and debtors.

Today the net savings rate has fallen to zero, and the major factor impairing effective demand is the diversion of revenue to service the economy's debt overhead. Paying interest and principal reduces the disposable income that debtors have available to spend on goods and services, while the financial institutions that receive this revenue do not spend it on goods and services. They lend out their receipts to enable the buyers to purchase assets that already exist.[1]

The National Income and Product Accounts (NIPA) define the amortization of debt principal as saving. Most of these repayments are lent out to new borrowers, including corporate business whose balance sheets have reached what Hyman Minsky called the 'Ponzi stage' of fragility: the point at which the debt overhead is carried by debtors borrowing the interest charges that are growing exponentially. In this respect 'debts cause saving'.

Today's problem of inadequate consumer demand and capital investment lies on the liabilities (debt) side of the balance sheet, not on the asset (saving) side. Keynes anticipated that, as economies grew and incomes rose, a rising proportion of S/Y would reduce consumption, leading to overproduction if employers did not cut back their own direct investment. This line of thought reflected the psychological theorizing of British marginal utility analysis rather than a financial view of the dynamics that determined the build-up of savings.

Keynes's discussion of savings led him to re-examine Say's Law, which described the circular flow of spending between producers and consumers. Under normal conditions producers would hire workers, who would spend their wages on buying what they produced. This was the basic meaning of the phrase 'supply creates its own demand'. But savings threatened to interrupt this circular flow by diverting the purchasing power of consumers away from the demand for goods and services, and that of employers away from the purchase of capital goods.

Keynes found saving to be the main culprit for the economic slowdown of the Great Depression on the ground that it led to reduced market demand, deterring new direct investment and hence slowing the growth of employment. But in today's US-centred bubble economy the problem has become more complicated. To the extent that savings are lent out (rather than invested out of retained earnings to purchase capital goods, erect buildings and create other tangible means of production), they divert future income away from consumption and investment to pay debt service. In this respect the growth of savings *in financial form* (that is, in ways other than new direct capital formation) adds to the debt overhead and hence contributes to debt deflation. This is what occurs with nearly all the savings intermediated and lent out or reinvested by the banks, insurance companies and other financial institutions.

Keynes did not devote much attention to the accrual of interest on past savings. His *General Theory* was ambiguous with regard to the specific forms that savings might take. They were identified simply as investment, so that on the macroeconomic plane, S = I. The implication by many Keynesians today is that savings actually cause investment. The reality is that savings not invested directly in new means of production were invested indirectly in stocks, bonds and real estate. Investment in securities and property already in existence had no positive employment effects. But there was not much growth in either borrowing or this kind of indirect investment back when the *General Theory* was published. The tendency was for savings to sit idle, as did much of the labour force.

THE SELF-EXPANDING GROWTH OF SAVINGS THROUGH THEIR ACCRUAL OF INTEREST

The financial system exists in a symbiosis with the 'real' economy. Each system has its own set of growth dynamics. Financial systems tend to grow exponentially at compound interest. The cumulative value of savings grows through a dynamic that Keynes had little reason to analyse in the 1930s – what Richard Price described as the 'geometric' growth of a penny invested at 5 per cent at the time of Jesus's birth, growing to a solid sphere of gold extending from the Sun out beyond the orbit of Jupiter by his day (1776). He contrasted this 'geometric' growth of savings invested at compound interest to the merely 'arithmetic' growth of a similar sum invested at simple interest. This was the metaphor that Malthus adopted to describe the growth of human populations in contrast to the means of subsistence.[2]

Many people saved money back in the time of Jesus, but nobody has obtained savings amounting to anywhere near a solid sphere of gold. The reason is that savings that are invested in debt tend to stifle economies, causing downturns that wipe out the debts and savings together in a convulsion of bankruptcy. This was what happened to the Roman Empire, and on a smaller scale it has characterized business cycles for the past two centuries. Yet this dynamic rarely has been related to the bankruptcy phenomenon, although it is a key factor countering the growth of savings.

Economies do grow faster than 'arithmetically', but not 'geometrically'. Their typical growth pattern is that of an S-curve, tapering off over the course of the business cycle. The exponential growth of savings and debts thus tends chronically to exceed that of the 'real' economy. Unless interest rates decline, the debt burden will divert income away from spending on goods and services, turning the economy downward (Figure 6.5 and Figure 6.6).

The *General Theory* recognized savings as arising out of current income, not as growing through the compounding of interest, doubling and redoubling at compound interest by their own inertia. They accrue interest independently of the course of incomes when invested in bonds or left in savings accounts, as well as accruing dividends if invested in stocks, or rental income if invested in property. This is especially true of 'forced savings' in the form of pay cheque withholding for social security, pension and retirement accounts, along with insurance policies segregated in a way that makes them unavailable for current spending.

Not being limited by the course of income or the ability to pay, the exponential growth of savings tends to exceed growth of the real economy. This is what occurs when economies are loaded down with debts, which could equally well be thought of as the savings overhead that is lent out. Rising savings on the asset side of the balance sheet connote a rising debt overhead on the liabilities side.

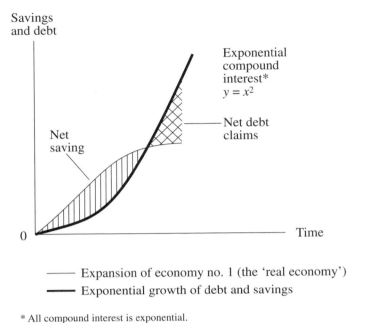

Note: * All compound interest is exponential.

Figure 6.5   How the rise in debt overhead slows down the business cycle

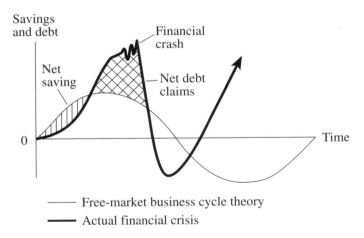

Figure 6.6   Financial crisis vs. business cycle

In this case saving does not necessarily reflect an increase of productive powers and the means of production, nor does it tend to employ labour. Rather, the debt service that results from lending out savings tends to shrink markets and employment.

It should be noted that, while the financial sector represents itself as providing credit to consumers and producers, it also absorbs income by charging interest, in amounts that are as large as the entire loan principal every doubling period: seven years at 10 per cent interest, 13 years at 5 per cent. Ultimately the financial sector extracts revenue from the economy. That is why it is in business, after all: to 'make money from money'.

Money cannot be made from money, of course. It is itself sterile, as Aristotle noted long ago. But it can charge interest from the rest of the economy that does perform the work. Levying interest, rent and other property and financial charges is not to be confused with making money through labour or capital investment. The perception of classical economics that the property and financial system is different has been lost in today's economic thought.

THE GROWTH OF NET WORTH THROUGH CAPITAL GAINS

The cumulative volume of savings also grows through a dynamic that Keynes had little reason to analyse in the 1930s: capital gains. Property and financial securities tend to appreciate in price over time. The main cause of this price appreciation is that the physical volume of assets grows slowly, while the financial volume of loanable funds grows exponentially.

Let us return for a moment to Richard Price's example of a penny saved at the time of Jesus being worth a sphere of gold extending from the Sun out to Jupiter. Few investors buy gold, as it does not yield an income. The largest investment – and the most heavily debt-financed asset these days – is land. More credit does not expand the volume of land, which is fixed, but it does raise its market price. A rising volume of savings is channelled to buy a fixed supply of land. The financial system thus creates capital gains as the finite volume of property and supply of buildings and financial securities expands more slowly than the potentially infinite volume of loanable funds.

Keynes did not anticipate that savings would be channelled in a way that bid up asset prices for securities and property without funding tangible capital formation. In the 1930s, net worth was built up mainly by saving, not by asset-price inflation such as is occurring today. In traditional Keynesian terms, revenue or credit spent on buying property in place represented hoarding, not investment.

Homeowners and investors imagine themselves growing richer as prices rise for their assets. Their net worth rises without their having to save. However, this rise tends to require more income set aside to pay debt service on the loans taken out to buy their property. Credit lent out in this way does not increase consumption and direct investment. It creates debts whose carrying charges shrink markets. Savings and debts rise together, so that there is no increase in *net* saving.

New saving does occur as financial institutions recycle the receipts of debt service into new loans, whose carrying charges absorb yet more future income. The result is that *gross* savings (and hence, indebtedness) rise relative to national income. Stated another way, saving for many homeowners takes the form of paying off their mortgages. This is not the same thing as hoarding (in Keynes's sense), but it plays much the same function, as it is not available for spending on current output.

As savings rise and are lent out, debt service absorbs more income. But the net economic surplus available to service these savings – by paying interest and dividends on the debts and securities in which they are invested – tends not to keep pace with their stipulated debt service. This debt problem therefore plays the deflationary economic role that Keynes attributed to savings.

HOW ASSET-PRICE INFLATION AGGRAVATES ECONOMIC POLARIZATION

Keynes favoured inflation as eroding the burden of debt. Calling for 'euthanasia of the *rentier*', he saw inflation as the line of least political resistance to wiping out the economy's debt burden. His idea was that inflation would leave more income available for consumption and for new direct investment. But asset-price inflation works in a different way. Instead of eroding the purchasing power of wealth relative to commodities and labour, it increases property prices without increasing consumer prices or wages. At least this has been the pattern since 1980. Wealth disparities have increased even more than have disparities among income brackets. The net worth for the wealthiest 10 or 20 per cent of the population has soared, while the rest of the economy has fallen more deeply into debt and many of its gains have turned out to be short-term.

Keynes recognized that rich and poor income and wealth brackets had differing marginal propensities to save. But today's financial polarization has gone beyond anything he anticipated, or what anyone else anticipated back in the 1930s, or for that matter even in the 1950s.

Long before the *General Theory*, economists recognized that wealthy people did not expand their consumption in keeping with their income growth. The image of widows and orphans living off their interest was relevant only for a small part of the economy. *Rentiers* always have tended to save their income and reinvest it in the financial and property markets. This occurs also with savings deposits, which banks lend out or invest directly in financial securities. Most of the interest and dividends credited to savers is thus left to grow by being lent out or ploughed back into indirect securities and property investment, increasing asset prices.

The ability to get an easy ride from the resulting asset-price inflation, coupled with an easy access to credit and favourable tax treatment, prompts investors to take their returns in the form of capital gains rather than current income. In real estate, the economy's largest sector, property owners use their rental income to pay interest on the credit borrowed to buy properties, leaving no taxable earnings at all. The same phenomenon characterizes the corporate sector, where equity has been retired for bonds and bank loans since 1980. Ambitious CEOs, managers of privatized public enterprises and corporate raiders have bought entire companies with debt-financed leveraged buy-outs. Interest charges have absorbed corporate earnings, leaving little remaining for new capital investment. The name of the game has become capital gains, which have been spurred more by downsizing and outsourcing than by new corporate hiring.

Prices for property, stock and bonds have soared relative to wages, forcing home buyers to spend a rising multiple of their annual incomes to buy housing. Also rising has been the cost of acquiring companies relative to corporate profits as price/earnings ratios increase.

Capital gains make the inequality of wealth and property more extreme than income inequality. The wealthiest layer of the population derives its power from capital gains, while using its income to pay interest – as long as interest rates are less than the rate of asset-price inflation. The ratio of wealth and property has risen relative to the value of goods and services, wages and profits, while the debt overhead has grown proportionally.

DOES ASSET-PRICE INFLATION 'CROWD OUT' NEW DIRECT INVESTMENT?

The FIRE sector has been expanding at the expense of the 'real' economy. It drains revenue in the form of interest, rental income and monopoly profits, which are paid out increasingly as interest and financial fees. This triggers a fresh cycle of saving and re-lending by the FIRE sector itself, not so much by the rest of the economy. The more interest accrues in the hands of creditors, the faster their supply of loanable funds increases, thanks to the 'magic of compound interest'. This revenue is lent out and accrues new interest ('interest on interest'), which is recycled into yet new loans.

This growth of savings and loanable funds in the hands of financial institutions is lent out mainly to buy property in place and financial securities, not to fund tangible capital formation. This financial dynamic spurs asset-price inflation, which in turn reduces the incentive to invest directly in capital goods, because it is easier to make capital gains than to earn profits.

These developments have prompted investors to seek 'total returns' – capital gains plus profits or earnings – rather than earnings alone. Under Federal Reserve Board Chairman Alan Greenspan as 'Bubble Maestro' in the 1990s, stock prices for dot.com and Internet companies soared without a foundation in earnings or dividend-paying ability. Balance-sheet manoeuvering was decoupled from tangible investment in the 'real' economy. Companies such as Enron prided themselves on not having any tangible assets at all, just a balance sheet of speculative contracts. People began to ask whether wealth could go on increasing in this way *ad infinitum*.

Keynes's analysis implied that the income 'multiplier' (Y/S, or 1/mps) would increase as prosperity increased and people consumed a smaller portion of their income. What was being multiplied, however, was not national income (wages, profits and other earned income) but the volume of credit and hence the pace of capital gains in the asset markets.

TAX POLICY AND FINANCIAL BUBBLES

Unlike the industrial sector, real estate does not report a profit – and hence, pays no income taxes. Property owners do pay state and local real estate taxes, to be sure, but they have been joined by the financial and insurance lobbies to shift local government budgets away from the land and onto the shoulders of labour, through income taxes, sales taxes and various user fees for municipal services hitherto provided as part of the basic economic needs and infrastructure.

Although land does not depreciate – that is, wear out and become obsolete – by far the bulk of depreciation tax credits are taken by the real estate sector. This is because the economic theory underlying tax obligations has become essentially fictitious. Each time a property is sold, the building is assumed to increase in value, rather than the land's site value generating the gain.

Nothing like this could happen in industry. Machinery wears out and becomes obsolete. (Think of computers and word processors bought a decade ago, or even three years ago.) Technological progress reduces the value of physical capital in place. But the prosperity that progress brings increases the market price of land.

In calling for 'euthanasia of the *rentier*' Keynes pointed to the desirability of preventing the diversion of income into the purchase of securities and property already in place. He hoped to restructure the stock market and financial system so as to direct savings and credit into tangible capital formation rather than speculation. He deplored the waste of human intelligence devoted merely to transferring property ownership rather than creating new means of production.

Today's financial markets have evolved in just the opposite direction from that advocated by Keynes. New savings and credit are channelled into loans to satisfy the rush to buy real estate, stocks and bonds for speculative purposes rather than into the funding of new direct investment and employment. Matters are aggravated by the fact that financial gains are taxed at a lower rate, thanks to the growing power of the financial sector's political lobbies. This prompts companies to use their revenue and go into debt to buy other companies (mergers and acquisitions) or real estate rather than to expand their means of production.

Going into debt to buy assets with borrowed funds experienced a quantum leap in the 1980s with the practice of financing leveraged buy-outs with high-interest 'junk' bonds. The process got under way when interest rates were still hovering near their all-time high of 20 per cent in late 1980 and early 1981. Corporate raiding was led by the investment banking house of Drexel Burnham and its law firm, Skadden Arps. Their predatory activities required a loosening of America's racketeering (RICO) laws to make it legal to borrow funds to take over companies and repay creditors by emptying out their corporate treasuries and 'overfunded' pension plans. New York's laws of fraudulent conveyance also had to be modified.

Tax laws promoted this debt leveraging. Interest was allowed to be counted as a tax-deductible expense, encouraging leveraged buy-outs rather than equity financing or funding out of retained earnings. Depreciation of buildings and other assets was permitted to occur repeatedly, whenever a property was sold. This favoured the real estate sector by making absentee-owned buildings and other commercial properties virtually exempt from the income tax. To top matters off, capital gains tax rates were reduced below taxes on the profits earned by direct investment. This diverted savings to fuel asset-price inflation. By the 1990s, the process had become a self-feeding dynamic. The more prices rose for stocks and real estate, the more mortgage borrowing rose for homes and other property, while corporate borrowing soared for mergers and acquisition.

Meanwhile, the more gains being made off the bubble, the more powerful its beneficiaries grew. They turned their economic power into political power to lower taxes and deregulate speculative finance, along with fraud, corrupt accounting practices and the use of offshore tax-avoidance enclaves, even further. This caused federal, state and local budget deficits while shifting the tax burden onto labour and industrial income. Markets shrank as a result of the fiscal drain as well as the financial debt overhead.

Abuses such as arrogance and outright fraud occurred in what became a golden age for Enron, WorldCom and other 'high flyers' akin to the S&L scandals of the mid-1980s. But free-market monetarism draws no distinction between tangible direct investment and purely financial gain-seeking. Opposing government regulation to favour any given way of recycling savings as compared to any other way, the value-free ethic of our times holds that making money is inherently productive regardless of how it is made. 'Free-market fundamentalism' came to shape neoliberal tax policy in a way that favoured finance, not industry or labour.

CAN ECONOMIES INFLATE THEIR WAY OUT OF DEBT?

Only a limited repertory of opportunities for profitable new direct investment exists at any given point in time. The exponential growth in savings tends to outstrip these opportunities, and hence is lent out. This lending (and its mirror image, borrowing) may become self-justifying at least for a time to the extent that it bids up asset prices. Homebuyers and investors feel that it pays them to go into debt to buy property, and this is viewed as 'prosperity', although it is primarily financial rather than industrial in character.

About 70 per cent of bank loans in the United States and Britain take the form of real estate mortgages. Most new savings and credit creation thus enables borrowers to bid up the price of homes and office buildings. The effect is to increase the price that consumers must pay to obtain housing, as new construction loans account for only a small proportion of mortgage lending. Overextended families become 'house-poor' as rising financial charges for housing diverts income away from being spent on new goods and services, 'crowding out' consumer spending and business investment.

Governments may try to mitigate the inflation of housing prices by raising interest rates. But this will increase the carrying charges for borrowers with floating-rate mortgages, as well as debtors throughout the economy. (Also, as Britain discovered in spring 2004, the increase in interest rates also raises the currency exchange rate, making its exporters less competitive in world markets.) For fixed-rate mortgages, higher interest rates may squeeze the banks, leading to losses in their portfolio values and prompting calls for the government to bail out losers (at least depositors, if not to rescue S&Ls and commercial banks).

Perception of this problem leads central bankers not to raise interest rates and take the blame for destroying financial prosperity by pricking the bubble. Instead, they try to keep it from bursting. This can be done only by inflating it all the more. So the process escalates.

Balance sheets improve as the pace of capital gains outstrips the rate of interest. Debt service can be paid out of rising asset values, either by selling off assets or by borrowing against the higher asset prices as collateral. The problem occurs when current income can no longer carry the interest charges. The financial sector absorbs more income as debt service than it supplies in the form of new credit. Asset prices turn down, but the debts remain on the books. This has been Japan's condition since its bubble peaked in 1990. It may result in 'negative equity' for the most highly leveraged mortgage borrowers in the real estate sector, followed by debt-ridden companies.

When interest charges exceed rental income, commercial borrowers hesitate to use their own money or other income to keep current on their debts. The limited liability laws let them walk away from their losses if markets are deflated, leaving banks, insurance companies, pension funds and other financial institutions to absorb the loss. Sell-offs of these properties to raise cash would accelerate the plunge in asset prices, leaving balance sheets 'hollowed out'.

Savings do not appear as the villain in such periods. The zero net savings rate has concealed the fact that gross savings have been re-lent to create a corresponding growth in debt. America's national debt quadrupled during the 12-year Reagan–Bush administration (1981–93). This increase in debt was facilitated by reducing interest rates by enough so that the unprecedented increase in credit rose without extracting more interest from many properties.

The natural limit to this process was reached in 2004 when the Federal Reserve reduced its discount rate to only 1 per cent. Once rates hit this nadir, further growth in debt threatened to be reflected directly in draining amortization and interest payments away from spending on goods and services, slowing the economy accordingly. Further debt growth would require a rising proportion of disposable personal income to be spent on debt service.

HOW LONG CAN BUBBLES KEEP EXPANDING?

The potential credit supply is limited only by the market price of all existing property and securities. The process is open-ended, as each new credit creation inflates the market value of assets that can be pledged as collateral for new loans.

Until bubbles burst, they benefit investors who borrow money to buy assets that are rising in price. Running into debt becomes the preferred way to make money, rather than the traditional first step toward losing the homestead. The motto of modern real estate investors is that 'rent is for paying interest' and this also applies to corporate raiders who use the earnings of companies bought on credit to repay their bankers and bondholders. What real estate investors and corporate financial officers are after is capital gains.

There is no inherent link with making new direct investment. Indeed, the after-tax return from asset-price inflation exceeds that which can be made by investing to create profits. Retirees, widows and orphans do best by living off capital gains, selling part of their growing portfolios rather than seeking a flow of interest, dividends and rental income. The idea begins to spread that people can live off capital gains in an economy whose incomes are not growing.

Asset-price inflation would be a rational long-term policy if economies could inflate their way out of debt via capital gains. The solution to debt would be to create yet more debt to finance yet more asset-price inflation. This dynamic is more likely to create debt deflation than commodity-price inflation, however. It is true that a consumer 'wealth effect' occurs when homeowners refinance their mortgages by taking new 'home equity' loans to spend on living, or at least to pay down their credit card debt so as to lower the monthly diversion of income for debt service. If this were to lead to a general inflation, interest rates would rise, prompting investors to shift out of stocks into bonds. Foreign investors and speculators bail out, accelerating the price decline. This threatens retirement funds, insurance companies and banks with capital losses that erode their ability to meet their commitments.

The more likely constraint comes from asset-price inflation itself as price/earnings ratios rise. Interest rates and other returns slow, making it difficult for pension plans and insurance companies to earn the projected returns needed to pay retirees. In any event, asset sales exceed purchases as the proportion of retirees to employees grows, causing stock and bond prices to decline. Pension funds must sell more stocks and bonds – or employers must set aside more of their revenue for this purpose, in which case their ability to pay dividends is reduced.

Asset-price inflation reaches its limit when interest charges absorb the entire flow of earnings. Debt-financed bubbles remove more purchasing power from the 'bottom 90 per cent' of the population than they supply. Debt spurs rising housing prices but reduces consumer demand as a result of the need to service mortgages. Likewise, financing for leveraged buy-outs, mergers and acquisitions may increase stock prices, but the interest charges absorb corporate earnings and 'crowd out' new direct investment and employment.

The drive for capital gains thus complicates the traditional macroeconomic Keynesian categories. Although these gains are not included in the national income statistics, they have become the key to analysing how asset-price inflation leads to debt deflation of the 'real' economy. Thus one may ask what sphere of the economy is more 'real' and powerful: that of tangible production and consumption, or the financial sector which is wrapped around it.

CAN THE DEBT AND SAVINGS OVERHEAD BE SUPPORTED INDEFINITELY?

Richard Price's illustration of the seemingly magical powers of compound interest is a reminder that many people saved pennies (and much more) at the time of Jesus, and long before that, but nobody yet has obtained an expanding globe of gold. The reason is that savings have been wiped out repeatedly in waves of bankruptcy.

The reason is clear enough. When savings, lending and 'indirect' financial investment grow by compound interest in the absence of new tangible investment, something must give. The superstructure of debt must be brought back into a relationship with the ability to pay.

Financial crashes occur much more quickly than the long build-up. This is what produces a ratchet pattern for business cycles: a gradual upsweep and sudden collapse of financial and property prices, leaving economies debt-ridden. Many debts are wiped out, to be sure, along with the savings that have been invested in bad loans – unless the government bails out savers at taxpayer expense.

Financial crises are not resolved simply by price adjustments. Almost all crises involve government intervention, solving matters politically. As the financial and property sectors gain political power relative to the increasingly indebted production and consumption sectors, their lobbies succeed in lowering tax rates on *rentier* income relative to taxes on wages and profits. Tax rates on capital gains have been slashed below those on 'earned' wages and profits, whereas the two rates were equal when America's income tax laws first were introduced.

Financial lobbies also have got lawmakers to adopt the 'moral hazard' policy of guaranteeing savings. Debtors may still go bankrupt, but savings are to be kept intact by making taxpayers liable to the economy's savers. Ever since the collapse of the Federal Savings and Loan Insurance Corporation (FSLIC) in the late 1980s a political fight has loomed over just whose savings are to be rescued. Unfortunately, the principle at work is that of 'Big fish eat little fish'. Small savers are sacrificed to the wealthiest savers and institutional investors.

The mathematics of compound interest dictates that such public guarantees to preserve savings cannot succeed in the long run. Financial savings and debts tend to grow at exponential rates while economies grow only by S curves, causing strains that cannot be supported as credit is used to buy assets rather than to invest in capital goods or buildings.

Financial strains become further politicized as large institutions and the 'upper 10 per cent' of the population account for nearly all the net saving, which is lent out to the 'bottom 90 per cent' and to industry. The balance-sheet position of the wealthiest layer increases as long as capital gains exceed the build-up of debt. The bottom 90 per cent also benefit for a while during the early and middle stages of the financial bubble. Workers are invited to think of themselves as finance capitalists-in-miniature rather than as employees being downsized and outsourced. But much of what they may gain in the rising market value of their homes (for the two-thirds of the US and British populations that are homeowners) is offset by the debt deflation that bleeds the production-and-consumption economy.

Throughout history societies that have polarized between creditors and debtors have not survived well. Rome ended in a convulsion of debt foreclosure, monopolization of the land and tax shifts that reduced most of the population to clientage. Third world countries today are being stripped of their public domain and public enterprises by the international debt build-up, while industry and real estate in the creditor nations themselves are becoming debt-ridden.

Today's bubble economy is seeing interest charges expand to absorb profits and rental income, leading to slower domestic direct investment and employment. Much as classical economists believed that rent would expand to absorb the entire economic surplus, it now appears that interest-bearing debt will play this role.

NOTES

1. Keynes noted that Malthus pointed out that landlords helped contribute to aggregate demand by spending their rental income on hiring servants. But banks lend to service producers and other labour, increasing the volume of debt.
2. I review how economists have treated this phenomenon in 'The Mathematical Economics of Compound Interest: A Four-Thousand Year Overview', *Journal of Economic Studies*, **27** (2000), 344–63.

7. Unit roots in macroeconomic time series and stabilization policies: a Post Keynesian interpretation

Gilberto A. Libanio

INTRODUCTION

The question of whether or not macroeconomic time series present a unit root has been exhaustively discussed within the *mainstream* of economics in the last two decades. The work of Nelson and Plosser (1982) is usually recognized as the starting point of this literature, with significant implications for econometric modelling, for business cycle theorizing, and for economic policy prescriptions.

The presence or absence of unit roots, to put it in a simple way, helps identify some features of the underlying data-generating process of a series. If a series has no unit roots, it is characterized as stationary, and therefore exhibits mean reversion in that it fluctuates around a constant long-run mean. Also the absence of unit roots implies that the series has a finite variance which does not depend on time (this point is crucial for economic forecasting), and that the effects of shocks dissipate over time.

Alternatively, if the series feature a unit root, they are better characterized as non-stationary processes that have no tendency to return to a long-run deterministic path. Besides, the variance of the series is time-dependent and goes to infinity as time approaches infinity, which results in serious problems for forecasting. Finally, non-stationary series suffer permanent effects from random shocks. As usually denominated in the literature, series with unit roots follow a *random walk*.

In sum, the existence (or not) of unit roots in macroeconomic time series brings about important implications, and this helps to explain why this topic has received a great amount of theoretical and applied research in the last two decades. There are many different issues in the unit roots literature that are somehow related but can be explored separately. To the question 'why do we care about unit roots in GNP?' Cribari-Neto (1996, p. 38) provides the following answer:

To a policymaker the answer could be: 'Because the policy implications are different.' To a macroeconomist, it could be answered that 'there are theoretical implications on several theories and models'. Finally, an econometrician would be satisfied with the answer: 'Because the asymptotics are different.'

On the other hand, the presence or absence of unit roots in macroeconomic time series has not received a great deal of attention from Post Keynesians, despite the possible implications of unit roots for theory and policy within the Post Keynesian paradigm, and despite the importance of this theme in macroeconomics research within the *mainstream*. This chapter tries to tackle this question and argues that the presence of unit roots in macroeconomic time series provides support to the general perspective adopted by Keynes and Post Keynesians on output and employment fluctuations, on the non-neutrality of money in the long run, and on some economic policy issues. Therefore, this chapter agrees with Cross (1993, p. 307) when he says that 'tests for unit roots (…) have surely offered insights into the nature of macroeconomic processes which do not entirely conflict with post Keynesian views'.

The main focus of this chapter will be the implications of unit roots in GNP time series for macroeconomic theorizing and for economic policies. In particular, the chapter analyses how different orthodox theories of macroeconomic fluctuations interpret the findings of unit roots, and it also offers an alternative interpretation, based on the work of Keynes and the Post Keynesians. The remainder of the chapter is organized as follows. The next section briefly describes the concept of unit roots in time series and the major unit root test in the literature. Sections three and four consider the implications of unit roots for *mainstream* business cycle theorizing, including the initial support for real business cycle theories, and the reactions to that perspective. Subsequently, I present an alternative perspective to the existence of unit roots in GNP time series, based on the Post Keynesian theory of output determination. The last section summarizes the arguments and suggests some economic policy implications of the analysis.

TESTING FOR UNIT ROOTS IN GNP SERIES

Consider two alternative models used to represent GNP time series:

$$y_t = a + bt + e_t, \tag{7.1}$$

$$y_t = a + y_{t-1} + e_t, \tag{7.2}$$

where y_t represents the natural logarithm of GNP at time t, t represents a time trend, b is a constant that gives the growth rate of the variable, and e is an error term with zero mean and finite variance.

The first specification implies that GNP equals the constant a at time zero ($y_0 = a$) and grows over time at a constant rate b, with the error term explaining deviations from the trend in each year. In other words, the variable y_t presents a stationary fluctuation around the time trend $a + bt$. Therefore, the variable is described as *trend-stationary* (TS), and stationarity is achieved by removing the time trend ('detrending'), that is, regressing y_t on t. Another feature of model (7.1) is that the variance of y_t is bounded by the variance of e_t, and the linear forecast of GNP converges to the time trend $a + bt$ as the forecast horizon increases. Finally, for the first specification, the effects of a shock at time t tend to zero over time, since the error term affects the outcome in the current period, but has no persistent influence in succeeding time periods.

Model (7.2), on the other hand, specifies that GNP grows at rate a from its previous value, with an error term playing a role every year. Despite the apparent similarity between the two models, they are indeed very different, and lead to different implications in many respects.

First, model (7.2) is non-stationary and cannot be made stationary through detrending. But note that the first difference of the series is given by $a + e_t$, a stationary process. So, stationarity can be achieved by differencing, and the model is said to be *difference-stationary* (DS). Model (7.2) is one of the simplest AR(1) processes, and can be described as a *random walk* with drift. The dependent variable displays a random fluctuation given by the error term e_t, in addition to the growth given by the drift term a. Contrarily to model (7.1), however, there is no tendency for y_t to return to a predetermined mean value, and its trajectory is given by an accumulation of disturbances. In other words, the error term affects not only what happens in the current period, but also what happens in all succeeding periods. In order better to visualize this point, we can substitute repeatedly for the lagged y_t value in equation (7.2) to get

$$y_t = y_0 + at + \sum_{i=1}^{t} e_i. \tag{7.3}$$

It is straightforward to see that the variance of y_t grows without bound over time, and that shocks to the system (captured by the error term) have a permanent effect on the series. Also the mean square error of the forecast of the DS model grows linearly with the forecast horizon.

Model (7.2) represents the *unit root hypothesis*, a terminology arising from the fact that the coefficient on y_{t-1} is unity. If this coefficient was less than unity, the series would be stationary (mean reverting) and random shocks would dissipate over time.[1]

In sum, the two models are indeed different and have different implications. Therefore it has become common practice to check whether a GNP series can be better described as a TS or a DS process. This is usually done by testing for the presence of a unit root in the autoregressive representation of the series. If a unit root is found, traditional estimation techniques cannot be used since, as is well known, spurious results are obtained when two variables with unit roots are regressed on each other: misleadingly high R squares and t statistics, and very low DW statistics.

There are different ways to test for the presence of unit roots. According to Elder and Kennedy (2001, p. 138), 'the augmented Dickey-Fuller (ADF) test has become the most popular of many competing tests in the literature'. It consists in estimating by OLS a model such as

$$y_t = a + bt + u. \, y_{t-1} + e_t,$$ (7.4)

in the form

$$\Delta y_t = (u - 1). \, y_{t-1} + a + bt + e_t,$$ (7.5)

and then testing for $u = 1$ (null hypothesis of unit root) using a t test.[2] Failing to reject the null is equivalent to failing to reject the existence of a unit root or stochastic trend in the data series.

Two major issues in performing ADF tests are the inclusion (or not) of an intercept term, a trend term, or both, and the selection of the truncation lag. ADF test results are very responsive to the presence of intercept and trend terms, and to the number of lags included. In general, including too many deterministic regressors results in lost power, whereas not including enough of them increases the probability of not rejecting the unit-root null.[3]

UNIT ROOTS AS A SUPPORT TO REAL BUSINESS CYCLE THEORY

The work of Nelson and Plosser (1982) is usually considered the starting point of a vast amount of research on unit roots in macroeconomic time series. Their paper uses long historical time series of annual data for 14 variables for the US economy, including measures of output, employment, prices, wages, money stock, and interest rates. Starting dates range from 1860 to 1909, and all series end in 1970. Nelson and Plosser's goal is to examine whether these time series are better characterized as TS or as DS processes.

In particular, they intend to question the traditional practice of decomposing output series into a secular component (long-run deterministic trend) and a cyclical component (stationary short-run fluctuations around trend). Nelson and Plosser argue that, if the series is non-stationary (that is, features a unit root in its autoregressive representation), then the secular component should be modelled as a stochastic process, responsible for any long-run non-stationarity observed in the series, since the cyclical component is assumed to be transitory. In other words, 'since cyclical fluctuations are assumed to dissipate over time, any long-run or permanent movement (non-stationarity) is necessarily attributed to the secular component' (ibid., pp. 139–40).

In this case, aggregate output is thought of as consisting of a non-stationary growth component plus a stationary cyclical component, being the total variation in output changes attributed to both components.

Nelson and Plosser (1982) then analyse sample autocorrelations and test for the existence of unit roots in the 14 long-run time series, and find that the null hypothesis of a unit root cannot be rejected at 5 per cent for most of the series. Nelson and Plosser acknowledge that non-rejection of the null hypothesis does not necessarily imply that the null is 'true'. This is particularly important in the case of unit root tests, since such tests usually have low power, that is, cannot differentiate between unit roots and a TS alternative with an AR root arbitrarily close to unity. However, they argue, if the deviations from a linear trend in the series are stationary, *'then the tendency to return to the trend line must be so weak as to avoid detection even in samples as long as sixty years to over a century'* (ibid., p. 152).

To sum up, Nelson and Plosser conclude that the evidence presented supports the DS representation of non-stationarity in economic time series, and that in this case economic fluctuations are better explained by movements in the secular component (caused mainly by real factors, such as changes in tastes and technology) than by the cyclical component.

In other words, the evidence of unit roots in GNP time series was interpreted by Nelson and Plosser (1982) as providing support for theories of fluctuations based on real (as opposed to monetary) factors. This argument has strongly influenced the direction of *mainstream* macroeconomic research since the 1980s.[4] Some authors argue that the advance of Real Business Cycle (RBC) models (full equilibrium models with emphasis on technology shocks as source of fluctuations) is mainly due to the empirical findings of Nelson and Plosser (1982). According to McCallum (2000, p. 119), 'the logical basis for the upsurge of the RBC movement can be viewed as principally empirical'. Or, as stated by Backhouse and Salanti (2000, p. 12): 'Although decisive tests are rarely possible, some papers cite one example where such a test occurred: the rejection of the hypothesis that monetary shocks were the cause of the business cycle. This led directly to the emergence of real business cycle theory.'

The argument used by Nelson and Plosser (1982) is that most of the fluctuations in output should be attributable to changes in the trend component, in a trend versus cyclical decomposition, which would presumably be unaffected by monetary factors. In other words, the existence of unit roots leads to the inference that movements in output are persistent; since the cyclical component is *assumed* to be stationary, it follows that output fluctuations are mostly associated with the secular component. The argument is completed by the idea that monetary shocks are necessarily temporary and so can only affect the cyclical component, and that the long-run path of the economy is mainly guided by real factors such as tastes and technology.

Nelson and Plosser's main conclusion in terms of macroeconomic theorizing follows directly from such reasoning, and can be summarized as follows:

> We conclude that macroeconomic models that focus on monetary disturbances as a source of purely transitory (stationary) fluctuations may never be successful in explaining a very large fraction of output fluctuations and that stochastic variation due to real factors is an essential element of any model of economic fluctuations. (Nelson and Plosser, 1982, p. 141)

It is worth noting that the argument rests on a number of implicit or explicit building blocks, all of them necessary for the final conclusions. First, Nelson and Plosser use the evidence of unit roots in GNP time series, although they recognize that none of the tests used can distinguish conclusively between a difference-stationary process and a trend-stationary process with an autoregressive root arbitrarily close to unity.

Second, it is inferred that innovations in the stochastic trend component have a larger variance than the innovations in the transitory component, and this leads to the conclusion that variations in the cyclical component of fluctuations are small in comparison with fluctuations in the trend component. Note that this inference is dependent upon the ability of the empirical analysis to differentiate between a DS and a TS process.

Third, the classical dichotomy between real and monetary variables is assumed. In particular, it is assumed that the cyclical component is stationary, and mainly affected by monetary factors, which are neutral in the long run.[5] In this respect, Nelson and Plosser acknowledge in a footnote that the theoretical possibility of a 'Tobin effect' of sustained inflation on the steady-state capital stock is ignored in their analysis. It is clear that, once money is allowed to play any significant role in the long-run path of the economy, unit roots do not necessarily support RBC theories (I will return to this point later). In addition, concerning the stationarity of the cyclical component, Nelson and Plosser admit it is a proposition that cannot be inferred from empirical analysis. However, they justify its use by saying that it is an assumption 'we believe most economists would accept' (ibid., p. 160).

The macroeconomic implications of the work of Nelson and Plosser (1982) are controversial, and have not gone uncontested. Many arguments in different directions have been developed in opposition to Nelson and Plosser's findings. In very general terms, two interrelated lines of criticism can be identified in the *mainstream* literature. The first one relates to an effort to reconcile the presence of unit roots in GNP time series with theories of output fluctuations other than RBC models; the other one contests the very existence of unit roots in the series or, more precisely, stress the inability of unit root tests to differentiate between TS and DS processes in data covering limited time spans.[6]

UNIT ROOTS AND NEW KEYNESIAN ECONOMICS

The first reactions to the conclusions of Nelson and Plosser can be seen as an attempt to promote New Keynesian models of aggregate fluctuations, in which GNP is expected to revert to a long-run trend, but in which the adjustment process can be very slow owing to imperfections in goods and labour markets. A number of papers were published during the 1980s with different arguments in this direction.

McCallum (1986) claims that the statistical evidence provided by Nelson and Plosser cannot be interpreted as providing support for RBC theory, since this evidence is equally consistent with other theories of business cycle. His criticism is primarily devoted to the second 'building block' mentioned before, that is, that the cyclical component of fluctuations has little importance relative to the secular component.

According to McCallum (1986) this point cannot be inferred from the data presented by Nelson and Plosser (1982), because it depends on the hypothesis that GNP series follows a DS process, which in turn is not guaranteed. McCallum points out and evaluates three types of evidence presented by Nelson and Plosser in favour of the hypothesis of non-stationarity. The first evidence is that the sample autocorrelations for annual GNP data are large and decay slowly. The second evidence is that the autocorrelations of annual GNP differences are positive and significant at lag one, but often not significant at longer lags. McCallum shows that both types of evidence are also compatible with the behaviour of a trend-stationary series with a root close to one, and concludes that it is not possible to determine with any degree of certainty if a series is difference-stationary or trend-stationary simply by inspection of the autocorrelation functions for levels and differences. The third evidence provided by Nelson and Plosser (1982) is formal tests of unit roots. Also in this case, McCallum argues, the evidence is far from conclusive, since unit root tests have low power to distinguish between a DS process and a TS process with an AR root close to unity.

In addition, McCallum (1986) shows that, if the decomposition of the series into cyclical and secular components assumes that the latter is given by a DS process when the process under study is actually one of the TS class with an AR root close to one, then it follows that the variability of the cyclical component will be underestimated. He concludes:

The time series evidence provided by Nelson and Plosser (1982) is inadequate to determine whether the relevant series are of the DS or TS class. This evidence itself, then, sheds little or no light on the issue of the relative variability of cyclical and secular components of typical macroeconomic time series – and consequently provides little or no support for the RBC hypothesis. (McCallum, 1986, p. 407)

The work of Campbell and Mankiw (1987) is also motivated by the findings of Nelson and Plosser (1982). Campbell and Mankiw assert that their goal is to question the view that economic fluctuations can be seen as temporary deviations from a deterministic trend. In view of that, their starting point is the assumption that, if output series are stationary and therefore mean-reverting, then a current shock should not change one's forecast of output in the long run (say, five to ten years). Campbell and Mankiw (1987) provide evidence of unit roots in post-war GNP time series, and suggest that persistence of shocks is an important aspect of the data, which 'should be used more widely for evaluating theories of economic fluctuations' (ibid., p. 858). However, they do not agree with the idea that the existence of unit roots is clear evidence that real, supply-side shocks are the main cause of the business cycle, or that fluctuations based on aggregate demand disturbances should be abandoned.

According to Campbell and Mankiw (1987), traditional theories of economic fluctuations accept two basic premises: (i) fluctuations are mainly caused by aggregate demand shocks; (ii) demand shocks have only short-term effects, and the economy reverts to the natural rate of output in the long run. They argue (p. 876) that Nelson and Plosser's 'extreme' conclusions follow from the abandonment of the first premise. Alternatively, they suggest that another way to cope with persistence of shocks is to abandon the second premise, the natural rate hypothesis. This would open the possibility of aggregate demand shocks having persistent effects on output, and this result could be explored in models of multiple equilibria. Campbell and Mankiw conclude: 'Perhaps models of temporary nominal rigidities (for example, Fischer, 1977) or misperceptions (for example, Lucas, 1973) could be reconciled with findings of persistence by abandoning the natural rate hypothesis in favor of some highly potent propagation mechanism' (Campbell and Mankiw, 1987, p. 877).

In sum, Campbell and Mankiw seem to provide a response to the work of Nelson and Plosser (1982). In other words, they point to the validity of some of the main aspects of 'traditional theories of business cycle' despite the findings of Nelson and Plosser. However, it is not clear how models such as Lucas (1973) and Fischer (1977) could survive without the natural rate hypothesis, and Campbell and Mankiw do not present any other suggestions in this direction. In order to reconcile such models with the finding that shocks are persistent, some sort of equilibrium rate of output would possibly need to be assumed in the long run, even if the process of return to trend is assumed to be very slow owing to rigidities and other forms of imperfections (as in many models in the new Keynesian literature). This means that the idea of a long-run natural rate of output would ultimately be maintained.

West (1988) offers an answer to this issue, contesting the evidence of unit roots in GNP time series, as well as the necessity to abandon the idea of a natural rate of output. His argument has two parts. The first is the well-known fact that unit root tests cannot discriminate between random walk and near random walk behaviour in finite samples. This implies, according to West (1988) that simple analysis of a single-country GNP data series is not sufficient to distinguish between stationarity and non-stationarity, and to evaluate the relative importance of nominal and real shocks; therefore, this type of empirical evidence is not sufficient to assert the usefulness of different theories of business cycle.

The second part of West's argument consists in showing that simple natural rate models in which nominal shocks are the main cause of fluctuations can generate results similar to a near random walk in GNP. In short, West (1988) builds a simple model with overlapping wage contracts in which monetary policy is the only source of disturbances. Intuitively, the wage contracts provide an endogenous source of persistence, since prices do not move instantaneously, and GNP fluctuations mimic a near random walk behaviour after a monetary policy shock. This is valid even if there is a long-run natural rate of output to which the economy eventually converges; all that is needed for the near random walk behaviour is a very slow process of adjustment. In sum, West's main point is that 'neither stationarity of the natural rate nor nominal shocks playing an important role in the business cycle are inconsistent with a root *very near to unity* being present in the GNP process' (ibid., p. 207, emphasis added).

It is clear that West minimizes the importance of unit roots in GNP series, based on the fact that random walk and near random walk behaviour cannot be distinguished. However, if the *actual* process behind GNP series is difference-stationary (although one cannot be sure of it), the concept of the natural rate of unemployment is called into question. Moreover, if the idea of near random walk is a valid description of the behaviour of GNP or, in other words, if GNP is trend-reverting but with a high degree of persistence, it seems that the concept of a natural rate unique and stable is not very useful anyway.[7] The target is still there, but the economy never reaches it, and successive shocks may drive economic fluctuations independently of what the natural rate is, since its attraction power is very low.[8]

UNIT ROOTS AND POST KEYNESIAN ECONOMICS

The existence of unit roots in GNP time series and the consequent persistence of shocks can also be used to support different non-mainstream views of economic fluctuations and economic growth, which emphasize the existence of multiple equilibria with the possibility of persistent involuntary unemployment, due to path dependence, hysteresis in labour markets, and non-neutrality of money in the long run, among other considerations.

In general terms, it can be argued that many theories in which aggregate demand influences the long-run equilibrium of the economy, or in which the concept of a natural rate of unemployment (unique and stable) is discarded, are compatible with the presence of unit roots in GNP. Examples include the type of multiple equilibria models developed by Hahn and Solow (1995), structuralist models *à la* Taylor (1991), and the Keynes–Post Keynesian approach to macro-economics, which is the focus of this chapter.

The main question our analysis is concerned with is how to reinterpret the findings of Nelson and Plosser (1982), that is, the existence of unit roots in GNP time series, in light of Post Keynesian ideas? In other words, how would their conclusions change if some of their main theoretical assumptions were abandoned?

It is important to remember a few essential assumptions of the work of Nelson and Plosser (1982), or RBC models in general: (i) cyclical fluctuations in the short run are stationary and mainly affected by aggregate demand disturbances; (ii) money is neutral, and only supply-side shocks (especially technological shocks) affect the long-run path of the economy; (iii) the classical dichotomy between real and monetary variables is valid; (iv) the economy is composed of fully rational agents maximizing an objective function over time, and fluctuations (caused by real shocks) are changes in the full (optimal) equilibrium position of the economy.

A Post Keynesian response to Nelson and Plosser's interpretation would not follow the same strategy pursued by New Keynesians and other mainstream macroeconomists, based mainly on a critique of the empirical results (as described in the previous section). Instead, it would consider a different set of assumptions and entail a completely different perspective on how actual monetary economies work. In this case, the question is: how do we interpret the proposition that GNP time series are non-stationary (and what implications can be derived) without the assumptions (i–iv) described above?

The properties of unit-root (non-stationary) series are well known and were briefly described in a previous section of this chapter. These properties are inter-related, but I will enunciate them in three separate propositions for analytical convenience. First, non-stationary processes have no tendency to return to a long-run deterministic path, and the trajectory of the dependent variable is given by an accumulation of disturbances. Second, shocks to the system are persistent, and alter the trajectory of the variable in the short and long periods. Third, it is not possible to make accurate predictions about the future behaviour of the variable, since the variance of the series is time-dependent and approaches infinity as the forecast horizon increases. All these features were taken by Nelson and Plosser (1982) as supporting RBC models, but they are also entirely compatible with a Post Keynesian view of how the real world works.

First of all, under the Post Keynesian paradigm, it is recognized that actual capitalist economies function in historical time. That is to say, economic events take place in a unidirectional sequence rather than instantaneously ('time is a device that prevents everything from happening at once'), and this implies that the timing and ordering of such events affect the nature of final economic outcomes. In other words, instead of considering an economic system which adjusts inevitably towards some determinate equilibrium, Keynes and the Post Keynesians take into account the idea that no equilibrium position can be independent of the trajectory of the economy towards it: history matters!

Moreover, some Post Keynesians explicitly discard the (neo) classical axiom of an ergodic economic environment, and emphasize that actual economic processes are non-ergodic (Davidson, 1994). It is clear that non-stationary systems are non-ergodic, since non-ergodicity implies that averages calculated from past observations may persistently differ from averages of future outcomes. As Davidson (1991, p. 132n) recognizes: 'Nonstationarity is a sufficient, but not a necessary condition, for nonergodicity.' Once again, time series with unit roots represent non-stationary processes and are, therefore, supportive of Post Keynesian views of economic processes.

Another important aspect of Post Keynesian economics is the emphasis on the uncertainty that surrounds decision making in a non-ergodic environment. Since economic agents make production and investment decisions based on expectations about an uncertain future, disappointment of expectations or changes in the environment may lead to sudden revisions of such decisions, which affect total expenditures and therefore alter the path of the economy, defining new equilibrium positions.[9] As Davidson (1993, p. 313n) puts it: 'the existence of uncertainty, *by definition*, assures that there never need exist a long-run statistical average about which the system will fluctuate as it moves from the present to an uncertain future'.

The role of expectations and the possibility of multiple equilibrium positions with involuntary unemployment are clearly described in the Post Keynesian literature. It is well known that Keynes used different assumptions about short-run and long-run expectations and their interaction. The so-called model of shifting equilibrium is considered to be Keynes's 'complete dynamic model' (Kregel, 1976, p. 215) and seems to provide the most accurate description of Keynes's views on the nature of decision making under uncertainty. In this model, short-period expectations may be disappointed and hence change, and such changes also affect long-period expectations.[10] The revision of long-term expectations given current outcomes implies, in turn, that the underlying determinants of aggregate demand (or the fundamental psychological variables: the propensity to consume, liquidity preference and the marginal efficiency of capital) are endogenous to the path of the economy. In this case, the long-run equilibrium will itself respond to short-run outcomes, and one should not expect the economy to converge to any predetermined path. According to Kregel (1976, p. 217),

> if (…) realization of errors alters the state of expectations and shifts the independent behavioral functions, Keynes's model of shifting equilibrium will describe an actual path of the economy over time chasing an ever changing equilibrium – it need never catch it.

On the other hand, persistence of shocks is a natural implication of Post Keynesian models, and it does not come as a surprise. Moreover, once the assumption of money neutrality is discarded, and the interdependence of real and monetary sectors is considered, the claim that real (technology) shocks are the only phenomena responsible for fluctuations in the long run does not make any sense. In the real world, money matters in the short and long run, and non-stationarity may be related to changes in monetary or real variables, and the consequent revision of expectations by economic agents.[11] This proposition also brings about important implications for stabilization policies: if monetary and financial variables influence the trajectory of the system in the short and long run, restrictive monetary policies that aim to stabilize the economy may have persistent negative effects that are usually neglected by the *mainstream* of the profession.

Concerning economic forecasting, the features of non-stationary series are also compatible with Post Keynesian perspectives. It is clear that the concepts of non-ergodicity and uncertainty imply that the future is not statistically calculable from past data. Keynes emphasized the fact that in many economic processes there is 'no scientific basis' for developing accurate inferences about the future: 'We simply don't know' (Keynes, 1937, p. 214).

CONCLUDING REMARKS

This chapter discussed the existence of unit roots in macroeconomic time series, and presented different interpretations for the idea that GNP series are non-stationary. The finding of unit roots in GNP was initially used to support real business cycles models, stressing the role of real (technological) shocks in aggregate fluctuations (Nelson and Plosser, 1982). This understanding has been contested by a number of authors, who argued that the empirical analysis of GNP time series was not conclusive and could equally support business cycle theories in which imperfections or rigidities imply a delayed adjustment process towards the natural rate of unemployment (for example, New Keynesian economics).

This chapter follows a different path and offers an alternative interpretation based on the work of Keynes and the Post Keynesians. Instead of contesting the validity of Nelson and Plosser's empirical findings, the chapter argues that these findings should be interpreted under different assumptions and that GNP time series with unit roots are compatible with the Post Keynesian perspective on economic fluctuations. In this case, some important elements are (i) path dependence and time irreversibility; (ii) multiple equilibria and the absence of a predetermined mean toward which the system converges; (iii) persistence of shocks and non-neutrality of money in the long run; (iv) uncertainty and the inability to have accurate predictions about the future behaviour of the variables.

I conclude by briefly mentioning some economic policy implications of the analysis. In general, GNP non-stationarity may lead to the defence of active macroeconomic policies for a number of reasons. First, if the system is not mean-reverting, and persistent underemployment equilibrium is possible, it follows that active monetary and fiscal policies may be needed to improve the performance of the economy, changing its path toward higher levels of output and employment.[12] Second, if the system follows a *random walk*,[13] 'Big Government' and 'Lender of Last Resort' (Minsky, 1986) may have a role to perform in providing floors and ceilings to constrain economic fluctuations. Third, macroeconomic policies also contribute to reduce uncertainty regarding future prospects of the economy and, therefore, promote faster recovery of investment and output levels after economic contractions.

On the other hand, inflation targeting mechanisms may also need to be reconsidered in the presence of non-stationarity since, in this case, it is clear that the anti-inflation policies typically adopted (for example, increase in interest rates) have persistent negative impacts on the economy. Therefore the use of monetary policy as an instrument to stabilize the price level must be accompanied by the recognition that the level of activity is also affected in the short and long run, and alternative policies should be considered in order to minimize such effects.

Finally, if there is a unit root in GNP, it is also possible to make a case against sharp contractions as a response to financial or currency crises in emerging economies, as is usually implicit in the recommendations of the IMF and other international financial institutions (Dutt and Ros, 2003). In this case, the negative effects of such policies do not tend to dissipate in the short run, and may even aggravate some of the problems they were supposed to alleviate.

NOTES

The author would like to thank Jaime Ros, Steve Fazzari and Jose Ricardo Costa e Silva for useful comments on an earlier draft. The usual disclaimer applies. Financial support from CNPq/Brazil is gratefully acknowledged.

1. The macroeconomic implications of unit roots will be addressed in more detail in the following sections.
2. Note that, under the null hypothesis, this t statistic is not asymptotically normally distributed, and therefore special critical values are required. Actually, critical values depend on the regression specification and on the sample size. Dickey and Fuller (1979), among others, provide tables with appropriate critical values for some cases.
3. A complete description of unit root tests is beyond the scope of this chapter. For a more detailed explanation, see Enders (1995, ch. 4).
4. The main effect can be seen as the advance of real business cycle models and the decline of new classical models – developed by Lucas, Sargent and Barro, among others, during the 1970s – in which monetary misperceptions were considered the major source of output fluctuations.
5. Indeed, Nelson and Plosser seem to consider a direct and unequivocal association between aggregate demand, monetary factors and stationary cycles, on one hand, and aggregate supply, real factors and stochastic trend components, on the other.
6. Other reactions to the work of Nelson and Plosser relate to the discussion of alternative procedures for performing unit root tests. In this case, one of the most important contributions is the work of Perron (1989), which considers the presence of exogenous structural breaks in the series, and allows for a differentiation between 'small' and 'large' shocks. This and other developments in econometric modelling are beyond the scope of this chapter.
7. For a broad discussion of the concept of the natural rate of unemployment, see Cross (1995).
8. Another line of argumentation in the unit roots debate – known as the 'we don't know, and we don't care' argument – claims that it is not really important for macroeconomic theorizing whether or not unit roots are detected in GNP time series. This branch of the literature has a lot in common with some arguments presented in this section, especially those by McCallum (1986) and West (1988), about the inability of unit root tests to distinguish between TS and DS processes in finite samples. In this case, however, the criticism seems to be even more profound; moreover, there is not a defence of any specific theories of economic fluctuations. See Christiano and Eichenbaum (1990), Rudebusch (1992), Diebold and Rudebusch (1999).
9. See Fazzari, Ferri and Greenberg (1998) for a model where negative shocks in aggregate demand imply changes in the optimal pricing and production decisions of firms in a monopolistically competitive environment, which lead to persistent effects in output and employment.
10. For formalizations of Keynes's shifting equilibrium model, see Dutt (1997) and Setterfield (1999). In both cases, the models provide several features which are compatible with non-stationary systems, such as path-dependence and no automatic adjustment to a given mean.
11. Note that 'external' shocks are not a necessary condition for economic fluctuations. In the Post Keynesian literature, there are many well-known attempts to explain fluctuations and instability that are endogenous to the system (for example, Minsky's financial instability hypothesis (1986). Also, money is considered to be endogenous, and therefore the idea of a 'monetary shock' cannot be directly transferred without some adaptation.
12. In this case, propositions denying the necessity, desirability and effectiveness of macroeconomic policies, such as the ones defended by Lucas, Barro and other New Classical proponents, are not valid.
13. According to Cribari-Neto (1996, p.40), random walks 'can take you anywhere'.

REFERENCES

Backhouse, Roger and Andrea Salanti (eds) (2000), *Macroeconomics and the Real World, Vol 1: Econometric Techniques and Macroeconomics*, New York: Oxford University Press.

Campbell, John and Gregory Mankiw (1987), 'Are output fluctuations transitory?', *Quarterly Journal of Economics*, **102**, 857–80.

Christiano, Lawrence and Martin Eichenbaum (1990), 'Unit roots in real GDP: do we know, and do we care?', *Carnegie Rochester Conference Series on Public Policy*, **32**, 7–62.

Cribari Neto, Francisco (1992), 'Persistência de Inovações e Política Econômica: A Experiência do II PND', *Revista Brasileira de Economia*, **46** (3), 413–28.

Cribari Neto, Francisco (1996), 'On time series econometrics', *Quarterly Review of Economics and Finance*, **36** (special issue), 37–60.

Cross, Rod (1993), 'Hysteresis and Post Keynesian economics', *Journal of Post Keynesian Economics*, **15** (3) (Spring), 305–8.

Cross, Rod (ed.) (1995), *The Natural Rate of Unemployment: Reflections on 25 Years of the Hypothesis*, Cambridge: Cambridge University Press.

Davidson, Paul (1991), 'Is Probability Theory Relevant for Uncertainty? A Post Keynesian Perspective', *Journal of Economic Perspectives*, **5** (1) (Winter), 129–43.

Davidson, Paul (1993), 'The Elephant and the Butterfly, or Hysteresis and Post Keynesian Economics', *Journal of Post Keynesian Economics*, **15** (3) (Spring), 309–22.

Davidson, Paul (1994), *Post Keynesian Macroeconomic Theory*, Cheltenham, UK and Brookfield, US: Edward Elgar.

Dickey, David and Wayne Fuller (1979), 'Distribution of the estimators for autoregressive time series with a unit root', *Journal of the American Statistical Association*, **74**, 427–31.

Diebold, Francis and Glenn Rudebusch (1999), *Business Cycles*, Princeton, NJ: Princeton University Press.

Dutt, Amitava (1997), 'Equilibrium, path dependence and hysteresis in Post-Keynesian models', in Philip Arestis, Gabriel Palma and Malcolm Sawyer (eds), *Markets, Unemployment and Economic Policy – Essays in Honor of Geoff Harcourt*, vol. 2, New York: Routledge.

Dutt, Amitava and Jaime Ros (2003), 'Contractionary effects of stabilization and long run growth', unpublished manuscript, University of Notre Dame.

Elder, John and Peter Kennedy (2001), 'Testing for unit roots: what should students be taught?', *Journal of Economic Education*, Spring, 137–46.

Enders, Walter (1995), *Applied Econometric Time Series*, New York: Wiley.

Fazzari, Steven, Piero Ferri and Edward Greenberg (1998), 'Aggregate demand and firm behavior: a new perspective on Keynesian microfoundations', *Journal of Post Keynesian Economics*, **20** (4) (Summer), 527–58.

Fischer, Stanley (1977), 'Long term contracts, rational expectations, and the optimal money supply rule', *Journal of Political Economy*, **LXXXV**, 191–205.

Hahn, Frank and Robert Solow (1995), *A Critical Essay on Modern Macroeconomic Theory*, Cambridge, MS: MIT Press.

Juselius, Katarina (2000), 'Models and Relations in Economics and Econometrics', in R. Backhouse and A. Salanti (eds), *Macroeconomics and the Real World. Vol. 1*, pp. 167–98.

Keynes, John Maynard (1936), *The General Theory of Employment, Interest and Money*, London: Macmillan.

Keynes, John Maynard (1937), 'The general theory of employment', *Quarterly Journal of Economics*, **51** (2) (February), 209–23.

Kregel, Jan (1976), 'Economic methodology in the face of uncertainty: the modeling methods of Keynes and the Post-Keynesians', *Economic Journal*, **86** (June), 209–25.

Lucas, Robert, Jr. (1973), 'Some international evidence on iutput–inflation tradeoffs', *American Economic Review*, **63**, June, 326–34.

McCallum, Bennett (1986), 'On "real" and "sticky-price" theories of the business cycle', *Journal of Money, Credit, and Banking*, **18** (4), November, 397–414.

McCallum, Bennett (2000), 'Recent developments in monetary policy analysis: the roles of theory and evidence', in R. Backhouse and A. Salanti (eds), *Macroeconomics and the Real World. Vol. 1*, pp. 115–39.

Minsky, Hyman (1986), *Stabilizing an Unstable Economy*, New Haven, CT: Yale University Press.

Nelson, Charles and Charles Plosser (1982), 'Trends and random walks in macroeconomic time series: some evidence and implications', *Journal of Monetary Economics*, **10**, 139–69.

Perron, Pierre (1989), 'The great crash, the oil price shock, and the unit root hypothesis', *Econometrica*, **57**, 1361–401.

Rudebusch, Glenn (1992), 'Trends and random walks in macroeconomic time series: a reexamination', *International Economic Review*, **33**, 661–80.

Setterfield, Mark (1999), 'Expectations, path dependence, and effective demand: a macroeconomic model along Keynesian lines', *Journal of Post Keynesian Economics*, **21**(3) (Spring), 479–501.

Smith, Ron (2000), 'Unit roots and all that: the impact of time-series methods on macroeconomics', in R. Backhouse and A. Salanti (eds), *Macroeconomics and the Real World*, pp. 199–218.

Snowdon, Brian, Howard Vane and Peter Wynarczyk (1994), *A Modern Guide to Macroeconomics*, Cheltenham, UK and Brookfield, US: Edward Elgar.

Solow, Robert (1986), 'Unemployment: getting the questions right', *Economica*, **53** (210), 23–44.

Taylor, Lance (1991), *Income Distribution, Inflation and Growth: Lectures on Structuralist Macroeconomic Theory*, Cambridge, MA: MIT Press.

West, Kenneth (1988), 'On the interpretation of near random-walk behavior in GDP', *American Economic Review*, **78** (1) (March), 202–9.

8. Mark-up determinants and effectiveness of open market operations in an oligopsonistic banking sector: the Mexican case

Noemí Levy and Guadalupe Mántey[1]

INTRODUCTION

Endogenous money theorists usually assume commercial banks operate in oligopolistic competition, and set the loan rate by adding a mark-up to the Central Bank rate. They are divided on what determines the mark-up, particularly on the role of liquidity preference, and the resulting slope of the credit supply curve.

The effect of the interest elasticity of deposits demand on loan rates has been neglected by Post Keynesian writers, because they emphasize that causality goes from credit to deposits, and also because financial deregulation and innovations have widened the possibilities for liability management.

For the circuitists, even the concept of deposits demand is meaningless, since they conceive cash balances as a residual variable in the monetary circuit. Accordingly, deposit interest rates are often assumed to be determined by a mark-down of the interbank rate, while the size of the spread is conditioned by administrative costs of cheque accounts (Palley, 1994).

In this chapter, we maintain that commercial banks have oligopsonistic power in their domestic deposit market which enables them to maximize profits by lowering deposit rates when the central bank raises the price of reserves, and banks aim to satisfy a trustworthy demand for credit.

Various factors account for bankers' oligopsony in the deposit market: first, bankers' high degree of concentration, and scale economies, which favour collusive behaviour; second, their strategic position in the payments system, since they are able to create money; and finally, their convenient locations, which enable customers to lower transaction costs. Oligopsony in bank deposit markets has hitherto been seldom investigated, and may modify the structuralist conception of an upward-sloping credit supply curve, when economic activity rises and/or bankers' liquidity preference increases.

The chapter is divided into three sections. First we describe three different versions of short-term interest rate linkages that are distinguishable among endogenous money theorists. In the second section, we present a fourth alternative, which includes oligopsony in bank deposit markets, and risks associated with the structure of banks' balance sheets, as additional variables that influence interest rate spreads.

In the third section, we investigate the causal linkages between short-term interest rates in Mexico, where institutional barriers exist to free competition between public and private short-term financial assets, thus favouring banking oligopsony. In Mexico, private financial intermediaries are simultaneously bidders in the primary market for government securities, and are exclusive dealers in the secondary market. The fact that at present Treasury bill rates are 2.5 times bank deposit rates, and loan rates are 3.1 times the latter, suggests that the bank deposit market is dominated by buyers.

In order to show the direction of causality, we present a VAR model wherein the endogenous variables are the interbank rate, the three-month Treasury bill rate, the rate on three-month bank deposits, the bank loan rate and the real exchange rate; the rate on eurodollar three-month deposits was introduced as an exogenous variable to represent the foreign rate of interest. We analyse the results of three cointegration and error-correction models obtained for the loan rate, the Treasury bill rate and the interbank rate, respectively, which provide support to our hypotheses on the existence of oligopsony in the Mexican bank deposit market, and the compensatory role of deposit interest rates in determining loan rates.

Finally, we summarize the conclusions of our research on monetary policy, and also conjecture regarding the relevance of Post Keynesian horizontalist and structuralist approaches to central bank behaviour, under the specific institutional setting considered.

SHORT-TERM INTEREST RATE LINKAGES WITH ENDOGENOUS MONEY

Following endogenous money and interest parity theories, we would expect that, in emerging economies with strong exchange rate pass-through, central banks would keep interest rates high enough to support the non-inflationary exchange rate. They could achieve this result, either by offering a limited supply of reserves (verticalists), or simply by raising the rate of interest at which they provide unlimited amounts of liquidity (horizontalists). Both approaches would deem Central Bank policy to be reflected in higher short-term market interest rates, although their respective expectations regarding interest rate differentials would be distinct.

We start our discussion assuming that banks demand liquidity from the Central Bank after they have taken into account their creditworthy demand for loans (Rochon, 1999; Wolfson, 1996), as well as market conditions for other sources of funding. The monetary authority, on the basis of its reaction function, may decide to accommodate the demand for reserves at the prevailing interest rate, or to supply the required reserves at a higher interest rate, depending on whether it assigns greater priority to guaranteeing the payment system or to monetary policy objectives (Padoa-Schioppa, 1994; Moore, 1985).

Whatever the decision, two distinct outcomes can follow, since the stability of market interest rates and lending terms largely depends on the smooth operation of the payment system (Fry *et al.*, 1999).

The Horizontalist Position

Horizontalists believe payments system safety is the primary responsibility of a Central Bank. Accordingly, they represent the base money supply curve as a horizontal line at the level of the interest rate exogenously determined by the monetary authority.

Interest rate exogeneity, in this approach, does not imply that the monetary authority can set it regardless of the level of international interest rates or domestic macroeconomic conditions (Moore, 1991). Rather it means that the monetary authority is free to make a choice on its level, according to conventional wisdom (Rochon, 1999), and on the basis of its reaction function. The fundamental idea is that the rate of interest at which the Central Bank supplies reserves to the banking system is not determined by market forces; rather it is a politically settled distributive variable (Eichner, 1987), and as such it cannot be linked to any concept of scarcity (Kaldor, 1983).

Thus Central Bank interest rates (on overdrafts, deposits and discount facilities) are the exogenous variables, and the quantity of base money is endogenously determined by commercial bank credit demand. Given that at the chosen price the quantity of reserves supplied will be perfectly elastic, market interest rates will tend to follow Central Bank rates, plus a mark-up. This is the well-known horizontalist position (Smithin, 1994).

Since the supply curve for reserves is horizontal at the exogenous interest rate set by the monetary authority, horizontalists see no reason why the bank credit supply schedule should be upward sloping, provided bank customers satisfy the solvency criteria established by the banker. Furthermore, if the Central Bank chooses not to accommodate fully the demand for reserves, and decides to provide required liquidity at a higher interest rate, there still will be no reason for an upward-sloping credit supply curve since, at the new interest-rate level, the supply curve for reserves will remain horizontal. In this latter case, horizontalists assume the bank credit supply curve will shift upwards, just as the base money supply curve does; and the curve will not have a positive slope because bankers will only grant credit to their trustworthy customers (that is those who fulfilled the solvency criteria established by the banker).

They also refuse to accept an upward-sloping credit supply curve on the grounds of the Kaleckian principle of increasing risk. They concede that, in a static situation, increasing leverage may discourage further bank lending. But they deny that this principle applies in a dynamic model, because in the long run profits and net worth grow; and the degree of leverage, for the economy as a whole, may decrease in spite of credit expansion (Lavoie, 1996).

Horizontalists emphasize that short-term credit facilities increasingly take the form of contingent credit lines, which involve stable interest rate differentials (Niggle, 1991). They also argue that banking markets operate under imperfect competition, so loan rates are determined by a mark-up over the Central Bank rate (Arestis and Eichner, 1988).The mark-up does not depend on economic activity, since credit is not extended on the basis of project profitability, but rather on customers' solvency, the collateral provided and the term of the loan, which are independent from the business cycle. The margin is assumed to be a function of bankers' state of confidence and their degree of monopoly. Rochon (2001) defines it as: $ia = [1 + m(e)]\ icb$ where ia is the loan rate, m is the margin associated with bankers' degree of monopoly, e is their state of confidence or liquidity preference, and icb is the Central Bank rate.

Horizontalists implicitly assume that the rate of interest paid on bank deposits is also a function of Central Bank rates, and does not depend on depositors' liquidity preference. They reject any causal relationship that goes from the liability side of banks' balance sheets to their asset side, since this implies a return to exogenous money supply theory (Rochon, 2001). Credit supply, in their opinion, can only be limited by the availability of trustworthy customers (Arestis and Eichner, 1988).

The monetary authority may supply the reserves demanded by commercial banks by direct credit loans to bankers (overdrafts), open market purchases of government bonds, or via the discount window. The rate at which the authority grants credit sets an upper limit to the interest rate on repurchase agreements (funding rate). Similarly, the rate of interest at which the monetary authority accepts deposits from commercial banks sets a floor for the rate of interest charged on interbank loans (Schwartz, 1998).

When the monetary authority accommodates the supply of reserves to commercial banks' demand for liquidity, horizontalists anticipate the following linkages between short-term interest rates:

1. Central bank interest rates on overdrafts, deposits and discount facilities determine interbank lending rates and the rate of interest for repurchase agreements on government securities (funding rate).

2. Funding and interbank lending rates determine commercial bank loan rates.
3. Funding and interbank lending rates determine commercial bank deposit rates.
4. Loan rate mark-up varies, but it is not directly associated with the level of economic activity.

An increase in the rate at which the Central Bank supplies reserves need not widen commercial banks' financial margin. This result contrasts with the adjustment expected in the conventional theory of exogenous money, where a rise in the base rate causes a fall in bank credit supply and, for this reason, reduces deposit rates (Rojas and Rodríguez, 1999).

Some horizontalists contemplate liability management as a permanent banking practice, which aims to minimize costs, and hence do not dismiss it even when the monetary authority accommodates the liquidity demand (Rochon, 1999). When this occurs, responses to changes in the exogenous rate of interest should be thought of as being conditioned by the costs and risks associated with all sources of bank funding, and the resulting substitution elasticities. We shall return to this point in the second part of the chapter.

The Structuralist Position

Structuralists agree that the monetary authority sets the rate of interest exogenously in the wholesale money market, and the quantity of reserves is endogenously determined (Wray, 1998). Nevertheless, they argue that it is unrealistic to assume that the Central Bank would be ready to provide an unlimited amount of reserves at the prevailing rate, as bank credit expands, since this could bring inflationary pressures and balance of payments disequilibrium (Pollin, 1991). Accordingly, structuralists expect the monetary authority to accommodate reserves demand by means of a combination of price and quantity adjustments, so that the supply curve for reserves will be upward-sloping. Money supply will still be endogenously determined by credit demand, but the credit supply schedule will also be upward-sloping.

Some structuralists argue that, even if the Central Bank followed a fully accommodating policy, commercial banks would not agree to supply an unlimited quantity of loans as their capital/asset ratio fell, or as their customers' degree of leverage mounted (Dow and Dow, 1989; Wray, 1990, 1992). They contend that, because credit risks rise with the volume of lending, interest rates on loans should include a higher mark-up on Central Bank rates, which would produce an ascending credit supply curve. The Central Bank sets the base rate, and the structure of interest rates is dependent on liquidity preference.

According to arguments proposed by structuralists, the following linkages between short-term interest rates can be expected:

1. The base money rate determines the interbank lending rate.
2. The interbank lending rate settles loan rates, with margins varying with economic activity.
3. Deposit rates depend on the interbank rate minus administrative costs.
4. Through liability management, commercial bankers equalize the marginal costs of alternative sources of funds (Chick, 1989; Palley, 1994).

Interest Rate Linkages with Asymmetric Expectations

As we have seen, the most important difference between horizontalists and structuralists, regarding linkages between short-term interest rates in banking markets, has to do with factors that influence the loan rate mark-up over the interbank lending rate. On this point, structuralists argue that increased economic activity inevitably causes liquidity strain, thus accounting for widening interest rate differentials. Horizontalists contend that varying mark-ups between market rates and the exogenously determined Central Bank rate have other causes, including changes in bankers' liquidity preference, but unrelated to any concept of scarcity brought by increased economic activity.

In his theory of credit rationing Wolfson (1996) offers an alternative explanation to the loan rate mark-up, on the basis of asymmetric expectations of commercial bankers and debtors. He argues that every loan rate depends on the reference rate plus a spread, which varies according to the degree of risk that

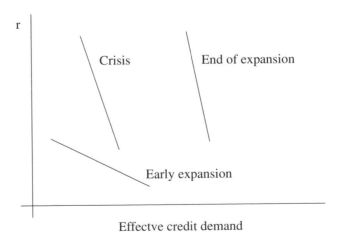

Figure 8.1   Cyclical changes in credit rationing

the banker attaches to the debtor. In addition to a wider mark-up, risky debtors face more severe contract terms, in the form of collateral demanded, loan period length and solvency conditionality.

Wolfson assumes that bankers' state of confidence varies with the economic cycle, and causes changes in the spread demanded as well as in the solvency criteria enforced. This involves changes in the position of the credit demand schedule, and not only movement along the curve (see Figure 8.1).

In an upswing of the economic cycle, interest rates are low, and effective credit demand (that is, from trustworthy customers) lies at the bottom left of the figure. Total demand for credit (notional demand) is larger, but bankers ration credit on the basis of their solvency criteria. As prosperity increases, profits grow, the credit demand schedules (notional and effective) move to the right and upwards, and their slopes increase. As the boom ends, profit growth declines, bankers' state of confidence deteriorates, credit rationing increases markedly, and the effective credit demand curve shifts to the left, thereby causing a credit crunch that leads to crisis (Wolfson, 1996).

Dow and Rodríguez-Fuentes (1998) have developed an explanation of bankers' behaviour on the basis of cyclical changes in liquidity preference analogous to Wolfson's theory. They envisage a money supply curve with two turning points, as credit expands along the economic cycle. The turning point M1 (see Figure 8.2) appears during an upturn of economic activity, and is produced by optimistic expectations that lead to more interest-inelastic credit demands. The second turning point, M2, appears at the end of prosperity, when interest rates have risen and credit is allocated in riskier projects. The credit supply curve the

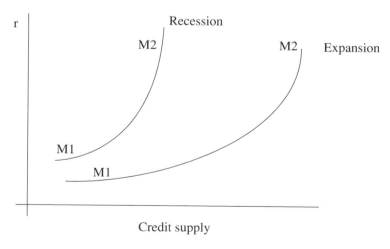

Figure 8.2   Cyclical changes in bankers' liquidity preference

authors describe does not represent a range of simultaneous possibilities, as is the case with the conventional money supply curve; rather they emphasize that it implies changes over time, so that it may be horizontal at low levels of interest rates and vertical at the highest levels. The authors also consider the possibility that increases in liquidity preference along the economic cycle change the slope of the whole curve, and shift it leftwards as the figure shows.

From these analyses we derive two conclusions: first, spreads cannot rise indefinitely without impairing bankers' solvency; hence we should expect that, once the loan rate reaches its maximum safe level (the *bank equilibrium rate*), the mark-up will cease to rise, and non-price mechanisms such as tighter solvency criteria will be employed to allocate credit among debtors. Second, it is unlikely that a positive significant relationship will appear between the banking mark-up and the level of economic activity over longer time periods.

Short-term interest rates linkages, with asymmetric expectations, may thus be described as follows:

1. Central bank rates settle the interbank rate.
2. The loan rate is determined by a spread over the interbank rate, which depends on bankers' state of confidence and the maximum safe level of lending rates.
3. The loan rate mark-up over the interbank lending rate may not be significantly associated with the level of economic activity, on account of bankers' reliance on non-price mechanisms for credit allocation, once interest rates reach the maximum safe level.
4. Bank deposit rates depend on the interbank lending rate and administrative costs.

SHORT-TERM INTEREST RATE LINKAGES WITH OLIGOPSONY IN DEPOSIT MARKETS AND DIFFERENTIATED FUNDING RISKS

When money is endogenous, the monetary authority sets the price of reserves, and bankers maximize profits by means of liability management. Bankers maximize profits when the marginal cost of all sources of funds (minus administrative costs) is equal to the interbank lending rate (Palley, 1994). This equilibrium condition determines the structure of the bank balance sheet.

If we admit that all sources of funds are affected by uncertainty and differentiated risks which influence their expected prices, we should incorporate the degree of oligopsony and the risks attached to the balance sheet structure as explanatory variables in loan rate and banking mark-up models. It would be unrealistic for a banker to charge the same rate of interest on loans fully backed by underpriced deposits in the same currency, as on loans in local currency supported by interbank credit lines in foreign currency.

Liability management may increase the risks of a bank portfolio, even if it does not affect the ratio of loans to reserves or the capital requirement, when banks raise funds in foreign currencies to lend in local currency, or when they issue short-term liabilities to make long-term loans. Exposure in foreign currency, and mismatching in the term structure of bank assets and liabilities, may exert significant pressure on mark-ups over interbank lending rates (Ghigliazza, 1994).

Neither of these causes of spread widening is necessarily linked to the level of economic activity; though both might be influenced by bankers' confidence levels. Mark-ups also vary according to credit users: big corporations are charged lower mark-ups than small firms, and consumer debts exhibit the highest spreads (ibid.). Post Keynesian writers have acknowledged oligopolistic competition in credit markets, but they have neglected imperfect competition in deposit markets, and its influence on mark-ups. Nonetheless, the effects of imperfect competition on interest rate spreads have also been analysed from other theoretical perspectives.

Cukierman and Hercowitz (1989) designed a monetarist model for the interest rate spread in an oligopolistic banking sector, focusing attention on the distinct consequences of inflation in deposit and credit markets. They showed that, in an oligopolistic market structure, an increase in inflation widens the spread between loan and deposit interest rates, because inflation raises firms' credit demand, and lowers households' demand for deposits; in their model, inflation also raises real interest rates, because bond transaction costs for firms are lower than for households, and household demand for bonds tends to decline more than the supply of bonds by corporations.

Neoliberal writers, like Gurley and Shaw (1979) and Galbis (1981), also paid attention to the effects of imperfect competition on interest rate spreads and credit supply. They warned against interest rate liberalization in oligopolistic banking markets, and rightly anticipated that market-oriented financial reforms, in imperfect markets, could widen interest rate differentials, and bring about a fall in credit volume; so, for this market structure, discretional monetary policies should be retained.

Free competition in deposit interest rates has also been considered dangerous, because it leads to higher loan rates which bring about adverse selection and moral hazard problems (Stiglitz and Weiss, 1981). Diaz-Alejandro (1985) recalled that, when bank oligopolies began to appear in Latin America, in the 1960s, their collusive behaviour led governments to set loan interest rate ceilings and deposit interest rate floors, in order to prevent banking profits from being maximized by widening spreads.

More recently, Kamin *et al.* (1998) pointed out that financial market segmentation, and oligopolistic bank structures may account for deposit and loan rates moving in different directions from central bank rates. They found that these domestic market distortions might prevail even if the interbank market is properly integrated into the international financial market.

Baglioni (2000) created an oligopoly model of the banking sector with liquidity risk, where banks accommodate random fluctuations of deposits and loans through liquidation of excess liquid reserves, or by borrowing from the Central Bank, through the discount window, when reserves are insufficient. Since the latter involves a penalty applied by the Central Bank, Baglioni maintains that banks should have some degree of market power in the deposit and/or the loan markets, in order to compensate such costs.

But it is Sarr (2000) who has recently explored in greater detail the effects of oligopsony in the banking sector. Interestingly, Sarr claims that oligopsony is not an undesirable phenomenon, nor does it entail inefficiency in financial resources allocation, because monopsony in the deposit market does not necessarily imply larger banking profits. He argues that bankers may lower deposit rates in order to subsidize non-intermediation services, because cheaper banking services attract corporate customers and thereby increase deposits.

In a banking system, where the share of non-intermediation banking services in bank proceeds is relatively small, and net income depends heavily on interest rate spreads, it is likely that bankers prefer to keep deposit interest rates low, because even a small increase in interest would significantly affect their profitability.[2] Sarr builds up a model to determine the optimal interest margin for a bank, which depends upon the latter's degree of oligopsony in the deposit market, its degree of monopoly in the loan market, its operational costs and its evaluation of credit risks.

It is conceivable that recent changes in the institutional framework of financial markets are affecting bankers' market power and their profit-maximizing behaviour. The degree of monopsony in the deposit market is likely to be strengthened by financial innovations such as plastic money and electronic transfer payments, which give rise to an interest-inelastic demand for deposits. We can expect their influence on mark-up behaviour to be more noticeable as the economy opens up, and the interest elasticity of domestic demand for credit increases.

On the other hand, structural changes in credit allocation can be used as a tool to offset increasing interest elasticity of credit demand as the economy opens up. Since corporate customers' demand for credit is more interest-elastic than consumer demand, a banker could consider a larger allocation of credit for consumption expenditures, instead of working capital or investment outlays, as a means of maximizing profits.

Thus the slope of the credit supply curve depends crucially on the behaviour of deposit interest rates, and also on whether credit is allocated to corporate customers or to finance consumer expenditures. The role played by the interest elasticity of bank deposits demand on the credit supply curve, as well as the effects of structural changes in credit allocation on its slope, have not yet been fully investigated.[3]

In an oligopsonistic banking system, where funding sources have differentiated risks, short-term interest rate causal linkages are likely to be the following:

1. Central bank rates on credit and deposits influence the rate on government bonds' repurchase agreements and the interbank lending rate.
2. The interbank rate determines the loan rate with a variable mark-up, which depends on the degree of oligopsony, bankers' state of confidence, and the risks attached to the balance sheet structure resulting from structural changes in credit allocation and liability management.
3. Deposit rates are conditioned by institutional arrangements and financial innovations.

In the following section, we attempt to test these hypotheses for the Mexican banking sector.

CAUSAL LINKAGES BETWEEN SHORT-TERM INTEREST RATES IN MEXICO

In order to disentangle the causal linkages between short-term interest rates in Mexico, we began by estimating an unrestricted VAR model for the interbank lending rate (TIIBP), the three-month Treasury bill rate (TCET3), the bank loan rate (TIAN2), the bank three-month deposit rate (TDB3), and the real peso-US dollar exchange rate (TICR80). The rate on eurodollar three-month deposits was introduced as an exogenous variable (see Table 8.1). This model was estimated with stationary series in first differences, in order to observe causality relationships (Spanos *et al.*, 1997).

Parameter estimates for lagged variables revealed that causality ran from the real exchange rate to short-term rates, but not the other way around, as conventional theory postulates. Similar results were systematically obtained from Granger causality tests with up to 12 lags (see Table 8.2). The influence of the external interest rate was not significant for all endogenous variables in first differences, but it was essential for obtaining cointegrating vectors.

From Table 8.1, we derived the following unexpected preliminary results:

1. There was no evidence of a significant relationship between the Treasury bill rate and the interbank lending rate.
2. There was a causal relationship from the loan rate to all interest rates, including the loan rate itself

Table 8.1   Unrestricted VAR estimates*

	TIAN2D	TICR80D	TIIBPD	TCET3D	TDB3ND
TIAN2D(–1)	–0.875239	–0.192889	–1.110113	–0.932382	–0.599980
	(–5.30798)	(–2.83093)	(–4.50926)	(–3.50230)	(–2.99003)
TIAN2D(–2)	–0.017861	–0.082466	–0.220187	–0.476798	–0.210911
	(–0.17912)	(–2.00137)	(–1.47897)	(–2.96159)	(–1.73808)
TICR80D(–1)	1.592395	0.273102	2.923024	2.825359	1.898954
	(5.01149)	(2.07998)	(6.16145)	(5.50740)	(4.91095)
TICR80D(–2)	–0.836517	0.066387	–0.322261	0.870020	0.822980
	(–2.38162)	(0.45740)	(–0.61452)	(1.53420)	(1.92540)
TIIBPD(–1)	0.372356	0.047152	–0.118228	0.128888	0.016816
	(2.73596)	(0.83844)	(–0.58184)	(0.58657)	(0.10153)
TIIBPD(–2)	–0.013070	0.068281	–0.095919	0.181179	0.135909
	(–0.11136)	(1.40791)	(–0.54739)	(0.95614)	(0.95157)
TCET3D(–1)	0.188541	–0.075489	–0.073754	–0.560590	–0.166796
	(1.05999)	(–1.02706)	(–0.27772)	(–1.95208)	(–0.77058)
TCET3D(–2)	0.276720	–0.083717	0.348107	–0.118494	–0.182679
	(1.58861)	(–1.16308)	(1.33851)	(–0.42134)	(–0.86178)
TDB3ND(–1)	0.617348	0.037156	0.689980	0.481774	0.194516
	(2.91304)	(0.42429)	(2.18066)	(1.40805)	(0.75423)
TDB3ND(–2)	0.235341	0.284364	0.526698	0.693955	0.551190
	(1.11851)	(3.27067)	(1.67664)	(2.04283)	(2.15268)
TEUDL3D	0.042437	0.017108	0.390422	0.548571	0.550091
	(0.11091)	(0.10820)	(0.68342)	(0.88798)	(1.18137)
Adj.R-squared	0.735387	0.117293	0.577166	0.363113	0.286514

Sample (adjusted): 1979:4 2001:2
Included observations: 87 after adjusting endpoints
t-statistics in parenthesis

Notes:
* Meaning of variables:
TIAN2D = Loan rate first difference,
TICR80D = Real exchange rate first difference,
TIIBPD = Interbank rate first difference,
TCET3D = 3-month Treasury bill rate first difference,
TDB3ND = Bank deposit rate first difference,
TEUDL3D = Eurodollar 3-month deposit rate first difference.

Table 8.2   *Granger causality tests on Treasury bill rate and real exchange rate variations (sample 1978.1–2001.4)*

Number of Lags	Null Hypotheses	
	Treasury bill rate does not cause real exchange rate (F probability)	Real exchange rate does not cause Treasury bill rate (F probability)
1	0.04090	0.00000
2	0.13219	0.00009
3	0.46703	0.00006
4	0.64064	0.00022
6	0.78322	0.00124
8	0.65716	0.00486
10	0.58449	0.00660
12	0.65180	0.02713

Note: The tests were carried out on stationary time series data for the Treasury bill rate (first difference) and the real exchange rate (first difference).

3.   There was a causal relationship from the real exchange rate to all interest rates.

Aside from the last finding, which could be explained by the inflationary effect of currency depreciation,[4] there was no straightforward interpretation of these results. They could be indicative of the pre-eminence of payment system safety over other objectives of monetary policy, but also of imperfect competition in the banking sector and possibly bank collusion.

The next step was to investigate the existence of cointegrating vectors, which provided a better insight on the adjustment mechanism of interest rates. We found cointegrating vectors with stable parameters and sound economic meaning for the loan rate, the Treasury bill rate and the interbank rate (see Statistical Appendix). From these long-run relationships, we derived the three error correction models that appear in Tables 8.3, 8.4 and 8.5 below.

Long- and Short-run Determinants of the Bank Loan Rate

The Johansen procedure indicated a long-run relationship of the loan rate with the other three interest rates and the real exchange rate, though the Treasury bill rate parameter was not significant. When the cointegrating vector was estimated by ordinary least squares, this variable became redundant. After deleting it from the equation, residuals remained stationary; hence we conjectured that there was an error-correction mechanism whereby variations in the loan rate contributed to sustain a long-run relation of this variable with the interbank rate, the deposit rate and the real exchange rate.

In the short run, however, changes in the interbank rate, either lagged or contemporaneous, were not statistically significant. This result was in line with our preliminary findings regarding the weak influence of monetary policy on credit terms.

Table 8.3 shows the best error correction model estimated. We can see that loan rate variations in the short run are positively related to changes in the rate of interest paid on deposits (which is a cost element for banks), lagged one period, and to contemporaneous and lagged real exchange rate variations. Loan rates also appear to be negatively influenced by changes in the money multiplier; this last result suggests an oligopolistic market structure in Mexican commercial banking.

Although loan rates appear to be positively influenced by deposit rates, this does not disprove oligopsony in the deposit market, because the average real deposit rate in Mexico over the sampling period was minus 1.7, and its median value was zero. This suggests rather that there is a floor to nominal deposit rates (dependent on the rate of inflation), which operates as a constraint on bankers' profit maximization; thus, when nominal deposit rates are lower than the rate of inflation, and bankers fear a run of deposits, they raise deposit and loan rates simultaneously.

Recent empirical research on the relationship between loan and deposit rates in Mexico provides support to this explanation. Martínez *et al.* (2001) found that the spread between the loan rate and the average deposit rate was significantly dependent upon the real ex ante Treasury bill rate; and it was inversely related to the output gap, as one would expect under oligopolistic competition. Since the average real loan rate over the last two decades was 10.2 per cent (median value was 11.8 per cent), the large size of the mark-up also suggests this interpretation.

Long- and Short-run Determinants of the Interbank Rate

The Johansen test reported a cointegrating equation for the interbank rate, in terms of the other three rates and the real exchange rate. Nevertheless, the coefficients for real exchange and bank deposit rates in the cointegrating vector were not significant. When the cointegrating equation was estimated by the ordinary least squares method, these two variables became redundant and were therefore deleted from the equation.

Consequently, the long-run behaviour of the interbank rate was only conditioned on the Treasury bill rate and the bank loan rate. This result was quite consistent with an expected intervention by the monetary authority to stabilize

Table 8.3   Error correction model estimated for the loan rate variation

Variable	Coefficient	Std. Error	t-Statistic	Prob.
TIAN2D(−1)	−0.325184	0.039959	−8.138025	0.0000
TDB3ND(−1)	0.661804	0.095505	6.929505	0.0000
TICR80D(−1)	0.717691	0.205251	3.496651	0.0008
TIAN2RES2(−1)	−0.475478	0.092934	−5.116311	0.0000
TICR80D	0.590514	0.178742	3.303717	0.0014
KD	−5.519762	2.203085	−2.505469	0.0143
DUMLIB	20.54028	4.281252	4.797726	0.0000
DUM87	14.25476	3.837408	3.714686	0.0004
DUM952	31.92237	4.516838	7.067415	0.0000

R-squared	0.907084	Mean dependent var.		−0.046023
Adjusted R-squared	0.897675	S.D. dependent var.		11.74393
S.E. of regression	3.756675	Akaike info criterion		2.743725
Sum squared resid.	1114.896	Schwarz criterion		2.997089
Log likelihood	−236.5905	F-statistic		96.40427
Durbin-Watson stat.	1.514016	Prob(F-statistic)		0.000000

Tests on residuals (F Probability):
Jarque-Bera = 0.98
LM(4) = 0.15
ARCH(4) = 0.15
White = 0.19

LS // Dependent variable is TIAN2D
Sample (adjusted): 1979:3 2001:2
Included observations: 88 after adjusting endpoints

Notes:
Key to variables:
TIAN2D = Loan rate difference,
TDB3ND = Deposit rate difference,
TICR80D = Real exchange rate difference,
TIAN2RES2 = Error correction mechanism obtained from cointegrating vector in Table 8A.2,
KD = Money multiplier difference,
DUMLIB = Dummy variable for interest rate liberalization. It takes value 1 in 1988.1, and zero everywhere else,
DUM87 = Dummy variable for 1987 stock market crash. It takes value 1 in 1987.3, and zero everywhere else,
DUM952 = Dummy variable to represent uncertain expectations on foreign inflows immediately after 1994 exchange rate crisis. It takes value 1 for 1995.1, and zero everywhere else.

Table 8.4   Error correction model estimated for the interbank rate variation

Variable	Coefficient	Std. Error	t-Statistic	Prob.
TIIBPRES3(−1)	−0.598515	0.081653	−7.329986	0.0000
TIAN2D	0.756297	0.055544	13.61628	0.0000
TIAN2D(−1)	−0.341597	0.043078	−7.929802	0.0000
TIAN2D(−2)	−0.123009	0.042791	−2.874618	0.0052
TDB3NDD(−1)	−0.300641	0.058989	−5.096560	0.0000
TDB3ND	0.531542	0.058874	9.028396	0.0000
TICR80D(−1)	0.751393	0.215656	3.484217	0.0008
DUM82	−10.91692	2.684293	−4.066964	0.0001
DUM85	14.56972	2.691235	5.413768	0.0000
DUMBONDES	22.80032	3.758430	6.066449	0.0000

R-squared	0.936309	Mean dependent var.	−0.097126
Adjusted R-squared	0.928864	S.D. dependent var.	13.95109
S.E. of regression	3.720934	Akaike info criterion	2.735732
Sum squared resid.	1066.092	Schwarz criterion	3.019169
Log likelihood	−232.4520	F-statistic	125.7730
Durbin-Watson stat.	2.382469	Prob(F-statistic)	0.000000

Tests on residuals (F Probability):
Jarque-Bera = 0.50
LM(4) = 0.23
ARCH(4) = 0.23
White = 0.73

LS // Dependent Variable is TIIBPD
Sample (adjusted): 1979:4 2001:2
Included observations: 87 after adjusting endpoints

Notes:
Key to variables:
TIIBPD = Interbank rate difference,
TIIBPRES3 = Error correction mechanism obtained from the cointegrating vector in Table 8A.2,
TIAN2D = Loan rate difference,
TDB3ND = Deposit rate difference,
TDB3NDD= Deposit rate second difference,
TICR80D = Real exchange rate difference,
DUM82 = Dummy variable to represent a period of exchange control. It takes value 1 for 1982.3 and 1982.4, and zero everywhere else,
DUM85 = Dummy variable to represent a liquidity shortage due to the effect of currency devaluation on reserves demand, which was unforeseen in the law whereby central bank domestic credit was frozen. It takes value 1 for 1985.2, and zero everywhere else,
DUMBONDES = Dummy variable to represent a liquidity shortage arising from the substitution of government long-term bonds for Treasury bills in commercial banks' portfolios. It takes value 1 in 1989.4, and zero everywhere else.

the payments system. In the error correction model, however, changes in the Treasury bill rate, either lagged or contemporaneous, were not significant (see Table 8.4). Short-run variations in the interbank rate are mainly dependent on the variables that influence commercial banks' financial margin, that is, deposit and loan rates.

These results, in conjunction with findings in the previous section, suggest that the monetary authority does not fully accommodate reserve demands from banks, but its interventions in the money market are ineffective in modifying bankers' behaviour in retail credit markets. We single out the following factors that may account for this outcome:

1. Financial margins are too wide in Mexican banks, and they have been growing steadily, particularly since 1988, after interest rates on deposits were liberalized (see Figure 8.3). In the period 1999–2002 loan rates have averaged 3.1 times deposit rates.
2. Commercial banks enjoy a privileged position in the short-term segment of the financial market, mainly as a result of artificial barriers erected in government security markets, whereby commercial banks are bidders in the primary market, and exclusive dealers in the secondary market. Commercial banks have been increasingly trading government securities in repurchase agreements with their largest customers, and through their own trust and investment funds, but do not sell them directly to investors. Hence short-term government securities do not compete with bank deposits, and deposit rates may be set well below the risk-free asset return. In the period 1999–2002, Treasury bill rates have averaged 2.5 times bank deposit rates.
3. Substitution of electronic money transfers for conventional paper money, and changes in payments practices, have generated a demand for current bank accounts, which is not very elastic to interest rates, thus enabling bankers to minimize the rate of interest paid on deposits. The Treasury bill rate and the bank deposit rate were approximately equal in 1992, and in 2002 the former was 2.5 times the latter (see Figure 8.4)

Long- and Short-run Determinants of the Treasury Bill Rate

Following Eichner and Wray, we consider that the monetary authority expresses its reaction function by means of the Treasury bill rate. Eichner (1987) separates monetary policy actions into two broad compartments: one for interventions aimed at stabilizing the payments system, which would smooth variations in the interbank rate; and the other for defensive operations in order to achieve other monetary policy goals. Wray (1998) argues that Central Bank intervention in the money market is defensive by nature, because the monetary authority

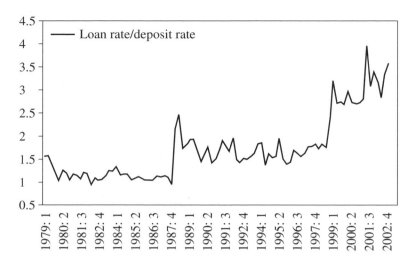

Figure 8.3   Financial margins increased steadily after the process of globalization

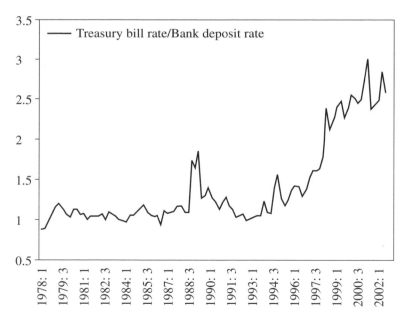

Figure 8.4   Financial margins increase due to increased treasury bonds rates and reduced deposit rates

Table 8.5   Error correction model estimated for Mexican 3-month Treasury bill rate variations

Variable	Coefficient	Std. Error	t-Statistic	Prob.
TCET3RES1(–1)	–0.031293	0.019288	–1.622357	0.1089
TDB3ND	0.989582	0.053952	18.34189	0.0000
TPCND	0.197122	0.040609	4.854096	0.0000
DUMCRIS	7.588165	1.359055	5.583412	0.0000
DUM89	–13.19020	2.253525	–5.853142	0.0000
DUM88	16.34740	2.156033	7.582168	0.0000
DUM86	–13.99591	1.478629	–9.465466	0.0000

R-squared	0.974979	Mean dependent var.	–0.212927
Adjusted R-squared	0.972977	S.D. dependent var.	12.64524
S.E. of regression	2.078708	Akaike info. criterion	1.544993
Sum squared resid.	324.0769	Schwarz criterion	1.750445
Log likelihood	–172.6977	F-statistic	487.0754
Durbin-Watson stat.	2.079364	Prob(F-statistic)	0.000000

Tests on residuals (F Probability):
Jarque-Bera = 0.78
LM(4) = 0.96
ARCH(4) = 0.99
White = 0.61

LS // Dependent Variable is TCET3D
Sample(adjusted): 1981:1 2001:2
Included observations: 82 after adjusting endpoints

Notes:
Key to variables:
TCET3D = 3-month Treasury bill rate difference,
TCET3RES1 = Error correction mechanism obtained from cointegrating vector in Table C.2 from Appendix,
TDB3ND = Deposit rate difference,
TPCND = Commercial paper rate difference,
DUM89 = Dummy variable to represent the end of external debt restructuring under the Brady Plan. It takes value 1 for 1989.3 and zero everywhere else,
DUM88 = Dummy variable to represent authorization for banks to place commercial paper in the stock market. It takes value 1 for 1988.4, and zero everywhere else,
DUM86 = Dummy variable to represent a policy change, by means of which the rate of return on Treasury bills was fixed, and the volume of securities sold was endogenously determined. It takes value (+)1 in 1986.3, value (–1) in 1986.4, and zero everywhere else.

sells and purchases government securities as a primary tool for draining or increasing reserves, in order to hit its interest rate target.

In keeping with conventional wisdom, we found that in Mexico the Treasury bill rate cointegrates with the government deficit, the real rate of exchange and the capital account of the balance of payments. All parameters in the cointegrating equation estimated with the Johansen method were significant, and exhibited the expected signs.

In the short run, however, contemporaneous and lagged changes in the variables entering the correction mechanism were not significant; and the short-run behaviour of the Treasury bill rate appeared to be heavily influenced by the terms on which commercial banks raise funds in the domestic market; that is, the rates of interest on deposits and commercial paper (see Table 8.5). Granger causality tests systematically indicated that changes in deposit rates preceded changes in the Treasury bill rate, and not the other way around (see Table 8.6)

Although this result was unexpected, it is reasonable given the hypothesis on commercial banks' collusion in an oligopolistic financial market. The short-run behaviour of the Treasury bill rate reflects commercial banks' profit-maximizing strategy of portfolio investment, while the long-run process indicates adjustments in fiscal policy that are endogenously determined by the Central Bank's stabilization policy. Our model suggests government deficit is the policy variable that adjusts the Treasury bill rate in the long run.

The short-run determinants of the interbank rate and the Treasury bill rate reflect the two different motives for banks' demand for reserves which Rochon

Table 8.6   Granger causality tests on Treasury bill rate and bank deposit rate (sample 1978.1–2002.4)

Number of lags:	Treasury bill rate does not cause bank deposit rate (F Probability)	Null hypotheses Bank deposit rate does not cause Treasury bill rate (F Probability)
1	0.319	0.074
2	0.129	0.042
3	0.524	0.046
4	0.161	0.023
5	0.022	0.007
6	0.037	0.018

Note: The tests were carried out on stationary time series data for three-month Treasury bill rate (first difference) and three-month bank deposit rate (first difference).

(2001) distinguishes. The equation for the interbank rate demonstrates bankers' demand for reserves in order to satisfy credit demands from trustworthy borrowers, while the equation for the Treasury bill rate reflects bankers' demand for money as a portfolio investment decision.

CONCLUDING REMARKS

We have argued that deposit market oligopsony and structural changes in bank balance sheets have not yet been given a proper place in the Post Keynesian controversy on the slope of the credit supply curve.

Financial innovations in payment practices, while reducing the interest elasticity of deposits demand, tend to increase the degree of oligopsony in deposit markets. Downward pressure on deposit interest rates may preclude loan rates from rising, despite increasing bankers' liquidity preference. On the other hand, financial-market deregulation and capital-account liberalization tend to increase the interest elasticity of large corporations' credit demands, thereby inducing bankers to maximize profits by increasingly allocating credit to satisfy consumers' demand, which is interest rate-inelastic.

The slope of the credit supply curve will depend on, among other factors, the relative importance of these two forces that influence the spread between loan and deposit rates. We note, however, that neither financial innovations nor structural changes in credit allocation are necessarily associated with the level of economic activity.

In countries where the institutional framework enhances deposit market oligopsony, the spread between loan and deposit rates may be so large that central banks are unable to influence credit market conditions by means of open market operations. Under these circumstances, we recommend that monetary authorities return to direct controls on credit expansion as a means of influencing aggregate demand.

NOTES

1. We gratefully acknowledge valuable comments and criticisms made by Arturo Huerta, Julio López, Basil Moore, Louis-Philippe Rochon and Jan Toporowski on an earlier version of this chapter. Remaining errors are our sole responsibility.
2. Since the spread between loan and deposit rates is usually the main source of bank earnings (around 80 per cent, according to Wong, 1997), it is reasonable to assume that this is the general case.
3. Some unexpected results of empirical research on loan rates and mark-up determinants, such as the inverse relationship between the prime rate and long-term deposit rates observed by Deriet and Seccareccia (1996) in the United States, could possibly be explained within this analytical framework.
4. In Mexico, the elasticity of inflation to currency devaluation is above unity.

REFERENCES

Arestis, P. and A.S. Eichner (1988), 'The post-Keynesian and institutionalist theory of money and credit', *Journal of Economic Issues*, **22** (4) (December), 1003–21.

Baglioni, A. (2000), 'Liquidity cost and interest rate spread in an oligopoly model of the banking sector', *Rivista Internazionale di Scienze Economiche e Commerciali*, **47** (4) (December), 559–77.

Chick, V. (1989), 'The evolution of the banking system and the theory of monetary policy', University College of London discussion paper 89-03, November.

Cukierman, A. and Z. Hercowitz (1989), 'Oligopolistic financial intermediation, inflation and the interest rate spread', Foeder Institute for Economic Research working paper no. 17-89, Tel-Aviv University, May.

Deriet, M. and M. Seccareccia (1996), 'Bank mark-ups, horizontalism and the significance of banks' liquidity preference: an empirical assessment', *Economies et Societés, Monnaie et production*, **10** (2–3), 137–67.

Diaz-Alejandro, C. (1985), 'Adiós represión financiera ¡Qué tal, crac financiero!', reprinted in L. Bendesky (ed.) (1991), *El Papel de la Banca Central en la Actualidad*, Mexico: CEMLA-Banco de España, pp. 215–41.

Dow, A.C. and S.C. Dow (1989), 'Endogenous money creation and idle balances', in J. Pheby (ed.), *New Directions in Post-Keynesian Economics*, Aldershot, UK and Brookfield, US: Edward Elgar, pp. 147–64.

Dow, S. and C. Rodríguez-Fuentes (1998), 'The political economy of monetary policy', in P. Arestis and M.C. Sawyer (eds), *The Political Economy of Central Banking*, Cheltenham, UK and Lyme, USA: Edward Elgar, pp. 1–19.

Eichner, A. (1987), *The Macrodynamics of Advanced Market Economies*, Armonk, NY: M.E. Sharpe.

Fry, M.J., I. Kilato, S. Roger, K. Senderowicz, D. Sheppard, F. Solís and J. Trundle (1999), *Payment Systems in Global Perspective*, London: Routledge–Bank of England.

Galbis, V. (1981), *Aspectos Teóricos de las Políticas de Tasas de Interés en Países en Desarrollo*, Mexico: CEMLA Ensayos.

Ghigliazza, S. (1994), 'El margen financiero', *Boletin CEMLA*, **40** (3) (May–June), 117–20.

Gurley, J.G. and E.S. Shaw (1979), *Money in a Theory of Finance*, Washington: The Brookings Institution.

Kaldor, N. (1983), 'Keynesian economics after fifty years', in J. Trevithick and G.N.D. Worswick (eds), *Keynes and the Modern World*, Cambridge: Cambridge University Press, pp. 1–28.

Kamin, S., P. Turner and J. Van't dack (1998), 'The transmission mechanism of monetary policy in emerging market economies: an overview', *Bank for International Settlements Policy Papers*, 3 (January).

Lavoie, M. (1996), 'Monetary policy in an economy with endogenous money', in G. Deleplace and E.J. Nell (eds), *Money in Motion: The Post-Keynesian and Circulation Approaches*, New York: St. Martin's Press, pp. 532–45.

Martínez, L., O. Sánchez and A. Werner (2001), 'Consideraciones sobre la conducción de la política monetaria y el mecanismo de transmisión en México', Banco de México Serie Documentos de Investigación no. 2001-2, March.

Moore, B. (1985), 'Contemporaneous reserve accounting: can reserves be quantity constrained?', *Journal of Post-Keynesian Economics,* **7** (1), 103–13.

—— (1991), 'Money supply endogeneity: "reserve price setting" or "reserve quantity setting"?', *Journal of Post-Keynesian Economics*, **13** (3), 404–13.

Niggle, Ch. S. (1991), 'The endogenous money supply theory: an institutional appraisal', *Journal of Economic Issues*, **25** (1) (March), 137–51.

Padoa-Schioppa, T. (1994), *Adapting Central Banking to a Changing Environment*, Washington: International Monetary Fund.

Palley, T.I. (1994), 'Competing views of the money supply process: theory and evidence', *Metroeconomica*, **45** (1) (February), 67–88.

Pollin, R. (1991), 'Two theories of money supply endogeneity: some empirical evidence', *Journal of Post-Keynesian Economics*, **13** (3) (Spring), 366–96.

Rochon, L.P. (1999), *Credit, Money and Production: An Alternative Post-Keynesian Approach*, Cheltenham, UK and Northampton, MA, USA: Edward Elgar.

—— (2001), 'Horizontalism: setting the record straight', in L. P. Rochon and M. Vernengo (eds), *Credit, Interest Rates and the Open Economy*, Cheltenham, UK and Northampton, MA, USA: Edward Elgar.

Rojas, E. and P.C. Rodríguez (1999), 'El papel de la estructura financiera en la transmisión de la política económica', *Monetaria*, **22** (1) (January–March), 1–37.

Sarr, A. (2000), 'Financial liberalization, bank market structure, and financial deepening: an interest margin analysis', IMF working paper WP/00/38, March.

Schwartz, M.J. (1998), 'Consideraciones sobre la instrumentación práctica de la política monetaria', Banco de México Documento de Investigación no. 9804, October.

Smithin, J. (1994), *Controversies in Monetary Economics: Ideas, Issues and Policies*, Aldershot, UK and Brookfield, US: Edward Elgar.

Spanos, A., E. Adrenou and G. Syrichas (1997), *A VAR Model for the Monetary Sector of the Cyprus Economy*, Nicosia: Central Bank of Cyprus.

Stiglitz, J.E. and A. Weiss (1981), 'Credit rationing in markets with imperfect information', *American Economic Review*, **71** (3) (June), 393–410.

Wolfson, M.H. (1996), 'A Post-Keynesian theory of credit rationing'. *Journal of Post-Keynesian Economics*, **18** (3) (Spring), 443–70.

Wong, K.P. (1997), 'On the determination of bank interest margins under credit and interest rate risks', *Journal of Banking and Finance*, **21** (2) (February), 251–71.

Wray, L.R. (1990), *Money and Credit in Capitalist Economies: The Endogenous Money Approach*, Aldershot, UK and Brookfield, US: Edward Elgar.

—— (1992), 'Commercial banks, the central bank and endogenous money', *Journal of Post-Keynesian Economics,* **14** (3) (Spring), 297–310.

—— (1998), *Understanding Modern Money: The Key to Full Employment and Price Stability*, Cheltenham, UK and Lyme, US: Edward Elgar.

STATISTICAL APPENDIX

Table 8A.1   Johansen test for the loan rate cointegrating vector

	Likelihood	5 per cent	1 per cent	Hypothesized*
Eigenvalue	Ratio	Critical value	Critical value	No. of CE(s)
0.300537	70.45954	59.46	66.52	None**
0.184133	39.36210	39.89	45.58	At most 1
0.148835	21.65724	24.31	29.75	At most 2
0.076621	7.637217	12.53	16.31	At most 3
0.008036	0.701983	3.84	6.51	At most 4

*(**) denotes rejection of the hypothesis at 5% (1%) significance level
L.R. test indicates 1 cointegrating equation(s) at 5% significance level

Normalized cointegrating coefficients: 1 cointegrating equation(s)

TIAN2	TDB3N	TIIBP	TCET3	TICR80
1.000000	–0.229976	–0.611197	–0.086408	–0.227556
	(0.10677)	(0.11269)	(0.16997)	(0.07136)

Log likelihood –997.4843

Sample: 1978:1 2001:4
Included observations: 87
Test assumption: No deterministic trend in the data
Series: TIAN2 TDB3N TIIBP TCET3 TICR80
Exogenous series: TEUDL3
Warning: critical values were derived assuming no exogenous series
Lags interval: 1 to 2

Notes:
Key to variables:
TIAN2 = loan rate,
TDB3N = deposit rate,
TIIBP = interbank rate,
TCET3 = 3-month Treasury bill rate,
TICR80 = real exchange rate peso–US dollar.

Table 8A.2   *Cointegrating vector for the loan rate estimated by ordinary least squares*

Variable	Coefficient	Std Error	t-Statistic	Prob.
TICR80	0.259237	0.069463	3.732014	0.0003
TDB3N	0.182319	0.088572	2.058429	0.0425
TIIBP	0.735464	0.084416	8.712350	0.0000

R-squared	0.926201	Mean dependent var.	44.19922
Adjusted R-squared	0.924504	SD dependent var.	26.73671
S.E. of regression	7.346307	Akaike info. criterion	4.021160
Sum squared resid.	4695.235	Schwarz criterion	4.104487
Log likelihood	−305.6567	F-statistic	545.9375
Durbin-Watson stat.	1.534802	Prob. (F-statistic)	0.000000

LS // Dependent variable is TIAN2
Sample (adjusted): 1979:1 2001:2
Included observations: 90 after adjusting endpoints

Notes:
Key to variables:
TIAN2 = loan rate,
TDB3N = deposit rate,
TIIBP = interbank rate.

Table 8A.3 *Preliminary results in loan rate error correction model estimation*

Variable	Coefficient	Std Error	t-Statistic	Prob.
TIAN2D(–1)	–0.530342	0.203580	–2.605081	0.0110
TIAN2D(–2)	0.034094	0.101761	0.335035	0.7385
TIIBPD(–1)	0.153704	0.156434	0.982551	0.3289
TIIBPD(–2)	–0.023699	0.110177	–0.215102	0.8302
TDB3ND(–1)	0.631512	0.142753	4.423816	0.0000
TDB3ND(–2)	0.306294	0.157737	1.941795	0.0558
TICR80D(–1)	1.401008	0.313018	4.475805	0.0000
TICR80D(–2)	–0.668806	0.339227	–1.971559	0.0522
TIAN2RES2(–1)	–0.457787	0.198862	–2.302027	0.0240

R-squared	0.772648	Mean dependent var.		–0.049425
Adjusted R-squared	0.749330	SD dependent var.		11.81196
S.E. of regression	5.913895	Akaike info. criterion		3.652307
Sum squared resid.	2727.984	Schwarz criterion		3.907400
Log likelihood	–273.3230	F-statistic		33.13500
Durbin-Watson stat.	1.975005	Prob. (F-statistic)		0.000000

LS // Dependent variable is TIAN2D
Sample (adjusted): 1979:4 2001:2
Included observations: 87 after adjusting endpoints

Notes:
Key to variables:
TIAN2 = loan rate,
TIIBP = interbank rate,
TDB3N = deposit rate,
TICR80 = real exchange rate peso–US dollar,
TIAN2RES2 = error correction mechanism obtained from cointegrating vector in Table 8A.2.

Table 8A.4   Johansen test for the interbank rate cointegrating vector

Eigenvalue	Likelihood Ratio	5 per cent Critical value	1 per cent Critical value	Hypothesized No. of CE(s)
0.290797	64.21998	59.46	66.52	None*
0.180036	34.32558	39.89	45.58	At most 1
0.140933	17.05651	24.31	29.75	At most 2
0.040935	3.840478	12.53	16.31	At most 3
0.002344	0.204167	3.84	6.51	At most 4

*(**) denotes rejection of the hypothesis at 5% (1%) significance level
L.R. test indicates 1 cointegrating equation(s) at 5% significance level

Normalized cointegrating coefficients: 1 cointegrating equation(s)

TIIBP	TCET3	TDB3N	TIAN2	TICR80
1.000000	0.134683	0.470531	−1.725707	0.486566
	(0.31158)	(0.19348)	(0.33300)	(0.14505)

Log likelihood −998.3297

Sample: 1978:1 2001:4
Included observations: 87
Test assumption: no deterministic trend in the data
Series: TIIBP TCET3 TDB3N TIAN2 TICR80
Lags interval: 1 to 2

Notes:
Key to variables:
TIIBP = interbank rate,
TCET3 = 3-month Treasury bill rate,
TDB3N = deposit rate,
TIAN2 = loan rate,
TICR80 = Real exchange rate peso–US dollar.

Table 8A.5   *Cointegrating vector for the interbank rate estimated with ordinary least squares*

Variable	Coefficient	Std Error	t-Statistic	Prob.
TIAN2	0.454758	0.056283	8.079795	0.0000
TCET3	0.586712	0.063381	9.256950	0.0000

R-squared	0.959423	Mean dependent var.		42.43633
Adjusted R-squared	0.958962	SD dependent var.		27.29052
S.E. of regression	5.528455	Akaike info. criterion		3.441789
Sum squared resid.	2689.616	Schwarz criterion		3.497340
Log likelihood	−280.5849	F-statistic		2080.733
Durbin-Watson stat.	1.499206	Prob. (F-statistic)		0.000000

LS // Dependent variable is TIIBP
Sample (adjusted): 1979:1 2001:2
Included observations: 90 after adjusting endpoints

Notes:
Key to variables:
TIIBP = interbank rate,
TCET3 = 3-month Treasury bill rate,
TIAN2 = loan rate.

Table 8A.6   Johansen test for the treasury bill rate cointegrating vector

Eigenvalue	Likelihood Ratio	5 per cent Critical value	1 per cent Critical value	Hypothesized No. of CE(s)
0.245613	46.65487	39.89	45.58	None **
0.182446	21.00659	24.31	29.75	At most 1
0.028879	2.675736	12.53	16.31	At most 2
9.95E-05	0.009059	3.84	6.51	At most 3

*(**) denotes rejection of the hypothesis at 5% (1%) significance level
L.R. test indicates 1 cointegrating equation(s) at 5% significance level

Normalized cointegrating coefficients: 1 cointegrating equation(s)

TCET3	BCAP	DEFGR	TICR80
1.000000	0.005374	–0.136726	–1.790077
	(0.00125)	(0.10675)	(0.22560)

Log likelihood –1577.433

Date: 12/02/02 Time: 21:00
Sample: 1978:1 2001:4
Included observations: 91
Test assumption: No deterministic trend in the data
Series: TCET3 BCAP DEFGR TICR80
Lags interval: 1 to 2

Notes:
Key to variables:
TCET3 = 3-month Treasury bill rate,
BCAP = capital account of the balance of payments (in dollars),
DEFGR = government deficit in real terms,
TICR80 = real exchange rate peso–dollar.

Table 8A.7   *Cointegrating vector for the treasury bill rate estimated with ordinary least squares*

Variable	Coefficient	Std. Error	t-Statistic	Prob.
TICR80	1.399327	0.106084	13.19074	0.0000
BCAP	−0.002217	0.000538	−4.117568	0.0001
DEFGR	0.185939	0.051832	3.587310	0.0005
R-squared	0.648355	Mean dependent var.		36.96128
Adjusted R-squared	0.640627	SD dependent var.		25.58425
S.E. of regression	15.33718	Akaike info. criterion		5.491954
Sum squared resid.	21405.85	Schwarz criterion		5.573123
Log likelihood	−388.5021	F-statistic		83.89196
Durbin-Watson stat.	0.745939	Prob. (F-statistic)		0.000000

LS // Dependent Variable is TCET3
Sample (adjusted): 1978:1 2001:2
Included observations: 94 after adjusting endpoints

Notes:
Key to variables:
TCET3 = 3-month Treasury bill rate,
TICR80 = real exchange rate peso–dollar,
BCAP = capital account of the balance of payments (in dollars),
DEFGR = government deficit in real terms.

9. The Washington Consensus and (non-)development

Hansjörg Herr and Jan Priewe

INTRODUCTION

In this chapter we deal with some principal issues of strategies for development. First, we focus on the role of macroeconomic policies in what has been coined as the 'Washington Consensus'. The term was invented by John Williamson (1990) to express what he thought would be the lowest common denominator of policy advice to Latin American countries by Washington-based institutions. Here, we detect some shortcomings and lack of clarity which reflect that there perhaps never really has existed a more or less clear Washington Consensus, especially concerning macroeconomic strategies. We conclude that macroeconomic policies have to play a much more important and comprehensive role especially in the area of monetary and exchange rate policy, and the balance of payment equilibrium.

After interpreting the Washington Consensus in the first section, we discuss some of its macroeconomic key shortcomings in section two. Section three gives a short overview of a positive and a negative development scenario, the latter leading to repressed growth in a broadly liberalized market economy. In the final section an alternative policy package is sketched briefly. The chapter attempts to give a comprehensive and summarizing critique and cannot go into details of the argumentation.

INTERPRETING THE WASHINGTON CONSENSUS

Whether it was or still is a consensus or not, there is probably a broad assent among many in the IMF and the World Bank that developing and transition countries need a mix of macroeconomic stabilization and structural adjustment. Williamson (1990) captured this idea in ten points.[1] Later it became a new consensus that especially institution building and poverty reduction had to be added to the original Washington Consensus. Rodrik summarized what he regards as the augmented Washington Consensus in another ten points.[2] These 20 points concern 'sound money' (= stabilization policy) and mainly improvements in the allocation of resources with the aim to increase productivity. Therefore privatization, improving property rights, enhancing competition, getting the prices right and abandoning all barriers to domestic and international flows of goods and finance are the focus. The aim is to implement what is conceived as a truly free and hence liberalized market economy. Whereas free capital movements were not part of the Consensus as Williamson explicitly pointed out, in the augmented version financial liberalization which includes more or less all capital account transactions has become an important ingredient reflecting the de facto policies of the Bretton Woods institutions. The vision of the Consensus is that macroeconomic policies have to provide the stable framework which allows improvements in allocation to unfold positively. Thus macro policies have to secure only the preconditions for economic growth which is triggered endogenously by improved allocation through structural adjustment policies.

The macro policies addressed in the Consensus can be summarized as follows: (a) absence of too high inflation, sometimes one-digit inflation rates are referred to as being tolerable (World Bank, 2003a), (b) balanced or close to balanced public budgets, (c) not too high current account deficits and (d) either flexible or fixed exchange rate regimes (corner solutions). The main instruments to achieve these goals are tight monetary policies in favour of the control of a broad money supply or to reach an inflation target and tight fiscal policies focusing on the retrenchment of government expenditures. The use of expansionary monetary and fiscal policies is excluded.

Furthermore, if both stabilization and adjustment policies are agreed upon and implemented, preferential loans by the Washington institutions and other donors can be offered. This type of finance is regarded as predecessor for private capital flows, comprising all kinds of finance such as bank credits, portfolio investment or FDI which make up for the shortcomings of the domestic financial sector and of domestic savings. So developing countries are seen as emerging markets which have to be enclosed in global finance. This will most probably lead to a net capital inflow reflected in a capital account surplus and a current account deficit for longer periods. Various theories underpin the necessity of net capital inflows: most prominently, the concept of a savings gap in the tradition of applied Harrod–Domar and Chenery and Strout (1966) growth theory and also the neoclassical growth theory which stipulates capital flows from the capital-rich to the capital-poor. Of course this requires removing barriers to capital mobility. This approach assumes a long phase of current account deficits and an accumulation of foreign debt in developing countries until the 'take-off' is reached. It should also be mentioned that the Washington Consensus is applied uniformly to all countries and only to a certain extent takes the specific local context of the countries into account (Rodrik, 2003; Stiglitz, 2002).

Recently Williamson (2004) has argued that the Washington Consensus of 1989 was a sensible though incomplete reform agenda. He had always rejected the widespread notion that this agenda is 'neoliberal' as it did not adhere to many typical convictions of market fundamentalists. However, its actual interpretation and application in practice in many cases (although not all) justified such accusations. Williamson had conceded that the Consensus had evaporated in the late 1990s, especially in dissent with the Bush administration (namely the US Treasury) concerning fiscal policy, income redistribution and capital account liberalization, to some extent also in the field of exchange rate policy. Besides redistribution, institution building including a more active role of governments and countercyclical fiscal policies Williamson today adds prudent control of the capital account and sequencing of reforms as important supplementary issues of the old Washington agenda, without hope of regaining a consensus.[3] In the following we confine our analysis to the macroeconomic ingredients of what we conceive as the de facto Washington Consensus.

SOME KEY SHORTCOMINGS OF THE 'WASHINGTON CONSENSUS'

We focus on six shortcomings related to macroeconomic aspects of the Washington Consensus and the asserted relationship between allocation and economic growth which is questioned here.

Inflation Analysis and Stabilization Policy

How much price stability do developing countries need? In the World Bank's 'PRSP Sourcebook' less than 10 per cent is considered to be sufficient (World Bank, 2003b). However, under conditions of global currency competition with free capital mobility and the pending risk of capital flight and dollarization, developing countries need a much higher degree of price stability. Even if they are too ambitious, the benchmarks are set by the dominant strong currencies and their inflation rates. Strong deviations from these benchmarks result in permanent devaluation, higher dollarization, aggravated foreign debt burdens in case the nominal exchange rate is defended by stimulating capital inflows, weakening of the domestic financial sector including higher interest rates, to mention some of the economic costs of too high inflation. In other words low inflation, as hard as it may be to achieve and sustain, needs much more consideration.[4] With capital controls the currency competition might be dampened somewhat.

Concerning the sources of inflation, the analyses should focus on the causes of cost-push inflation accommodated by the monetary authorities in almost all developing countries; especially in an economic crisis there is by definition no excess real aggregate demand.[5] Non-accommodation of cost-push inflation leads to an extreme degree of tightness of monetary policy which prevents development and endangers the functions of the domestic financial system. Contrary to the traditional viewpoint, devaluations and wage-price spirals are the most prevalent sources of inflation in developing countries. The stronger the integrated international goods markets and the higher the import-GDP share, the stronger the pass-through from devaluation to inflation (see Rojas-Suarez, 2003, pp. 146ff.). The higher the degree of dollarization – for example in case of indexation of domestic prices and wages in foreign currencies – the more direct is the pass-through (Ize and Parrado, 2002; IMF, 2003; Fischer, Sahay and Végh 2002). In many developing countries with low growth rates, a devaluation–wage–price spiral in combination with a restrictive monetary policy to fight inflation leads to low domestic demand and/or even stagflation. The muddling-through between the fight against inflation with restrictive macro policies and the need to reduce aggregate demand typically leads to a situation of repressed growth and continuing inflationary problems (stagflation). Hence inflation control obviously requires stable exchange rates.

Exchange Rate Regimes

The inflationary process can be stopped by using stable nominal exchange rates as nominal anchor and a complementary nominal wage anchor. If these two anchors hold, monetary policy can be less restrictive or even expansionary. Adjustments of exchange rates should be possible; arrangements like currency boards or absolutely fixed nominal exchange rates are too rigid and can become too costly in certain economic constellations.

Orthodox monetarist theory is in favour of flexible (that is, floating) exchange rates, whereas the Washington Consensus admitted that absolute tight exchange rates, for example currency boards, might also be feasible. The macroeconomic guideline is not very clear on this point, especially as it remains unresolved how to maintain fixed exchange rates once this regime is chosen (Baliño, Bennett and Borensztein 1999). Foreign reserves will only suffice in the short run, and even very high interest rates can hardly defend exchange rates once the confidence in the domestic currency has vanished, as experienced in many countries. The traditional bipolar view on either fixed or flexible regimes seems somewhat removed from reality and practice, since almost all countries avoid (and must avoid) too high fluctuations of the exchange rates. There is much evidence for open economies that devaluations are closely linked to inflation (see above). Therefore permanent and/or strong devaluations have to be avoided. So the floating option with high volatility contradicts the emphasis on price stability and 'sound money' as stipulated in the Consensus.

Capital Account Liberalization or Control?

International capital movements between the developed and underdeveloped world have been unstable.[6] Very often, capital flows into developing countries and builds up a fragile macroeconomic constellation, then follows the sudden return of the capital to the developed world and a subsequent currency crisis. The strength of such capital flows is intensified by contagion after a crisis in one country has started. The capital inflow and outflow waves can roll over one part of the developing world after the other. This happened, for example, when in the early 1990s capital moved to Central America; in 1994, during the Mexican crisis, the wave left Central America and hit some transition countries such as the Czech Republic and Asian countries such as Thailand or Indonesia. In spring 1997, the Czech model collapsed in a currency crisis and in the autumn of the same year the Asian crisis shocked the world when capital came back into the developed world. Such types of capital movements make it extremely difficult even for developing countries following sound economic policies to avoid large exchange rate changes. In developing countries supportive capital controls to stabilize the exchange rates seem to be necessary to avoid destabilizing capital inflows and outflows.

Risks of Current Account Deficits and External Debt

In most developing countries there is simply no domestic savings gap. In spite of the weak empirical and theoretical background of the savings gap model it is still widely used in international institutions and ministries (Easterly, 1999). In principle, import goods can be financed by export proceeds; external debt[7] does not necessarily improve investment and, even if it does so temporarily, debt has to be repaid (and portfolio investment and FDI can be withdrawn). When depreciations cannot restore international competitiveness, if the Marshall–Lerner conditions do not apply, a market failure exists that requires special remedies as exceptional cases. A balance of payment regime with long-lasting current account deficits has fundamental disadvantages. In the 1990s, the average (unweighted) current account deficits in low and lower middle income countries were 5.9 per cent of GDP. Among the 99 countries with data available (out of 117 in these groups) there were only 12 surplus economies (Herr and Priewe 2004, p. 77; see Figure 9.1). That such deficits can hardly be regarded as sustainable is ignored or repressed by the proponents of the Washington Consensus. In other words, there is no coherent balance of payment concept within this Consensus.[8]

With the current account deficits, external debt is built up, denominated in hard currency. This 'original sin' (Eichengreen and Hausmann, 1999; Eichengreen, Hausmann and Panizza, 2002), which cannot be overcome by developing countries, leads to a high vulnerability of the indebted country. The higher the

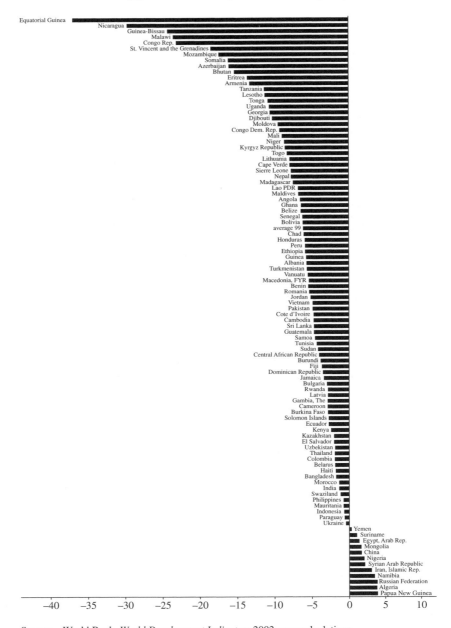

Source: World Bank, *World Development Indicators* 2002, own calculations.

Figure 9.1   Current account balance in per cent of GDP, 99 low and lower middle-income countries, 1990–2000 (gross) indebtedness, the higher the danger that indebtedness will lead to financial crises. There are two patterns:

1. A country with high foreign debt is confronted with an abrupt refusal of creditors to roll over credits and/or a sudden outflow of capital. The resulting devaluation then leads to an epidemic domestic liquidity and solvency crisis (Jeanne and Zettelmeyer, 2002). Kaminsky and Reinhart (1999) have found that, particularly in developing countries, exchange rate crises typically lead to systemic banking crises as firms and banks in countries with high foreign debt in cases of devaluation break down.[9] It should be emphasized that current account deficits (even high ones) combined with high growth may sometimes prevail for quite long periods, especially if the deficits are used to import investment goods. However, the seeming link between growth and current account deficits is deceptive; the longer the imbalance is sustained, the more risks will emerge that ultimately trigger off strong and often sudden devaluations.[10]

2. Most low-income countries, let alone highly indebted poor countries (HIPC), have little access to commercial capital markets and rely more or less on credits from international institutions and foreign governments, apart from the low level of FDI. These capital flows are relatively stable as donors normally do not stop to issue credits. The problem of these countries is that their current account situation is not sustainable and that they grow slowly in a situation of over-indebtedness. Debt relief in HIPC-countries improves the situation until after some time over-indebtedness returns (Easterly, 2002).

As rational economic agents know, the disastrous consequences of overindebtedness and devaluations, high current account deficits and high gross foreign debt will weaken the reputation of the domestic currency. This leads to a risk premium with substantially higher real interest rates[11] in developing countries. The result is low growth and a less equal income distribution as compared to the developed world.

Countries with high foreign debt in foreign currency fear to devalue and thus tend to delay devaluations even if they have huge current account deficits and the situation will become unsustainable. Such a policy is detrimental to exports and the reputation of the local currency. Capital flight has to be reduced or necessary capital imports have to be stimulated by high interest rates. Countries in such a situation are caught in a difficult dilemma. Devaluation will destroy the domestic financial system because of high foreign debt, and not to devalue will lead to even higher foreign debt and low growth. Since the current account deficits in such countries are typically partly paid by policy loans or donations, soft budget constraints can delay necessary adjustments.

Debates about poverty reduction and debt relief remain at the surface of the problems, insofar as new foreign debt is created even in the case that international institutions give credits. The discussions have focused too much on so-called 'good' or 'bad' foreign debts; for example private foreign debt is conceived as 'good' compared to budget deficits in foreign currency. It has been overlooked that high foreign debt makes a country vulnerable against shocks which in developing countries cannot be avoided, independent of the individual debtor. Prudence in financial liberalization is mentioned in the Washington Consensus, but actual policy by international institutions and Western governments much too often presses developing countries to open up the capital account too early. The avoidance of a current account deficit and of a substantial gross foreign debt is the best basis for developing in a world with volatile international capital movements and an unstable world economy. It also has to be recognized that countries with high foreign debt in foreign currency lose the exchange rate as an adjustment instrument. Especially if the exchange rate in developing countries cannot be kept stable and frequent economic shocks need exchange rate adjustments to (re-)establish international competitiveness, foreign debt should be low. To avoid vulnerability and to keep a certain degree of economic policy autonomy are convincing arguments for preventing substantial net and gross foreign debt in developing countries. The best constellation for development is to prevent a current account deficit, limit foreign gross debt and strive for a stable nominal exchange rate (see below). If it is not possible for a country to combine a stable exchange rate with a balanced current account, the second best option is to realign the exchange rate by a once-off devaluation and thus rebalance the current account. To maintain the option to devalue, a high level of foreign and domestic debt in foreign currency has to be avoided.

However, if external debt is regarded as necessary or unavoidable, it should be confined to beneficial or less risky flows. FDI are preferable and should be advised (mainly because of the lack of a currency risk for the recipient country and the desired technology transfer); rollover risks in the case of loans should be minimized through long-term contracts or political guarantees. Again in such cases appropriate capital controls can help avoid the unfavourable sources of inflows and destabilizing exchange rate volatility due to volatile capital flows.

The Neglect of Dollarization

Dollarization is the unofficial or official use of hard currency within a country for holding wealth, giving credit or expressing the price for wages and goods. Here we focus on unofficial dollarization. It is a sign that agents do not trust the national currency as they expect high inflation and/or high devaluation. Dollarization is a double-edged sword, as it makes the domestic banking system inherently fragile:

1. Dollarization produces dangerous currency mismatch, as banks, firms, households and the government may have debts in dollars and revenues in domestic currency.
2. For countries with high dollarization a lender of last resort (for example the Central Bank always providing sufficient liquidity for the banking system) exists only for the part of the financial system working with domestic currency.
3. Because of currency mismatch there is a high incentive for banks to invest collected foreign currency deposits abroad. In addition the typically high stock of cash hoarding in foreign currencies disrupts bank intermediation and is lost for domestic credit supply.
4. The higher the dollarization the smaller the room to manoeuvre for monetary policy. In a state of high dollarization financial wealth in domestic currency can only increase in line with the increase in wealth in foreign currency. If there is an increase in domestic monetary wealth (due to credit creation in domestic currency), according to the degree of dollarization, domestic wealth will be exchanged in foreign currency. Particularly in developing countries, nominal devaluations are risky and will further increase dollarization. Thus the volume of money creation and credit expansion in the domestic economy may become so small that credits for investment are almost non-available. If they are available, then they are extremely costly or their volume may be even too small to prevent a permanent lack of liquidity. Increasing dollarization is identical to portfolio shifts from domestic to foreign currency. If there are no sufficient capital imports, which lead to the negative effect of higher indebtedness in foreign currency or sufficient current account surpluses, any domestic credit expansion and/or an increasing degree of dollarization will lead to devaluation, inflation and finally to higher domestic interest rates. Overall, dollarization reduces the availability of domestic credit and increases interest rates for credits in foreign and local currency, as compared with a situation where dollarization is lower (Honohan and Shi, 2003).[12]

Obviously the issue of dollarization has been neglected in development macroeconomics and is regarded as an intricate issue of minor impact. There are plenty of publications stressing the disadvantages of dollarization (for example, World Bank, 2002a; IMF, 2003), but there seems to be no clear commitment in the Washington Consensus to seriously fight dollarization as a precondition for a stable financial system and for sustainable development.

A country that cannot provide a domestic currency with sufficient trust will hardly be able to establish coherent economic mechanisms. Instead the economy will be divided into a domestic currency segment, a foreign currency segment and – owing to a restrictive monetary bias of the regime and a lack of credit –

barter and subsistence segments. In the case where the domestic currency segment is inflationary, the erosion of the monetary system continues and dollarization increases. If the domestic currency sector in respect to inflation is stable, credit expansion in this sector is likely to be so much restricted that growth is repressed and, in extreme cases, the shortage of liquidity stimulates barter and subsistence segments in the economy.

The Underestimated Domestic Financial System

Although the domestic financial sector using domestic currency is one of the main strategic sectors in developing countries to stimulate investment, there are severe theoretical shortcomings which are not yet seriously addressed in mainstream development strategies. In traditional theories finance automatically follows the real economy. The question of finance was often simply ignored. Much of the discussion about structural adjustment in the financial sector is focused on the debates on repressed versus liberalized finance. The bipolar view is not very conducive, as both alternatives involve shortcomings. We call for more attention to the macroeconomic framework of the financial sector and appropriate institution building including adequate regulations. Prior to facilitating cross-border opening of financial flows, a stable domestic financial system has to be shaped. As dollarization makes a financial system inherently vulnerable, the degree of dollarization has to be reduced to low levels as a precondition for a sound financial system.

We agree with Chenery and Strout (1966) (and many others) that investment is the key to growth and development.[13] In line with investment, human capital formation must and can take place. But we disagree that investment should be financed by foreign sources (except FDI). Basically, a domestic financial system always has the potential to finance investment with domestic credit. Among others it was Schumpeter (1934) who argued that development is only possible if innovative entrepreneurs get credits from banks to invest. What is necessary is *new* credit created first of all by the banking system with the help of the Central Bank. Saving in such an approach will be created out of the new income stimulated by investment.[14] From a macroeconomic point of view, prior saving (say in period t_0, without respective investment in the same period) as a precondition for investment (say in t_1) is logically impossible. The paramount role of finance-led growth is also stressed by the World Bank (2001). Indeed there is an impressive correlation between domestic bank credits to GDP and the development of countries. Low-income countries have a low ratio of domestic bank credits to GDP, whereas in developed countries the ratio is three times higher. There is no clear relation between the trade balance and this ratio (cp. Table 9.1). Russia, for example, has a high trade (and current account) surplus and a poorly developed financial system.[15] Uganda, often regarded as a model econ-

*Table 9.1   Domestic credit provided by the banking sector and the trade
balance in the year 2002 (% of GDP)**

	Domestic credit as percentage of GDP	External balance of goods and services as percentage of GDP
Low-income countries	48.6	0.4
Middle-income countries	82.9	3.4
High-income countries	168.5	0.0
Latin America and Caribbean	42.7	2.8
China	166.4	3.0
Belarus	17.5	−4.4
Uganda	15.4	−15.4
Vietnam	44.8	−4.0
Mozambique	13.2	−14.7
Nigeria	25.3	−5.9
Russian Federation	26.6	10.8

Note: * Domestic credit includes domestic credit in foreign currency.

Source: *World Development Indicators* (2004), Washington, DC: World Bank.

omy in Africa, relies heavily on foreign finance and reforms have not improved the outreach of the domestic financial systems. China as a developing country is an exception. The ratio of bank credits to GDP is nearly as high as in developed countries;[16] China had the highest growth rates of all the countries listed in the table mainly because of the domestic investment dynamics fuelled by state-owned banks and state-owned enterprises (cp. Herr and Priewe, 1999), despite severe shortcomings in the allocation of resources.

SCENARIO OF UNDERDEVELOPMENT AND 'REPRESSED GROWTH' VERSUS GROWTH SCENARIO

The most important single macroeconomic factor contributing to development is a stable domestic currency, which is broadly accepted by domestic households, banks and firms.[17] This is a necessary precondition for a workable financial sector which can offer sufficient credit and low interest rates. It is evident that especially currencies issued in developing countries have problems in competing with the world's leading currencies even if they are stable.

Figure 9.2 shows a typical regime of underdevelopment and 'repressed growth'.[18] The country has a current account deficit and thus an increasing debt in foreign currency. Such a constellation can be stable for a long time – theoretically, even the sustainable correlation between the current account deficit as a percentage of GDP, the growth rate of GDP, the interest rate and foreign debt to GDP can be calculated. But the point is that the fragility of the economy increases with increasing gross foreign debt. Rational economic agents expect that any external shock from the world economy or from inside the country – and shocks are especially likely in developing countries with their often fragile economic, social and political system – may lead to devaluation and inflation and the weakening (in some cases destruction) of the domestic banking system indebted in foreign currency. In such a situation economic agents will prefer to keep financial wealth in foreign currencies. If it is kept abroad there is capital flight; if it is kept inside the country there is dollarization. The results are high interest rates and an unstable domestic banking system. To put it differently, the country is not able to issue a domestic currency which is sufficiently accepted by economic agents, with the result of high interest rates due to a high country risk premium, high dollarization and a lack of credit supply. The overall effect

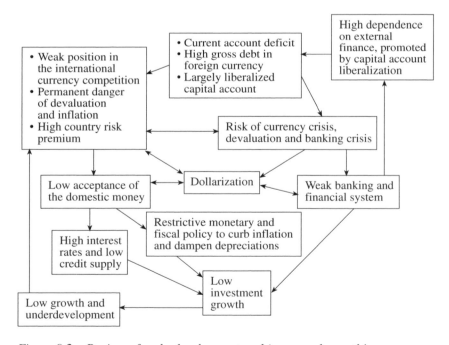

Figure 9.2   Regime of underdevelopment and 'repressed growth'

is low investment and low growth. The bad economic performance of the country gives no scope to improve the acceptance of the domestic currency. Even a stable price level and a stable exchange rate may not be able to improve the quality of the domestic currency, reduce dollarization and give the Central Bank the option to cut interest rates and stimulate credit supply. The 'wait-and-see' attitude, stressed by Dornbusch (1990), prevents the (re)vitalization of the acceptance of the domestic money and the country is stuck in an underdevelopment path. It should be emphasized that this constellation of 'repressed growth' likely occurs with floating exchange rates, liberalized capital account and deregulation of the domestic financial sector. It is one of the typical Washington Consensus regimes (see Herr and Priewe 2004, chapter 2),[19] maybe even the most typical one.

A positive macroeconomic scenario is the reverse of the repressed growth regime (see Figure 9.3). Policies are geared towards the most vital point for development: the creation of an accepted national currency. A high quality of the domestic currency can only be achieved if *price-level stability, exchange-rate stability and sufficient growth* can be realized over a longer period. Price-level

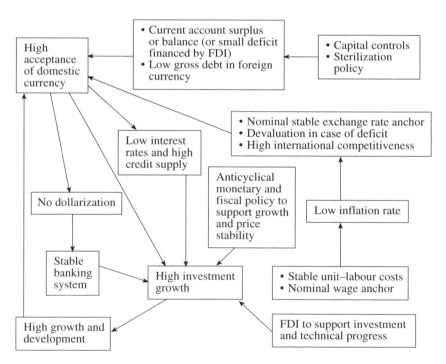

Figure 9.3   Regime of development and growth

stability and the accumulation of trust in the domestic currency in developing countries are directly related to nominal exchange-rate stability as the exchange rate is the best indicator for a currency to survive in the international currency competition. Nominal exchange-rate stability and high international competitiveness (the latter also a precondition for development) can only be achieved simultaneously if domestic unit–labour costs are stable, which is identical to the notion that nominal wage increases follow an average productivity growth (plus target inflation rate). Ideal for a single country is a constellation of surplus in the current account and appreciation expectations, which keep the domestic interest rate low. The higher the acceptance of the domestic currency, the lower the domestic interest rate and the higher domestic investment as the reputation of the domestic currency is built up and fears of devaluation and systemic domestic failures in the banking systems vanish.

In our positive scenario we did not stress improvements in the allocation of productive factors which are so much at the centre of policy recommendations of international institutions. In contrast to neoclassical thinking, improvements in allocation do not automatically trigger growth. In some areas there might even exist a trade-off between improved allocation and macroeconomic stability. This does not mean that we do not want a better allocation or the improvement of institutions. But we believe that only a stable macroeconomic development and integration into the world economy, which make the country no longer dependent on unstable international capital movements, are capable of paving the way to deepening allocation improvements. Allocation reforms, known as structural adjustments, without a stable macroeconomic constellation are doomed to fail and may even lead to disastrous economic crises (as for example in Russia in the early 1990s).

A NEW WORLD ORDER FOR ECONOMIC DEVELOPMENT

It has been argued above that a current account surplus is an important part of a positive development strategy; many of the most successful countries after World War II were in such a constellation. Many of them – for example Japan, Germany, Taiwan, the People's Republic of China – followed or still follow an aggressive neomercantilist strategy. Obviously not all countries in the world can have a surplus in the current account and can follow the ideal development strategy of a single country. If all countries in the world strive for current account surpluses the world economy attains a restrictive and destabilizing bias (Robinson, 1937; Vandenbroucke, 1985; Herr, 1997). There are several ways that this problem can be solved.

Global Competition for Achieving Surplus, Unfavourable for the Majority of Developing Countries

In the present world economy there is a tough economic competition between surplus and deficit countries. Deficit countries try to improve through real depreciations (nominal devaluations, if possible, and/or reduction of unit–labour costs and/or low domestic growth), but in many cases fall involuntarily into deficits; surplus economies try to maintain or increase their surpluses. It is almost only the USA that has accepted deficits to a certain degree since the early 1980s as its external debt is in domestic currency and even strong exchange rate fluctuations do little harm to the US economy and the reputation of the US dollar. Unfortunately, the current account deficit of the US is not (fully) reflected in surpluses of countries in the developing world (such as China) as to a large extent it reflects surpluses of other developed countries (such as Japan). Most developing countries are caught in the regime of underdevelopment and have to fight against current account deficits, overindebtedness, dollarization, capital flight and stagnation.

Global Balance of Payment Clearing Mechanism

The world economy would create fewer destabilizing shocks for developing countries if there were more exchange rate stability between the US dollar, euro and yen,[20] *and* if at the same time there were a mechanism which could keep current account balances of developing and developed countries in check. A worldwide regime with an equilibrium mechanism is only possible if there is a supranational institution which organizes cooperation between countries and is able to stimulate adjustment mechanisms in case current account deficits occur. Such a supranational institution could follow ideas of the international 'Clearing Union' proposed by Keynes after World War II (Keynes, 1969; cp. Davidson, 1999).[21] This would require a new world currency system, something like a Post Keynesian Bretton Woods II.

Surplus for Developing and Deficits for Developed Countries

The most favourable constellation for developing countries is current account deficits of the bloc of developed countries, especially the United States, European Union and Japan, and current account surpluses of the bloc of developing countries. In such a constellation developing countries could stimulate their economies by dynamic export performance and at the same time strengthen the reputation of their currencies. This requires undervaluation policies in the developing countries vis-à-vis hard currencies and overvaluation policies in the bloc of developed countries vis-à-vis developing countries; furthermore, goods markets would have to be fully opened in developed countries to imports from poorer countries.

There may be a group of some 50 very poor countries which completely depend on foreign aid to survive. Clearly, such countries are on the drip and have to be further financed by rich countries. They can only develop as transfer economies in dependence on their donors. A sharp increase in foreign aid for this country group, as proposed vigorously by Jeffrey Sachs and others, can be of strong direct help but corroborates many macroeconomic distortions and will probably result in long-term economic and political dependence. Instead a new orientation in development strategy including a policy to stimulate exports from developing countries and lower current account deficits is gradually needed to overcome the existing development blockade of many overindebted countries in the South. Such alternatives – for example grants instead of loans, or loans to be repaid in local currency, and exchange rate stabilization aid – cannot be discussed here.

CONCLUSIONS

Theoretically, even the best allocation (or perfect performance in structural adjustment) does not induce enduring aggregate demand, and hence growth and capital accumulation. Allocation improvements can even go along with low growth or recession; long-run positive effects may never be realized if short-run problems cannot be overcome and a 'bad' development path is followed. Contrariwise, there can be high growth due to favourable macroeconomic conditions despite suboptimal allocation (see Herr and Priewe, 1999, for the case of China). Furthermore, to find out what 'optimal' allocation really is will take a long time and depends on the specific circumstances of countries (the simple model of perfect competition can be misleading); structural adjustments including institution building are time consuming, as may be studied in the economic history of developed countries. Therefore increased attention has to address the macroeconomic forces of growth separately from adjustment issues at a micro level. Of course improvements at the micro level also have to take place continuously to remain on a path of high growth (Rodrik, 2003).

In the field of development it is very often not possible to realize quickly the first best solution. Typically there are trade-offs. For example, in the case of a conflict between stabilization and growth on the one hand and optimal structural adjustment on the other, there is no doubt that growth is more important in the short run and high growth improves the economic, social and political conditions for structural reforms which require a long period of time.

Capital controls are a good example. They are commonly regarded as an awkward and old-fashioned instrument from the age preceding the globalization of finance. If stable exchange rates, a current account surplus or at least a balanced current account and low foreign debt are regarded as a necessary (although not sufficient) precondition for growth and development, there is a conflict of goals. Capital import controls (rather than capital export controls) can help to keep the balance of payment in equilibrium. Furthermore, the liberalization of the capital account should progress gradually as it did over many decades in the now developed countries. Premature liberalization of cross-border capital flows can smash or suffocate the domestic financial sector which, however, is crucial for development. Premature liberalization of the capital account prevents the development, in most countries, an immature and distorted local financial sector, thus inducing high opportunity costs. Highly developed global finance without any restriction for mobility may conflict with the need to secure macro stability in less developed economies (Eichengreen, 1999; Stiglitz, 1999). In the augmented Washington Consensus, prudent capital account opening is mentioned, but international institutions much too often recommended and pressed for quick capital account liberalization, rather than consider that developed countries, even after World War II, needed decades and not years.

To sum up, an alternative macroeconomic policy package to the old or augmented Washington Consensus should comprise the following objectives and policies as long as there exists no new global currency and balance of payment clearing system:

1. low inflation near to the inflation rate in hard currency countries in the case of an open capital account with unfettered currency competition;
2. current account surplus via stimulating exports (first best) or balance or small deficit financed only by FDI inflows (second best) or moving gradually towards these goals (third best); avoiding forced current account balance through low growth and austerity policies;
3. low gross external debt;
4. stable nominal (though adjustable) exchange rates backed by stable unit–labour costs as two interlinked nominal anchors for the price level; real undervaluation of the currency (first best);
5. low real interest rates, through reduced currency risk premium;
6. repressed dollarization;
7. sustainable budget deficits in local currency;
8. capital account controls (temporary or permanent) to (a) curb current account imbalances, (b) stabilize exchange rates, (c) dampen dollarization, (d) extend leeway for domestic monetary policy, (e) shelter the domestic financial sector;
9. foreign aid: grants instead of preferential loans, debt relief with new conditionality according to the abovementioned policies.

NOTES

1. Williamson mentioned fiscal discipline, redirection of priorities in public expenditures, tax reforms to lower marginal rates and a broader tax base, interest rate liberalization, competitive exchange rates, trade liberalization, liberalization of foreign direct investment (FDI) inflows, privatization, deregulation and secure property rights (cp. Williamson, 1990, 2000; Kuczynski and Williamson, 2003).
2. Rodrik (2003) proposed the 'augmented' Washington consensus as the previous ten items plus the following ten: corporate governance, anti-corruption, flexible labour markets, adherence to WTO disciplines, adherence to international financial codes and standards, 'prudent' capital account opening, non-intermediate exchange rate regimes, independent Central Bank/inflation targeting, social safety nets and targeting poverty reduction.
3. See Williamson (2004) and his further explanations at the conference in Berlin, 'Searching for Alternatives – Beyond the Washington Consensus', 22–3 September 2004.
4. In a cross-country analysis, Bruno and Easterly (1995) found out that below an inflation rate of 40 per cent there is no clear link between inflation and per capita growth. Dornbusch and Fischer (1993) found that inflation rates over 30 per cent become unstable. We believe inflation rates of 30 or 40 per cent are too high for stable development. Firstly, cross-country regressions are based on weak methodological grounds. They do not take into consideration individual country circumstances such as the existence of capital controls, the political situation, the effectiveness of government policies and the whole institutional structure of a country (Arestis and Demetriades, 1997). Secondly, during the last decade the degree of dollarization in developing countries increased, capital controls were reduced and liberalization was pushed. In such an environment the currency competition between the currencies of developing countries and the leading world currencies (US dollar and euro) becomes more intensive. Substantially higher inflation rates in developing countries than in industrial countries would certainly induce more capital flight, higher dollarization, devaluation and higher real interest rates in developing countries. Such a constellation would not foster a stable sustainable growth process.
5. The idea of cost inflation goes back to Keynes (1930). Keynes distinguishes between cost inflation and demand inflation. For him cost inflation is in the centre of inflationary processes (see also Herr and Priewe, 2003; Herr, 2002).
6. There is no economic model available that can explain the volatile exchange rate movements between the leading world countries since the early 1970s. The purchasing-power-parity theory in all its forms is certainly not helpful to explain these exchange rate swings (Isard, 1997). Instead, foreign exchange markets should be regarded as asset markets without a stable equilibrium determined by fundamentals, but governed by unstable short-term expectations and jumping from one short-term equilibrium to another.
7. External debt is interpreted here in a broader sense, including portfolio and foreign direct investments. Portfolio investment includes shares and debt securities. In the case of the latter, foreign debt in foreign currency is built up. In principle, FDI and portfolio investment in the form of shares can be regarded as external debt, too (liabilities vis-à-vis foreign wealth owners), however the exchange rate risk is borne by the foreign investor.
8. As a rule of thumb, in many instances practitioners regard deficits up to 5 per cent of GDP as tolerable, in particular if they are rooted in non-budget deficits. There is not one glimmer of theory backing such rules. If deficits are considered too high, mostly restrictive macro policies are advised to dampen GDP and imports.
9. The Asian crisis in 1997 and the Russian crisis in 1998 are good examples among many of the effects pointed out. In both cases the Central Bank could not help and the financial systems broke down. For an overview of such twin crises, cp. Kaminsky and Reinhart (1999).
10. Such strong devaluations are predominantly real devaluations which increase the real burden of external debt as well as domestic debt in foreign currency in the case of debt dollarization.
11. Even worse is the predominant fact that long-term credit is often not available.
12. High market-determined interest rates in liberalized credit markets lead to a distorted credit

allocation as good debtors drop out and risk-prone debtors are selected (Stiglitz, 1992). This effect is usually not discussed when the liberalization of financial systems is recommended.

13. Hence we disagree with Easterly and others who claim that physical investment is irrelevant for long-run growth because they assert that only technical progress drives growth. This assumes the notion of disembodied technical progress which is a rare phenomenon in reality.

14. Keynes (1937) developed similar arguments and the modern circuit models drawing on Schumpeter and Keynes see banks as necessary 'circuit starters' for investment and production (Bossone and Abdourahmane, 2002).

15. In Russia, the banking system, highly indebted in foreign currency, was nearly wiped out in the currency crisis of 1998.

16. Even if the estimated amount of non-performing loans is deducted, the ratio is outstanding in the developing world.

17. We certainly do not claim that a stable and accepted currency is the only factor for development. Human capital, innovative entrepreneurs, rule of law and so on are also of eminent importance. But without stable domestic money these factors cannot unfold their positive effects.

18. Here the term 'development' is used in the sense of sustained growth. We are, of course, well aware that development is more than just growth.

19. GDP per capita grew in the 1990s in low-income countries (unweighted average) by −0.5 per cent and by 1.4 per cent in lower middle-income countries (Herr and Priewe, 2004, p. 84; the figures refer to 100 out of 117 countries in these categories because of data availability. The data is based on the *World Bank Indicators*).

20. For a long time, Paul Davidson has been arguing for more stable exchange rates (Davidson, 1982).

21. Keynes proposed three obligatory options for severe surplus countries: (a) increasing imports from clearing union member countries, (b) additional FDI and (c) unilateral capital transfers to deficit countries.

REFERENCES

Arestis, Philip and Panicos Demetriades (1997), 'Financial development and economic growth: assessing the evidence', *The Economic Journal*, **107**, 683–799.

Baliño, Thomás J.T., Adam Bennett Adam and Eduardo Borensztein (1999), 'Monetary policy in dollarised economies', IMF occasional paper 171, Washington, DC.

Bossone, Biagio and Sarr Abdourahmane (2002), 'A new financial system for poverty reduction and growth', IMF working paper WP/02/178, Washington, DC.

Bruno, Michael and William Easterly (1995), 'Inflation crises and long-run growth', National Bureau of Economic Research working paper no. 5209, Cambridge, MA.

Chenery, Hollis B. and Alan M. Strout (1966), 'Foreign assistance and economic development', *American Economic Review*, Sept., part 1 of 2, **56** (4), 679–733.

Davidson, Paul (1982), *International Money and the Real World*, London: Macmillan.

Davidson, Paul (1999), 'Global macro policies for reducing persistent high unemployment rates in OECD countries', in W. Filc and C. Köhler (eds) (1999), *Macroeconomic Causes of Unemployment: Diagnosis and Policy Recommendations*, Berlin: Duncker and Humblot, pp. 97–116.

Dornbusch, Ruediger (1990), 'From stabilization to growth', National Bureau of Economic Research, working paper no. 3302, Cambridge, MA.

Dornbusch, Ruediger and Stanley Fischer (1993), 'Moderate inflation', *World Bank Review*, **7**, 1–44.

Easterly, William (1999), 'The ghost of the financing gap. Testing the growth model used in the international financial institutions', *Journal of Development Economics*, **60** (2), 423–38.

Easterly, William (2002), 'How did heavily indebted poor countries become heavily indebted? Reviewing two decades of debt relief', *World Development*, **30** (10), 1677–96.

Eichengreen, Barry (1999), *Towards a New International Financial Architecture. A Practical Post-Asia Agenda*, Washington, DC: Institute for International Economics.

Eichengreen, Barry and Hausmann, Ricardo (1999), 'Exchange rates and financial fragility', National Bureau of Economic Research working paper no. 7418, Cambridge, MA.

Eichengreen, Barry, Ricardo Hausmann and Ugo Panizza (2002), 'Original sin: the pain, the mystery, and the road to redemption', paper prepared for the conference 'Currency and Maturity Matchmaking: Redeeming Debt form Original Sin', Inter-American Development Bank, 21–2 November, Washington, DC.

Fischer, Stanley, Ratna Sahay and Carlos A. Végh (2002), 'Modern hyper inflations', *Journal of Economic Literature*, **15**, 836–80.

Herr, Hansjörg (1997), 'The international monetary system and domestic policy', in D.J. Forsyth and T. Notermans (eds), *Regime Changes. Macroeconomic Policy and Financial Regulations in Europe from the 1930s to the 1990s*, Cambridge, MA: Berghahn Books, pp. 124–68.

Herr, Hansjörg (2002), 'Wages, employment and prices. An analysis of the relationship between wage level, wage structure, minimum wages and employment and prices', Business Institute Berlin at the Berlin School of Economics working paper no. 15, Berlin, accessed at www.fhw-berlin.de/fhw2000/lehre_und_forschung/working paper15.pdf.

Herr, Hansjörg and Jan Priewe (1999), 'High growth in China – transition without a transition crisis?', *Intereconomics*, **34** (6), 303–16.

Herr, Hansjörg and Jan Priewe (2003), 'The macroeconomic framework of poverty reduction. An assessment of the IMF/World Bank strategy', Business Institute Berlin at the Berlin School of Economics working paper no. 17, Berlin, accessed at www.fhw-berlin.de/fhw2000/lehre_und_forschung/working_paper_17.pdf.

Herr, Hansjörg and Jan Priewe (2004), 'Macroeconomic policies and financial development within the framework of poverty reducing development strategies – with case studies', unpublished manuscript, Berlin.

Honohan, Patrick and Anqing Shi (2003), 'Deposit dollarization and the financial sector in emerging economies', in James A. Hanson, Patrick Honohan and Giovanni Majnoni (eds), *Globalization and National Financial Systems*, Oxford: Oxford University Press.

IMF (2003), 'Financial stability in dollarized economies', document of International Monetary Fund SM/03/112, Washington, DC.

Isard, Peter (1997), *Exchange Rate Economics*, Cambridge: Cambridge University Press.

Ize, Alain and Eric Parrado (2002), 'Dollarization, monetary policy, and the pass-through', IMF working paper 02/188, Washington, DC.

Jeanne, Oliver and Jeromin Zettelmeyer (2002), 'Original sin, balance sheet crises and the roles of international lending', IMF working paper 02/234, Washington, DC.

Kaminsky, G.L. and Carmen Reinhart (1999), 'The twin crises: the causes of banking and balance of-payments problems', *The American Economic Review*, **89** (3), 473–99.

Keynes, John M. (1930), *A Treatise on Money, Volume I, The Pure Theory of Money*, London and Basingstoke: Macmillan.

Keynes, John M. (1937), 'The "ex-ante" theory of the rate of interest', *Economic Journal*, **47**, December, 663–9.

Keynes, John M. (1969), 'Proposals for an international clearing union', in J.K. Horsfield (ed.), *The International Monetary Fund 1946–1965, Vol. III, Documents*, Washington DC.

Kuczynski, Pedro-Pablo and John Williamson (eds) (2003), *After the Washington Consensus: Restarting Growth and Reform in Latin America*, Washington, DC: Institute for International Economics.

Robinson, Joan (1937), 'Beggar-My-Neighbour Remedies for Unemployment', in Joan Robinson (ed.), *Contributions to Modern Economics*; reprinted London: Blackwell, 1978, pp. 190–200.

Rodrik, Dani (2003), 'Growth Strategies', in Philippe Aghion and Steven Durlauf (eds), *Handbook of Economic Growth 2005*, vol. 1 part A, Amsterdam: North-Holland, pp. 967–1014.

Rojas-Suarez, Liliana (2003), 'Monetary policy and exchange rates: guiding principles for a sustainable regime', in P. Kuczynski and J. Williamson, pp. 123–56.

Roy, Tobias (2000), *Ursachen und Wirkungen der Dollarisierung von Entwicklungsländern*, Marburg: Metropolis.

Schumpeter, Joseph A. (1934), *The Theory of Economic Development. An Inquiry into Profits, Capital, Credit, Interest and Business Cycle*, Cambridge, MA: Harvard University Press.

Stiglitz, Joseph E. (1992), 'Capital markets and economic fluctuations in capitalist economies', *European Economic Review*, **36**, 269–306.

Stiglitz, Joseph E. (1999), 'Reforming the global economic architecture: lessons from recent crises', *The Journal of Finance*, **54** (4), 1508–21.

Stiglitz, Joseph E. (2002), *Globalisation and its Discontents*, New York and London: W.W. Norton & Co.

Teunissen, Jan Joost and Age Akkerman (2003), *The Crisis That Was Not Prevented: Lessons from Argentina*, The Hague: IMF.

Vandenbroucke, Frank (1985), 'Conflicts in international economic policy and the world recession: a theoretical analysis', *Cambridge Journal of Economics*, **9**, 15–42.

Williamson, John (1990), 'What Washington means by policy reform', in John Williamson (ed.), *Latin American Adjustment: How Much Has Happened?*, Washington, DC: Institute for International Economics.

Williamson, John (2000), 'What should the World Bank think about the Washington Consensus?', *The World Bank Research Observer*, **15** (2), 251–64.

Williamson, John (2004), 'The Washington Consensus as policy prescription for development', Institute for International Economics manuscript, Washington, DC.

World Bank. (2001), 'Finance for growth. Policy choices in a volatile world', World Bank policy research report, Washington, DC.

World Bank (2002a), *World Development Indicators 2002*, Washington, DC.

World Bank (2002b), *World Development Report 2002*, Washington, DC.

World Bank (2003a), 'Financial stability in dollarized economies', International Monetary Fund document, SM/03/112, Washington, DC.

World Bank (2003b), 'Macroeconomic Issues', in *PRSP Sourcebook*, Washington, DC: World Bank.

World Bank (2003c), *World Development Report 2003*, Washington, DC: World Bank.

10. Competition, low profit margin, low inflation and economic stagnation

Arturo Huerta

FINANCIAL LIBERALIZATION IMPOSES EXCHANGE-RATE STABILITY

Developing countries (particularly in Latin America) undertook liberalization of their financial markets in order to attract foreign funds to cover internal funding shortages, problems with the current-account deficit of the balance of payments, and problems related to economic growth. Limitations on short-term capital flows were eliminated to allow unrestricted movement, a prerequisite imposed by capital in order for funds to flow into a particular country. Yet the free flow of capital tends to bring changes in the currency, capital and money markets. With financial liberation, changes in expectations for the economy, or exchange rate behaviour, or internal versus external interest-rate differentials, can lead to rapid reversals of capital flows.

Financial liberalization requires stability in the exchange rate in order to avoid speculative practices and losses in financial capital, which occur when the currency in which investment occurs is devalued. Thus bringing down inflation and exchange-rate stability go hand-in-hand with financial liberalization. The latter cannot happen without conditions of stability being met, insofar as, in a context of uncertainty regarding the exchange rate or profitability of investments in a country, the free movement of capital would act against currency and financial markets, which in turn would deepen exchange-rate instability and provoke a crisis.

Thus countries with liberalized financial markets have been forced to seek low inflation, exchange-rate stability and conditions of domestic profitability, in order for capital to flow into a country and remain there. The economic situation today in Latin American countries is determined by consequences derived by liberalization and inflation-reducing policies.

When a country lacks the productive, financial and macroeconomic conditions to achieve exchange-rate stability and low inflation, it endeavours to implement contractionary monetary and fiscal policies (increasing the interest rate and restricting public spending), made possible by the autonomy granted to the Central Bank. It also implements fiscal discipline to lessen demand-led pressures on prices and on the foreign sector, thus eliminating expectations of inflation and devaluation.

Within the neoclassical framework, economic growth brings inflationary pressures, and subsequent policy decisions, aimed at avoiding pressure on prices, contract economic activity. Hence policies of fiscal discipline and high interest rates are the norm.

Economic policy makers make decisions hoping to provide low inflation and stability in the exchange rate, that would create the confidence needed to stimulate capital inflows. Economic policy management is sacrificed in favour of growth, in order to maintain the stable exchange rate sought by international financial capital.

Contractionary policies are accompanied by a process of privatization and internationalization of corporations and assets in order to widen the sphere of influence and profitability of private capital and encourage capital inflows. Thus the supply of hard currencies is increased, and demand restricted, in order for the exchange rate to appreciate. This rate is flexible vis-à-vis capital flows, but not with respect to the differential between domestic and foreign prices. Exchange-rate appreciation acts in favour of financial capital profitability since, upon exiting, it wants hard currencies at a lower price, and thus to increase profits already made internally.

Yet the decrease in inflation is not a result of increases in productivity, but rather exchange-rate appreciation, which cheapens imports, generating a competitive process, forcing domestic producers to lower their prices. In addition there is a restrictive fiscal policy – dampening domestic demand – and so too demand-led pressure on prices. The lowering of labour costs needs to be mentioned, since salary increases are lower than productivity gains and price hikes.

INFLATION-REDUCING POLICIES AND FALLING PROFIT MARGINS

Policies geared to stimulate trade, such as reducing tariffs and appreciating the exchange rate, which lower inflation by making imports cheaper, generate a process of inequitable competition that affects domestic producers and exporters, given their low productivity levels.

Appreciation of the exchange rate makes imports more competitive vis-à-vis domestic companies, which become price takers. In other words they make adjustments in response to prices determined by imports, and thus sacrifice their profit margin (price–cost relationship), because of greater competition from imported products. Thus the inability of domestic producers to compete against imported products reduces their degree of monopoly, as well as their share of the domestic market, given their displacement by imports.

Prices are no longer fixed by the most inefficient domestic companies, as was the case when protected markets existed in the economy, which allows the larger, more efficient companies to obtain high profit margins. In the context of trade openness and exchange rate appreciation, domestic companies lack the conditions to fix prices according to average costs, plus a profit margin goal to guarantee conditions of endogenous financing. They can no longer shift all cost increases to prices, given the competition they face. Companies must absorb higher costs by cutting profit margins, to avoid losing even more productivity and presence in the markets, vis-à-vis imports.

The share of imports in the domestic market has increased not only as a result of the appreciation of the exchange rate but also because of low productivity of domestic companies, in addition to productive lags attributable to lower investment, resulting from restrictive monetary and fiscal policies that accompany the appreciation in the exchange rate. Domestic companies are less competitive, while exports by multinational corporations, mostly intra-firm commerce, are unaffected since they are traded in their (home country's) currency. Thus the exchange-rate appreciation does not harm them but, on the contrary, allows them to buy imported inputs cheaply. Owing to their high import coefficient, exchange-rate appreciation is functional and profitable for exporters.

The law of a single price ceases to hold when priority is given to an appreciated exchange rate for the purpose of lowering inflation and guaranteeing more profitable conditions for international financial capital. The price distortion brought about by exchange-rate appreciation, together with differences in productivity and interest rates, internal versus external, and lower trade tariffs, leads to sales by domestic companies that are lower than production, preventing the profit incorporated in sales to be realized and thus lowering the rate of return.

Trade liberalization, together with anti-inflationary policies, characterized by exchange-rate appreciation and restrictive monetary and fiscal policy, has reduced domestic producers' competitiveness, lowered profit margins and dampened growth of the domestic market. This raises levels of idle capacity and pressures on the foreign trade deficit, generating problems of high domestic and foreign debt, and brings on a recession. In spite of a lower degree of monopoly power and, therefore, the need to sacrifice profit margins given import competition, domestic companies must also face a drop in their share of the domestic market and rate of return.

DECREASES IN PROFIT MARGINS, GREATER IDLE CAPACITY AND LESS INVESTMENT

Domestic producers are forced to work with lower profit margins in order to survive in an environment of trade openness, exchange-rate appreciation and imports, but are unable to counteract their loss of competitiveness, or to maintain or increase the demand for their products or market share. Productive capacity drops, productive chains are broken, and pressure on manufactures' foreign-trade deficit increases, reducing the domestic multiplier effect of demand and investment, given the higher percentage of imports.

Thus the drop in inflation comes with a process of deindustrialization, higher levels of debt, problems with the foreign trade sector and a rapid increase of foreign holdings in the economy.

Analyses by M. Kalecki and J. Steindl regarding monopolization conclude that a greater degree of monopolization brings a tendency towards stagnation (see King, 1999, p. 252). It is their understanding that higher profit margins can be obtained, but at the cost of lowering the share of wages in value added, which lowers wage earners' demand and so too economic growth. Therefore economic growth comes by lowering the degree of monopolization and profit margins in order to improve wages and demand for goods in order to jump-start the economy. Still, this does not happen in developing economies that have opened their markets and have no competitiveness against imports. This has reduced the degree of monopolization of domestic producers, but without favouring economic growth.

Competition unleashed by imports has not encouraged investment since domestic firms are at a disadvantage, and many of them prefer to distribute imported products instead of modernizing plant and equipment. Lower profit margins do not lead to higher real salaries, or to greater purchasing power for workers that would increase consumption and demand, and thus counteract the negative impact that lower profit margins have on profits. This is due to the fact that salaries are readjusted below increases in productivity and prices, both because domestic producers try in this way to counteract the problems of competitiveness they face with imports, but it is also due to the unemployment resulting from the downturn in production and investment.

When domestic producers begin to decrease real salaries to compensate for their lack of competitiveness, they end up affecting the dynamic of the rate of return and growth of the economy, owing to the fact that a lower profit margin compounds a contraction of domestic demand coming about from a drop in real salaries, which puts a brake on economic activity. Thus lower profit margins, notwithstanding their role in reducing inflation, do not lead to greater purchasing power for the population. This then means that a drop in inflation does not increase company or household income, rather it lowers their income. Thus a drop in both demand and company sales ensues, which prevents the realization of greater profits. In the words of Tracy Mott, 'a drop in investment not compensated by a rise in consumption expenditures is the cause of the cycle and long-term stagnation' (Mott, 2002, p. 160), which is exactly what happens when the drop in profit margins does not favour domestic workers, but rather is the consequence of a loss of competitiveness vis-à-vis imports. Therefore the drop in investment (coming from lower profits), as well as lower consumption (resulting from lower real salaries and greater unemployment), recreate an environment of economic stagnation.

The drop in the degree of use of productive capacity is a consequence of the loss of competitiveness vis-à-vis imports, leading to lower domestic sales and production, thus reflecting the fact that profits in this sector are not being realized, thus dampening the growth of investment and of the economy. Lavoie, following Kalecki, tells us that 'companies' rate of return depends on the rate of use of [installed] capacity and of the effective profit margin' (Lavoie, 2002, p. 175). Under conditions of reduced demand, displacement of domestic production by imports, lower profit margins and a higher level of idle capacity, there is no chance of increasing investment and economic activity. Accordingly, Steindl affirms that 'This depresses utilization and profits, and therefore tends to lower the growth rate even further' (Steindl, 1990a, p. 157).

Worth noting is the fact that the degree of monopolization, that is, the price–cost ratio, drops for domestic producers, but not for imports, and even less so in a context of an appreciation of the exchange rate, which acts in favour of the latter. The degree of monopolization and profits is transferred to foreign producers. They, by means of their exports (our imports), increase their share in the domestic market and their profits, at the expense of a drop in domestic companies' income, family income and aggregate demand.

Given the lack of domestic competitiveness to face imports, globalization has sentenced the economy to work with increasing idle capacity, external deficits, a high rate of indebtedness, credit restrictions and less investment, all of which brake economic activity, increase unemployment, reduce tax flows and increase pressure on public finances.

AS ITS PROFIT MARGIN DROPS, THE DOMESTIC FIRM IS UNABLE TO DETERMINE ITS FINANCING AND GROWTH

The process of inequitable competition that domestic producers face vis-à-vis imports means they lose the ability to determine prices and ensure the profit margins needed to finance investment. Domestic companies, given their low competitiveness with respect to imports, and their loss of market share, no longer have the ability to guarantee, by means of prices and high profit margins, the internal financing of their investments. On the contrary, they are forced to lower prices and profit rates because of the competition, thus sacrificing income and endogenous investment financing, leading to reduced ability to grow and, in fact, growth is now determined by the capacity to take on debt. This in turn is determined by the company's ability to pay, now dampened because it is a taker of price and profit structures. Wolfson writes, 'the price of a product can affect its ability' to get a credit (Wolfson, 1996a, p. 463).

In the context of economic liberalization, if domestic companies opt to increase prices to increase their profit margins and self-financing, they will be easily displaced in the market by imports. Thus inflation is reduced at the expense of a lower profit margin and internal financing conditions for domestic companies. Trade-opening and stabilization policies reduce inflation at the expense of placing domestic producers at a disadvantage with foreign competitors, straining their realization of profits and share of the domestic market.

The link between prices and investment changes within a context of economic liberalization and exchange-rate appreciation. In an open economy with inequitable competition, domestic prices are no longer determined by the need to generate the funds necessary for investment, but are now determined by the prices of imported products and, since these are lower in price than their domestic counterparts, they lower profit margins and dampen investment financing.

Domestic companies are hit not only by lower prices and profit margins but also by lower production insofar as they are displaced in the domestic market by imports. This brings an increase in the balance-of-trade deficit and idle capacity, leading to a drop in profits of companies in the productive sector, leaving them without self-financing, and forcing them to take on debt in order to solve their financial problems and/or to decapitalize.

Companies put themselves in a fragile financial situation by no longer having conditions by means of which to increase their profit margin and income in order to guarantee payments, and thus cease being creditworthy.

A recurring scenario ensues of lower profits (income) and credit restrictions, since, as internal funds dry up (an important factor in obtaining financing and strengthening investment growth) and as the debt ratio climbs [companies'], ability to obtain credit diminishes, deepening their growth-related problems. Fazzari and Variato point out that 'the ability of a firm to undertake an investment project may depend not only on the fundamentals of the project under consideration, but also on the firm's financial condition' (Fazzari and Variato, 1994, p. 355).

The increase in the foreign trade deficit and the increasing demand for inflows of capital lead authorities to exercise increasingly stringent monetary and fiscal policies in an effort to decrease pressure on the trade deficit and the exchange rate, which could discourage inflows of capital. A situation arises where a firm's income grows at a rate below the cost of its debt, so then credit availability is restricted and, consequently, so too investment and economic activity. Wolfson, following Friedman, argues, 'the sharp drop in price, and rise in interest rates which these actions cause are characteristic of financial crises' (Wolfson, 1986, p. 182).

The economy has come to depend on increased capital inflows to be able to cover the financing of the foreign trade deficit and the lack of internal financing. These capital inflows have not brought a greater growth of investment or productive capacity, which might improve competitiveness or the foreign trade balance. Rather, they have contributed to exchange-rate appreciation. This, in turn, has an impact on decreased competitiveness, and consequently reduced profit margins, while increasing the foreign trade deficit. As a result, the economy is less able to make payments on financial obligations deriving from capital inflows, leading to a greater current-account deficit in the balance of payments, putting a brake on economic activity and making the economy even more dependent on capital inflows.

FALLING PROFIT MARGINS AND WORKERS

According to M. Kalecki, income distribution between wages and profits depends on firms' degree of monopolization and workers' negotiating strength (Kalecki [1943] 1990). High profit margins stimulate trade unions to negotiate higher salary adjustments (Sawyer, 1982). Nonetheless this changes in the context of an open economy, where domestic producers cannot compete adequately with imports. This situation reduces the degree of monopolization and increases the foreign trade deficit. Domestic firms' lower profit margins weaken the hand of trade unions, given that the situation brings company closures, greater idle capacity and unemployment, which, given the fear of job losses, leads workers to refrain from demanding wage increases. This is due to the firms' weaker financial situation brought about by both competition and the smaller market they face. Workers have fewer possibilities of reducing domestic firms' already weakened degree of monopolization by changing income distribution towards consumption and, in this manner, stimulating economic growth. We ought to remember that, for Kalecki, 'stagnation could be avoided only by a substantial redistribution of income from profits to wages and a huge expansion of public expenditure' (see King, 1999, p. 252).

Wage earners' weakened negotiating power does not bring about increased profits for domestic producers since, in addition to falling profit margins and displacement by imports, producers face reduced demand due to the drop in real salaries.

When domestic producers' degree of monopolization drops and when workers' negotiating power is weakened, both sectors lack conditions to determine and increase their income through prices and wages, respectively. In other words, decreased income among domestic producers goes hand-in-hand with lower wages for workers. Warren Mosler tells us that workers' strength parallels the strength of domestic producers, in that 'a strong labor force requires strong businesses. In today's competitive market businesses are not strong, and therefore workers have little power' (Mosler, 1997). So long as domestic production is weak vis-à-vis imports, workers lack conditions in which to obtain greater benefits.

Exchange-rate appreciation brings a drop in inflation, at the expense of falling profit margins and real salaries, meaning that domestic producers and workers shoulder the brunt of the drop in inflation, as seen by the decapitalization of the productive sector, increasing unemployment and lower real wages.

The drop in income of domestic producers and workers is the result of prevailing anti-inflationary policies that dampen demand and reduce domestic producers' share of the local market. This contradicts Casseti's claim that 'a drop in profits' share is the only change with an expansionary effect while reducing inflation' (Casseti, 2002, p. 202). The drop in the degree of monopolization of domestic producers, vis-à-vis foreign competition, does not imply an expansionary effect for workers' purchasing power, or for demand or domestic economic activity, since it occurs alongside a drop in real wages. When real wages fall, rather than boosting the margin and amount of profits, they work against the latter, since demand, the degree of use of productive capacity and domestic economic activity also drop, given that exports do not counteract either import growth or the contraction of the domestic market.

Economic authorities are able, therefore, through economic liberalization and stabilization policies, to reduce domestic producers' degree of monopolization and workers' wage negotiating strength, thus restricting monetary demands provoked by prices and wages, allowing authorities to maintain restrictions on the monetary supply and thus send favourable signals of stability to international financial capital in order to stimulate inflows.

A redistribution of income takes place to the detriment of domestic producers and workers, and in favour of producers from the country of origin of our imports. Funds are transferred abroad, as a result of the foreign trade deficit, greater unemployment and lower income of domestic producers and families, which decreases investment, family purchasing power and thus demand, thereby affecting the dynamics of the economy.

Granted, inflation is reduced when domestic producers and workers are unable to determine prices and wages. The cost of lower inflation is the drop in profits in the productive sphere and in real wages, with the resulting decapitalization of the domestic productive sphere and greater control of foreign entities of the economy, in addition to restrictions on credit availability, on production and on employment, as well as increased vulnerability of the economy vis-à-vis capital flows.

Reducing inflation by means of the aforementioned policies works against productive capacity and economic growth, and weakens the economy's competitiveness, thus perpetuating the stagnation into which it has fallen.

Foreign producers control the degree of monopolization, thus affecting economic growth, since the situation brings a greater foreign-trade deficit, thus restricting economic activity. Renewed economic growth is made more difficult in this context, owing to the fact that the conflict is not so much between domestic producers and workers, but rather between domestic producers and foreign competitors, since the situation has brought a decapitalization of the domestic productive process and transfers of resources abroad.

LOW INFLATION BASED ON AN APPRECIATED EXCHANGE RATE IS NOT COMPATIBLE WITH ECONOMIC GROWTH

The Mexican government has tried to foster conditions of sustained economic growth by reducing inflation. Still, its policies in this regard have ended up braking domestic economic activity, making the economy highly vulnerably from abroad, and at the mercy of the behaviour of external variables (exports and capital flows).

The drop in inflation brought by monetary-exchange rate stabilization policies does not stimulate economic growth. Rather, such policies play an important role in weakening real variables, since they increase the competitive disadvantage in which domestic producers find themselves vis-à-vis imports. Inflation is reduced at the cost of decapitalizing the productive sector, of increased levels of indebtedness, and a greater foreign-trade deficit, all of which produce a recessive tendency, and increase the demand for domestic and foreign financial resources.

The pressure on the foreign sector forces the government to emphasize fiscal and monetary restrictions to dampen demand and pressures on the foreign sector and the exchange rate, thus recreating a recessive vicious circle. This makes the high cost of reducing inflation in this manner abundantly clear. A vicious circle is created since these policies continue to pressure the current account deficit in the balance of payments and work against profits and productive investment.

By suppressing demand and profits in the productive sector, the government tries to reduce inflation and stabilize the exchange rate, which is beneficial to capital flows, since it guarantees the value of financial capital. Such an economic policy generates improved conditions of profitability in the financial sector, to the detriment of the productive sector, leading to capital outflows from the latter and reinvested in the former, bringing down economic growth. Steindl tells us that 'More recently, the monetarist policy has reinforced the tendency of industrial firms to convert themselves into renters and speculators' (Steindl, 1990b, p. 178).

A situation arises in which the asking price for capital assets is less than the price offered for them, that is, a disincentive to investment, owing to the fact that projected income is insufficient to cover investment costs.

Inflation is reduced at the expense of prioritizing restrictive monetary and fiscal policies and enhancing the exchange rate, which leads to a drop in domestic and foreign demand, affecting investment decisions and economic activity. Domestic demand is increasingly met by imports, and foreign demand is supplied by producers from other countries in a better competitive position than Mexico's. Stagnation arises with the growing presence of imports in the domestic market, and the drop in exports, that manifests itself by a rise in unemployment and a drop in production.

With inflation-reducing policies, the economy is starved of public and private expenditures and investment necessary for the domestic market and to counteract the drop in exports. Likewise, there is no monetary policy that would generate the liquidity necessary to reactivate the economy, or production and profits in the productive sector.

Restrictive monetary and fiscal policies are given priority – and therefore a choice is made in favour of stagnation – to drop demand pressures below supply, and thus decrease pressure on prices, imports and the exchange rate, which could affect international financial capital.

LOW PROFITS, HIGH DEBT LEVELS, CREDIT RESTRICTIONS AND THE DROP IN INVESTMENT

The loss of competitiveness of domestic firms, vis-à-vis imports, not only reduces their share in the domestic market and profits, but also increases their level of debt as firms struggle to solve their financial problems. This debt ratio increases as a result of the prevailing restrictive monetary policy. The growing weight of debt servicing that this implies, together with firms' diminished income (as a result of stabilization policies that decrease their competitiveness and market growth) make it more difficult to meet financial obligations. Firms then proceed to cut expenses and investment, with a negative impact on economic activity and, therefore, on their income, thus falling into a vicious recessive circle. Ndikumana points out that 'debt service has a negative effect on investment beyond the fact that cash payment commitments reduce cash flow.

Debt payments not only reduce internal finance but also make outside finance more costly and scarce' (Ndikumana, 1999, p. 456).

Seeing that their income is reduced and that they cannot pay their debts, many firms lose capital, or are forced to seek foreign partners and/or sell assets to pay for liabilities, thus increasing the leverage of creditors. When conditions of general profitability and sufficient income to repay debts fail to appear, banking operations are threatened, as well as the availability of credit to guarantee financing and investment of the productive sector. In this regard Minsky stated that 'Profits are that part of prices that support the financial system and the structure of financial relations by providing the cash flows that validate past financial commitments. Profits are also the signals for investments and current financial commitments' (Minsky, 1985, p. 26).

Domestic firms' financial problems worsen both because of a drop in profits, as well as a prevailing high debt ratio, and also because of the banks' unwillingness to offer credit in light of existing insolvency problems. In a scenario of a high debt ratio (debt/income) ratio, of lower profits, and high uncertainty, creditors are reluctant to lend money, and eschew risk. Banks restrict credits when debtors cannot guarantee loan repayment. Pessimistic expectations act against monetary expansion by the banks, owing to their attitude of restricting credit. Moore points out that 'the supply of credit money thus varies pro-cyclically with changes in the demand for bank credit' (Moore, 1989, p. 26).

Thus both creditors' and debtors' risks contribute to the drop in credit supply and demand, and investment, creating a vicious circle, since these factors contract economic activity and profits, deepening liquidity and insolvency problems even further. These problems worsen as the Central Bank tightens monetary policy and increases the interest rate to avoid a rise in the preference for liquidity in a context of uncertainty. Such a policy increases the lack of liquidity and deepens financial problems.

The lack of internal financing for firms and the lack of credit cannot be reversed by accessing the stock market, given that doing so depends on solvency and the ability to grow. In other words, in a context of low profits and little hope of increasing them, firms have less chance of issuing stock to obtain funds, thus bringing a drop in investment and economic activity. In such a situation the ability to issue debt and create money on the part of banks and non-banks drops, because it is believed that this will bring even more problems of insolvency and speculative activity. The demand for credit and the ability of banks to create credit and money depend on expectations. Minsky reminds us that 'Anticipated cash flows from business operations determine the demand for and supply of debts to be used to finance positions in capital assets and the production of new capital assets (investment output)' (Minsky, 1985, p. 39). When expectations change, the demand for credit and the ability of banks to create credit and money falls. If sufficient future income for debt payments is not foreseen, the risks for creditors and debtors rise, and no one wants to borrow or lend. Supply and demand of credit is restricted. Money ['defined as a debt issued primarily to transfer purchasing power from the future to the present' (Wray, 1992)] cannot be created in a context of expectations of insolvency, given that it would be difficult to guarantee purchasing power (sufficient income) to pay debts.

Firms try to avoid losing their collateral and assets if projected profits are not realized to the extent needed to cover loans, and thus will not increase their risk. Wolfson writes, 'One might think that the higher risk projects would deter borrowers who fear bankruptcy' (Wolfson, 1996a, p. 445). Firms prefer to decrease investment and demand for debt in order to reduce risk. Sherman argues that, 'If insufficient demand causes expected losses, then why would any rational business-person wish to borrow at any positive rate of interest?' (Sherman, 1991, p. 56). In this context investment is forgone, thus financing is not required and the demand for credit drops.

Investment contracts in the absence of sufficient profitability and access to credit which, in turn, defers the repayment of debt. Minsky pointed out that 'profit expectations are consistent with financed investments, the profit flows must be sufficient to validate debts (that is, business will be able to fulfill their cash payment commitments embodied in their liability structure)' (Minsky, 1985, p. 37). As investment contracts, income and profits drop further, problems of insolvency deepen, and the possibility of bankruptcy becomes real. Steindl says that 'If business tries to remedy this [their indebtedness] by cutting down on investment in the next period, it will only bring about a fall in profit and further increase in the debt ratio. In this way, a cumulative downward process will be started' (Steindl, 1990c, p. 209).

If the productive sector has low profits, and low ability to pay off debt, the financial (banking) sector will also have further problems. The behaviour of the banking system depends on the productive sector. Malcom Sawyer writes that 'the financial system has a largely passive relationship with the real sector and the main action arises from the real sector (fluctuations in investment) rather than from the financial system. It is recognized that the financial system has to provide credit if the real sector is to expand' (Sawyer, 1999, p. 307). Problems travel from the productive sector to the financial sector even though the latter can repossess assets as a last resort.

To achieve better performance from both sectors, the economy needs to generate profitable conditions to encourage productive investment and meet payments, in order to decrease creditors and debtors' risk and thus increase the supply and demand of credit. Since firms cannot count on improved expectations of profits and financial conditions to invest, they will be unable to modernize their productive plant to improve competitiveness and profit. Actually the opposite occurs, a process of deindustrialization deepens, and so too the pressure on the foreign sector, which increases the economy's vulnerability.

DOMESTIC FIRMS' LOW PROFITS AND HIGH LEVELS OF DEBT BENEFIT FINANCIAL CAPITAL

Domestic firms' low profits and high debt levels place them in a subordinate position vis-à-vis banking capital, which only deepens when the cost of debt rises faster than the ability to make payments. Income distribution shifts in favour of creditors and against debtors. Domestic productive sectors with problems of overindebtedness and difficulties in making payments turn over control of assets and resources to creditors. Felix argues, 'in conjunction with the rising debt/income ratios from increased debt leveraging, the rentier's share of national income has therefore been rising persistently' (Felix, 1997–8, p. 214). The high levels of debt mean that company and family income is increasingly transferred to the rentier.

The rentier's increase in income does not stimulate productive investment, or consumption, since rentiers abound in the financial sphere, and their consumption is easily satisfied, so transfers to them work against a dynamic economy. In a scenario of low inflation, brought about by an appreciation of the exchange rate and high growth of imports, domestic and foreign creditors win out, given the prevailing high levels of debt. Wolfson points out that 'one effect of either a decline in prices or a decline in inflation is to transfer wealth from debtors to creditors' (Wolfson, 1996b, p. 317). Also US exporters (our principal suppliers) have been favoured, as have purchasers of profitable domestic assets, given that assets are being sold off in order to encourage capital inflows and maintain a stable (appreciated) exchange rate and low inflation.

NO GOVERNMENTAL POLICY EXISTS TO COUNTERACT THE DROP IN PROFITS IN THE PRODUCTIVE SECTOR, AND THE GOVERNMENT OPTS FOR STAGNATION AS THE BEST OPTION FOR BRINGING DOWN INFLATION

The government avoids policies that would counteract the drop in profits of domestic firms. It does not modify its trade or exchange-rate policies, nor does it increase the domestic market by means of public expenditure, because doing so would mean redefining the country's insertion in the globalization process. The government has no intention of devaluing the exchange rate so as to improve the competitiveness of domestic production, given that this would affect financial capital within the country, indispensable for financing the deficit in the current account. Similarly it will not raise public expenditure or the fiscal deficit to act countercyclically to reactivate the economy, given the drop in exports, since it fears that this would increase inflation and pressures on the foreign sector that would destabilize the exchange rate and affect international financial capital in the country. It thus insists on restrictive monetary and fiscal policies to decrease demand pressures on prices and the foreign sector. It continues to emphasize reducing inflation, instead of solving the problems associated with a dampened dynamic in the rate of return and lacklustre demand that continue to restrict economic growth and job creation. Although these policies feed expectations of low inflation for entrepreneurs, they do not generate conditions of profitability and growth for them that would encourage investment. Rather these policies end up working against competitiveness, both because an appreciated exchange rate is maintained and because greater production lags accumulate. Thus the stabilization policy acts in a procyclical way, worsening recessive problems in the national economy. Low productivity continues, productive lags and distortion in relative prices (internal vs external) continue, and thus the economy lacks the conditions to prevail in competition with imports, which would increase income and bring down pressure on the foreign-trade deficit, thus increasing the need for capital inflows to finance this deficit. This forces the government to maintain its contractionary monetary and fiscal policies in order to lower these pressures, as well as to lend confidence and attract capital into the country. So the drop in inflation does not lead to lower interest rates, or flexibility in fiscal and credit policies, that would favour economic growth. Tracy Mott tells us that 'the capitalist economy is condemned to cyclical movements around a level of activity below full employment, if countercyclical policies are not employed' (Mott, 2002, p. 164). The problem is that, in a context of free capital movements and uncertainty, the governments of developing countries are unable to make economic policies more flexible, since, given their theoretical framework, this would encourage speculative practices that would destabilize the financial markets.

The context of economic liberalization and exchange-rate appreciation makes it difficult for developing countries to achieve macroeconomic conditions for growth, that is, fiscal deficits and/or a surplus in the foreign trade balance. Only in this manner would the private sector be able to improve its financial situation (Kalecki, 1969) to cover the service of its debt and increase investment, thus breaking out of the rut of credit restrictions and economic stagnation.

THE UNSUSTAINABILITY OF EXCHANGE-RATE STABILITY AND ECONOMIC LIBERALIZATION

Given that stability of the exchange rate and low inflation rests on capital inflows, it ends up being unsustainable, as productive firms face increasing financial problems. Also pressures mount on the balance of payments, for reasons both of the deficit in foreign trade, and of the financial obligations that come with capital inflows themselves. We have stated that firms' low income generates high levels of debt, problems of insolvency and restrictions on credit, investment and employment. In addition, the economy lacks security of capital inflows to finance the external deficit and exchange-rate stability, meaning that problems of stagnation and pressure on the exchange rate are latent.

Capital inflows have been stimulated by privatization and they increase foreign participation in the economy. The problem is that profitable assets subject to sale run out sooner rather than later. This means that exchange-rate stability becomes fragile, and even more so in a context of uncertainty when the economy ceases to offer conditions of profitability and debt repayment. In this context, when agents' expectations change, capital flows out, leading to exchange-rate instability, and financial and economic crises. Laski points out, 'When debt grows in relation to the GDP, debtor confidence in the local currency is increasingly eroded. When these expectations prevail, capital flight begins and can lead to a panic' (Laski, 2001).

Uncertainty regarding the future – heightened because the domestic economy is not growing despite the recovery of the US economy in 2003, and because of pressure on the foreign sector and domestic public finances, along with the difficulty that the Mexican government is having in Congress to open the electrical and energy sectors to foreign investment – ends up lowering external demand for local currency and lowering capital inflows, which negatively affects the exchange rate, capital markets and the economy, making it clear that this modality of financial liberalization is unsustainable.

REFERENCES

Casseti, M. (2002), 'Conflict, inflation, distribution and terms of trade in the Kaleckian model', in Mark Setterfield (ed.), *The Economics of Demand-Led Growth. Challenging the Supply-Side Vision of the Long Run*, Cheltenham, UK and Northampton, MA, USA: Edward Elgar, pp. 189–211.

Fazzari, S.M. and A.M. Variato (1994), 'Asymmetric information and Keynesian theories of investment', *Journal of Post Keynesian Economics*, **16** (3) (Spring).

Felix, D. (1997–8), 'On drawing general policy lessons from recent Latin American currency crises', *Journal of Post Keynesian Economics*, **20** (2) (Winter).

Kalecki, M. (1969), *Theory of Economic Dynamics*, New York: A.M. Kelley.

Kalecki, M. (1943 [1990]), 'Political aspects of full employment', in J. Osiatynski (ed.), *Collected Works of M. Kalecki*, vol. I, Oxford: Clarendon Press, pp. 347–56.

King, J.E. (1999), 'Introduction', *Review of Political Economy*, **11** (3).

Laski, K. (2001), 'External constraints on sustainable growth in transition countries', WIIW research papers no. 281, edited by Kazimierz Laski, October.

Lavoie, M. (2002), 'The Kaleckian growth model with target pricing and conflict inflation', in Mark Setterfield (ed.), *The Economics of Demand-Led Growth. Challenging the Supply-Side Vision of the Long Run*, Cheltenham, UK and Northampton, MA, USA: Edward Elgar, pp. 172–88.

Minsky, H. (1985), 'The financial instability hypothesis: a restatement', in P. Arestis and T. Skouras (eds), *Post Keynesian Economic Theory*, Brighton: Wheatsheaf.

Moore, B. (1989), 'A model of bank intermediation', *Journal Post Keynesian Economics*, **12** (1) (Fall).

Mosler, W. (1997), 'Exchange rate policy and full employment' accessed at www.mosler.org/docs/docs/exchange_rate_policy_and_full_em.htm.

Mott, T. (2002), 'Longer-run aspects of Kaleckian macroeconomics' in Mark Setterfield (ed.), *The Economics of Demand-Led Growth: Challenging the Supply-Side Vision of the Long Run*, Cheltenham, UK and Northampton, MA, USA: Edward Elgar, pp. 153–71.

Ndikumana, L. (1999), 'Debt service, financing constraints, and fixed investment: evidence from panel data', *Journal of Post Keynesian Economics*, **21** (3) (Spring).

Sawyer, M. (1982), 'Towards a PostKaleckian Macroeconomics', in *Thames Papers in Political Economy*, London: North East London Polytechnic.

Sawyer, M. (1999), 'The Kaleckian analysis and the new millennium', *Review of Political Economy*, **11** (3).

Sherman, H.J. (1991), *The Business Cycle: Growth and Crisis Under Capitalism*, Princeton, NJ: Princeton University Press.

Steindl, J. (1990a), 'Distribution and growth', in Josef Steindl, Economic Papers 1941–88, London: Macmillan, pp. 149–65.

Steindl, J. (1990b), 'From Stagnation in the 30s to Slow Growth in the 70s', in Josef Steindl, *Economic Papers 1941–88*, London: Macmillan, pp. 166–79.

Steindl, J. (1990c), 'Saving and Debt', in Josef Steindl, *Economic Papers 1941–88*, London: Macmillan, pp. 208–15.

Wolfson, M.H. (1986), 'A Business-Cycle Model of Financial Crises', in *Financial Crises: Understanding the Postwar US Experience*, Armonk, NY and London: M.E. Sharpe.

Wolfson, M.H. (1996a), 'A Post Keynesian theory of credit rationing', *Journal of Post Keynesian Economics*, **18** (3) (Spring), 443–70.

Wolfson, M.H. (1996b), 'Irving Fisher's debt–deflation theory: its relevance to current conditions', *Cambridge Journal of Economics*, **20** (3) (May).

Wray, R. (1992), 'Commercial banks, the central bank, and endogenous money', *Journal of Post Keynesian Economics*, **14** (3) (Spring), 297–310.

11. Foundering after floating? Exchange rate management and the Mexican stock market, 1995–2001

Jesús Muñoz and P. Nicholas Snowden

INTRODUCTION

Domestic financial deficiencies have received increasing attention in diagnoses of the emerging market currency crises of the 1990s. Pegged exchange rates, together with moral hazard in the banking sector, are thought to have promoted both unhedged inflows and unsustainable indebtedness for bank borrowers. Broad consensus on the importance of these linkages has helped to promote a parallel accord on the need to replace pegged with floating exchange rates and to ensure strict prudential regulation of domestic banks. An implication of this reform agenda is that the comparative reliance of entities on bank debt finance will need to be reduced. Although force of circumstance renders this inescapable when banks become disinclined to lend in the aftermath of exchange rate re-alignments, longer-term considerations lead to a similar conclusion.

With flexible exchange rates thought to be essential in the presence of international financial flows, reliance on floating interest rate lending exposes heavily geared enterprises to sudden variations in debt service burdens when international financial conditions change. A shift from such borrowing towards equity (or fixed interest bond) finance would therefore be desirable, not least for the increased freedom conferred on the monetary authorities to operate policy according to inflation or exchange rate stabilization needs. The purpose of the present study, therefore, is to examine the disappointing contribution of equity finance in the recovery from the first of the sequence of emerging market financial crises experienced in the 1990s: that of Mexico after the collapse of the peso peg in December 1994.

The following section provides information on Mexican stock market developments (the Bolsa Mexicana de Valores, hereafter BMV) before reviewing its marginal contribution to the financial needs of a growing economy. While institutional deficiencies undoubtedly provide some of the explanation for this outcome, the focus below will be on mechanisms of potentially wider relevance.

In the third section an examination of market price behaviour is conducted in order to explore systematic influences acting on the demand for equities. Attention is drawn to the relationship between equity returns and fluctuations in the value of the peso, especially in the subperiod following 1997. An interpretation of this behaviour is offered in the fourth section and evidence consistent with it is then provided both at an aggregate and an enterprise level.

Finally, policy implications of the main findings of the study will be discussed; these may be stated briefly as follows. Equity stakes in indebted firms which are likely to be of limited appeal to domestic investors under a regime of managed floating and institutional weaknesses, to which attention has been drawn in the Mexican case, must be addressed in the context of this fundamental difficulty. Essentially, while firms in emerging economies need access to equity markets in order to reduce their gearing, investors are more likely to emerge when gearing has already been reduced.

THE BMV AND EQUITY FINANCING AFTER 1994

Summary indicators of the evolution of the BMV after the 'Tequila Crisis' are provided in Table 11.1. The performance of the market appears not to have reflected the comparatively robust performance of the economy. Although the BMV had been one of the more dynamic of the emerging stock markets since 1989, with the market capitalization to GDP ratio reaching a peak of 49.7 per cent in 1993, the table confirms that it failed to gain ground subsequently. Despite increasingly buoyant conditions in world equity markets, the rather steady decline in the number of listed firms and modest overall price to book

Table 11.1   BMV indicators, 1994–2001

Year	Market cap./GDP (%)	Number of listed firms	Price/book value ratio (%)
1994	45.17	206	—
1995	38.04	185	1.85
1996	33.21	193	1.76
1997	39.77	198	2.32
1998	23.59	195	1.61
1999	31.79	190	2.41
2000	21.90	177	1.98
2001	19.86	172	1.39

Source: Banco de México (2002); BMV (2002).

value ratios indicate a marginal role for the market in the post-crisis years. A similar impression is gained from firm-level data. While 24 public offers were made on the BMV in 1994, a review of the records suggests there were only 35 between 1995 and 2000 (one in 1995, 11 each in 1996 and 1997, three in 1998, five in 1999 and four in 2000).[1] (BMV, 2001).

Although capitalization languished in relation to GDP, realized returns when measured in $US were generally positive in the years following 1995. This discrepancy, reflecting the recovery of the (real) peso exchange rate, is confirmed in the $-adjusted returns for the market as a whole. Calculating annual dollar returns from the logarithmic trend for the monthly indices after prior division by the peso/$ exchange rate, the implied mean value for the IBMV (market index)[2] firms was 11 per cent from May 1995 to August 2001. The comparable value for the Standard and Poors 500 index was 17.5 per cent, whereas the volatility of the latter (measured by the *monthly* standard deviation of returns) was considerably lower (4.8 per cent against 10.5 per cent).

Underlying this overall performance, the subindices of the IBMV reveal large disparities in the fortunes of shares in the different industrial sectors. Table 11.2 displays the proportion of overall market capitalization represented by each sector just before the Tequila Crisis (the average for the month of December 1994) and during December 2000 (near the world equity market peak). An intermediate observation at the end of 1998 is also supplied, together with the average annual dollar returns (and monthly standard deviation) by sector; in this case computed over the interval May 1995–August 2001 for comparability with overall IBMV performance noted above.

The manufacturing sector appears to have been a clear beneficiary of the immediate post-crisis period of peso weakness, although these gains were

Table 11.2   Sector composition of the BMV

Date	Manuf.	Const.	Other	Retail	Services	Trans. & Comm.
Dec. 94	18.0	13	12.0	11.5	20.6	21.9
Dec. 98	27.2	9.2	9.5	15.9	10.7	24.3
Dec. 00	18.4	6.7	5.7	14.7	16.9	35.8
Mean annual $ returns (monthly volatility) 95/5–01/8	1.6 (7.9)	0 (11.8)	−4.9 (11.7)	12.2 (11.2)	10.0 (14.4)	22.0 (11.4)

Source: BMV (2002) and own calculations.

subsequently reversed as the currency began to strengthen again in real terms. A central bank index recorded a value of 120 for the real exchange rate in 1995 (1990 = 100) against 111 countries with real appreciation (lower values) in the subsequent years. Reaching 88.2 in 1998, the index fell to 65.6 by 2000 (Banco de Mexico, 2002). Construction, although incorporating cement producers with a significant international presence, is often regarded as reflecting the non-traded sector of the economy. While real appreciation and economic recovery (average annual real GDP growth was around 5.5 per cent over 1996–2000 inclusive) might have been favourable for the sector, the decline in its comparative valuation was unbroken in the second half of the decade. The sector labelled 'other' experienced a parallel decline, although the constituent firms defy categorization into tradable and non-tradable activities. They are typically holding companies and conglomerate enterprises that are characterized by comparatively high levels of indebtedness, as were several firms in the construction sector.

The retail sector is heavily influenced by a single company (Walmex), a subsidiary of Wal-Mart. In 1997, the US firm acquired a majority holding in its Mexican former joint venture partner and the rise in comparative importance of the sector by 1998 is substantially attributable to its subsidiary. Walmex was the second-largest company by capitalization and accounted for almost 11 per cent of the IBMV index in 2001.

The services sector is dominated by the main banks that were substantially undermined by the peso collapse in 1995. The recovery indicated after 1998 coincides with the increasing interest of foreign banks in moving into the sector. While the Spanish group Bilbao-Vizcaya had acquired four Mexican institutions in 1995 and 1996, Hong Kong and Shanghai, Santander and Citigroup all entered the market during 1997. Further external purchases took place in 1999 and 2000, resulting in some recapitalization. Finally, Telmex, the telecommunications firm, which accounted for around 18 per cent of the index in 2001, dominates the transport and communications sector. Like Walmex, it has a high 'profile' for international investors.

The relatively unfavourable performance of the BMV in the later 1990s may help to explain why there is little evidence that firms substituted equity finance for debt during these years. A summary indicator of developments in gearing (debt/equity) ratios is provided below in the form of a simple average for those 23 constituent (non-bank) firms of the BMV index for which continuous values for the years 1996 to 2000 were available from the publication *Expansión* (Table 11.3).

The impression that gearing ratios have tended to deteriorate rather than to improve remains unchanged after reference to most of the individual cases. While a number of index firms display relatively stable ratios, only three suggest any coincidence between initial or primary public share offers on the exchange

Table 11.3   Mean debt–equity % ratios, 1997–2000 (23 IBMV firms)

1997	1998	1999	2000
80.9	92.7	90.6	130.2

Source: *Expansión* (2000).

and a reduction in their gearing between 1997 and 2000. It is of some interest that these three cases had comparatively modest initial ratios.[3]

Whether or not the lacklustre performance of the BMV has discouraged new issues, the comparatively long period since the peso crisis permits empirical investigation of the reasons for the limited role of the stock exchange in the country's subsequent financial rehabilitation. See the following section.

EQUITY RETURNS AND THE EXCHANGE RATE: AN INITIAL EXAMINATION

Among the reform measures involving the BMV during the 1990s those that were intended to facilitate the participation of foreign investors appear to have enjoyed some success. By 1999, it was estimated that holdings by foreign investors accounted for around 43 per cent of market capitalisation (BMV, 2001). In this context, and with the establishment of a floating exchange rate regime, a natural starting point for an empirical enquiry into the performance of the exchange is an examination of the relationship between Mexican equity returns and an external yardstick. The basic relationship to be estimated is as follows:

$$R_i = \alpha + \beta t_1 R_{SP500} + \beta t_2 \Delta e_{Pesos/\$} + \varepsilon \qquad (11.1)$$

Denoting α, βt_1 and βt_2 as the parameters to be estimated, R_i is the monthly peso return on the relevant BMV index (calculated as the first difference of the natural logarithm of the index). The equivalent \$US return, denoted as R_{SP500}, is that on the Standard & Poors 500 index (calculated in the same manner). The second explanatory variable, Δe, is the percentage change in the peso/\$ exchange rate and ε is a random error.

If the Standard & Poors index (SP500) represented adequately a 'world' market portfolio, the equation would be compatible with those widely used to test the international version of the capital asset pricing model (CAPM) as applied, for example, by Solnik (1974). In the present case, it is chosen as the most relevant comparison since US investors and institutions dominate external interest in the Mexican market whereas Mexican investors are thought to be sensitive to equity returns in the USA. While uncertainty exists in the literature over the appropriate choice both of exchange rate and of 'world market' indices for estimating equations of this form, the US orientation adopted here appears consistent with the realities of the Mexican case.

Assuming, therefore, that the returns on the SP500 capture adequately the external influences acting on the Mexican market, presumably with a positive coefficient, the response of peso returns to exchange rate changes may, in principle, lie in either direction. Since these changes normally imply real movements, at least in the short term, it is likely that peso share prices will be related to changes in the parity. In the case of an exporting firm, an appreciation of the peso is likely to reduce export profitability with negative implications for the share price. Such firms have 'operational' (trading) exposure to a weakening of the dollar (strengthening of the peso) and the coefficient β_2 would be expected to be positive. In contrast, a domestically oriented Mexican enterprise with a substantial 'short' position in the dollar (for example, external debts) might experience a rise in its share price as the peso strengthened on the foreign exchanges. In this case, β_2 would be negative as a result of 'contractual' (balance-sheet) exposure.

In a study covering eight economies, and using methodology similar to that to be described below, Domínguez and Tesar (2001) find that the influence of exchange rate movements on equity returns is, in relation to expectations arising from the market efficiency hypothesis, surprisingly high. Their finding that in four of the eight countries (France, Japan, Netherlands and the UK) 60–70 per cent of firms exhibited positive exposure to the exchange rate is of particular interest in connection with the results to be reported here. While cases of positive and negative exposure were found about equally in a further three countries (Chile, Germany and Italy), the positive form characterizes the Mexican case. The authors define positive exposure to imply that an increase (fall) in the value of the home currency against foreign currencies results in a rise (fall) in firm share values. Firms would be exposed in these terms if the sensitivity of their returns were to exceed that implied by the relationship between movements in the exchange rate and in the overall market index in the firm's country of domicile.

A related study that focuses on the Mexican case attempted to construct a 'shadow exchange rate' index for the (pegged) peso in the period leading up to the crisis at the end of 1994. The approach adopted was to use an event study methodology to identify groupings of Mexican shares that exhibited abnormal (positive or negative) returns prior to the abandonment of the peg. Abnormal returns were then transformed into a shadow exchange rate index through division by a calculated exchange rate 'beta'. The latter was estimated for a selected 'portfolio' of shares from weekly data covering the initial year of the floating peso (Becker *et al.*, 2002). The 'difference' portfolio selected for calculation of the beta was 'long' in the shares of high net export firms and 'short' in those of low net export firms in the non-bank sectors. Albeit with one week's lag, this portfolio displayed significant negative exchange rate exposure with a weaker peso implying improved returns on the shares of firms with a high net export profile. Recalling its 'short' component, the result also suggests that returns on the shares of the more numerous non-bank firms with a low net export profile would tend to decline with a weaker peso. This is consistent with the results to be reported below.

The present investigation covers the extended period beginning with the resolution of the 'Tequila Crisis' in May 1995 until late August 2001. This interval, while it involved no further crises for Mexico, was marked by a sequence of currency collapses elsewhere: in Asia after July 1997, Russia in August 1998 and Brazil in early 1999. Recognizing the likely influence of these exogenous events, the estimation of equation (11.1) for the IBMV and subsector returns was examined for parameter variation over the chosen period. Visual inspection of the recursively estimated values for the coefficients suggested that such influences had possibly arisen, with the coefficient on the exchange rate tending to rise markedly in some sectors after mid-1997.

Recursive estimation of the Chow (forecast) test was applied to the individual indices and there was strong evidence of a structural break in April 1997 for both the services and the 'other' sectors. Manufacturing also provided weak evidence for a break at this time. The retail sector provided clear evidence of a slightly later break in July 1997 (possibly influenced by the Wal-Mart takeover referred to earlier), whereas the transport and communication sector highlighted July 1998 as the most likely date for an interruption of the estimated relationship.

Table 11.4 below therefore reports the estimation of equation (11.1), twice for each sector, to cover the periods before and after the identified breaks. While the recursive forecast test did not indicate a structural break for the IBMV, or for the construction and manufacturing sectors, the significant results for the alternative Chow breakpoint test (CB) in these two subsectors suggest that a disturbance arose at that time. The levels of significance for an F test of the breaks identified by the recursive Chow forecast test (CF) are indicated in the same manner as for the individual coefficients (adjacent to the sector name). In all cases, the second subperiod results incorporate the month in which the break occurred.

The contrast between the two subperiods in the results is striking from two perspectives. Although the number of observations is especially limited for the period before May 1997, the relationship estimated was very weak for that interval. The SP500 nevertheless exerted a noticeable influence on retail and transport and communication, two sectors where a single, internationally known, firm dominates the index (Walmex and Telmex, respectively). Exchange rate

Table 11.4 External sensitivity of returns before and after identified breaks (1995:5–2001:8)

Sector	Date of break	Before break				After break			
		β_1	β_2	Adj. R²	D.W.	β_1	β_2	Adj. R²	D.W.
IBMV	97/5	0.602 (1.47)	−0.341 (−1.15)	0.06	2.31	1.2 (6.9)***	−1.12 (−3.05)***	0.59	2.01
Construction	97/5, CB*	0.31 (0.51)	−0.574 (−1.31)	0.00	2.13	0.936 (4.71)***	−1.88 (−4.45)***	0.53	1.92
Manufacturing	97/5, CB**	0.497 (1.67)*	−0.31 (−1.45)	0.11	2.2	0.67 (5.11)***	−0.87 (−3.16)***	0.48	2.11
Other	97/5, CF***	0.482 (1.33)	−0.472 (1.8)*	0.11	2.36	1.11 (5.61)***	−1.85 (−4.4)***	0.59	2.24
Retail	97/8, CF**	0.788 (2.26)**	−0.856 (−3.09)***	0.35	2.6	0.884 (4.08)***	−1.6 (−3.58)***	0.45	2.31
Services (Banks)	97/5, CF ***	−0.00104 (−0.00)	−1.15 (3.81)***	0.35	1.65	1.25 (5.17)***	−2.7 (−5.25)***	0.59	1.83
Transport and Communication	98/8, CF**	1.37 (4.37)***	−0.422 (−1.37)	0.34	2.24	1.53 (5.58)***	0.0958 (0.16)	0.48	2.04

Notes: *, ** and *** indicate significance at 10%, 5% and 1% respectively. Figures in parentheses are 't' ratios; N = 24 and 52 for May 1997 break; CB and CF indicate Chow forecast and breakpoint tests; the (insignificant) constant terms are not reported to conserve space.

influences were also noticeable in the 'other' and retail sectors, with the greatest sensitivity indicated in the bank-related services sector. The results for the period after mid-1997, however, suggest a much more pronounced influence of external factors with all sectors reacting strongly to the SP500. It is the substantial increase in exchange rate sensitivity, however, that is most marked with four sectors (construction, other, retail and services) confirming that a given percentage appreciation of the peso is associated with a more than proportional increase in equity returns. Once again, the large coefficient for the services sector suggests that bank shares became especially sensitive to exchange rate movements.

Referring to the second sub-period in Table 11.4, application of the recursive Chow test procedure to these estimates revealed two further significant breaks at the sector level: construction in October 1998 and in services in April 1999. Figure 11.1 relates these dates to *levels* of the exchange rate (expressed here in terms of $/Peso) and the Cetes/US Treasury Bill interest differential over the period since mid 1995.

The rather general break identified earlier in May 1997 is shown in the figure to have arisen as the short-term interest differential between Mexico and the USA had reached its minimum value following the aftermath of the 1994 devaluation crisis. The two later breaks in the equity returns/exchange rate relationship identified in construction (October 1998) and services (April 1999) capture the duration of a substantial 'spike' in the interest differential and renewed peso weakness in the subperiod following the Russian bond default in August 1998.

To assess the extent to which the observed increase in exchange rate sensitivity after mid-1997 may have been attributable to these disturbances, Table 11.5

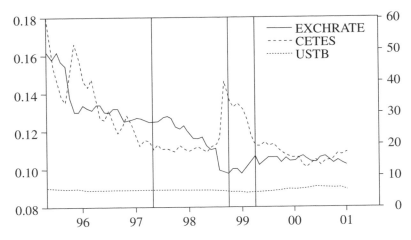

Figure 11.1   Interest differentials and the exchange rate

Table 11.5 External sensitivity of equity returns before and after the Russian crisis (1997:05–2001:08)

Sector	Date of break	Before break				After break			
		β_1	β_2	Adj. R^2	D.W.	β_1	β_2	Adj. R^2	D.W.
IBMV	99/4	1.27 (3.96)***	-1.46 (-2.59)**	0.69	1.93	1.13 (5.19)***	-0.16 (-0.28)	0.48	1.93
Construction	98/10, CB**	1.26 (4.36)***	-2.28 (-4.16)***	0.88	2.1	0.692 (2.68)***	-0.938 (-1.44)	0.19	1.84
Manufacturing	99/4	0.914 (3.78)***	-0.863 (-2.03)**	0.64	1.89	0.422 (2.64)***	-0.523 (-1.24)	0.2	2.17
Other	99/4	1.319 (3.39)***	-2.07 (3.02)***	0.68	2.33	0.87 (3.63)***	-1.13 (-1.78)	0.35	2.03
Retail	99/4	0.666 (1.48)	-1.87 (-2.43)**	0.45	2.24	1.004 (3.87)***	-1.4 (-2.05)*	0.4	2.49
Services (Banks)	99/4, CB***	0.959 (2.62)**	-4.01 (-6.22)***	0.81	2.16	1.31 (4.21)***	-0.47 (-0.58)	0.37	1.45

Notes: N = 23 and 29, except Construction, where N = 17 and 35. Transport and communication omitted owing to absence of exchange rate influence reported in Table 11.4.

217

repeats the procedure adopted earlier. With the exception of the construction sector the break point of April 1999 is chosen (identified initially in the services sector) to capture the return of calmer financial conditions as suggested by Figure 11.1. The two further subperiods are therefore 1997:05–1999:03 and 1999:04–2001:08. For construction, the two subperiods are defined as 1997:05–1998:09 and 1998:10–2001:08.

In general, the two years from May 1997 appear to have been characterized by an exceptionally high degree of sensitivity of Mexican shares both to the US market and to variations in the peso/$ exchange rate. This conclusion is highlighted by the loss of significance of the latter variable in the comparative international calm of the final subperiod, even with respect to the bank-dominated service sector that was increasingly under the management of foreign institutions.

Brief consideration of the results by sector serves to emphasize the extent to which Mexican equity returns and exchange rate fluctuations were linked over the two years. The results suggest that a 1 per cent depreciation of the peso would have been associated with a negative equity return of between 2 and 2.3 per cent in the domestically oriented construction and retail sectors for the month involved. Although the more internationally exposed manufacturing sector shows lower (roughly proportional) sensitivity, the implication remains that peso weakness undermines the sector's returns. The comparative exchange rate sensitivity of returns in the services (bank-dominated) sector became especially clear during the May 1997–May 1999 period with a 1 per cent depreciation of the peso apparently associated with a 4 per cent negative return for the month.

Although exceptional, the exchange rate sensitivity of bank shares also underlines the overall conclusion that peso weakness undermines equity returns, even in the sector that might be thought likely to benefit from a weaker currency: internationally exposed manufacturing. Whereas considerations of operational exposure would have predicted the opposite outcome, the dominance of balance sheet (or contractual) exposure involving a net 'short' position in foreign exchange (for example, through indebtedness) would be compatible with the negative relationships evident here. Before reporting evidence that levels of indebtedness were, indeed, relevant to equity price behaviour, however, the following section offers a more general theoretical perspective on the relationship between equity returns and exchange rate movements. The purpose is to provide a framework in which considerations of debt at the level of the firm may be related to the damping of exchange rate movements under a managed floating regime.

EXCHANGE RATE MOVEMENTS AND EQUITY RETURNS ON THE BMV: A PORTFOLIO BALANCE PERSPECTIVE

The elevated exchange rate exposure, relative to the overall BMV index, of certain Mexican equity returns between mid-1997 and mid-1999 is not readily reconciled with the international CAPM. Nor is the latter's underlying assumption that investors have homogenous expectations about asset returns clearly descriptive of the international integration process of an emerging stock market. Information imperfections, and differences in the array of investment opportunities considered, might be thought more typical with the state of external investor interest having substantial implications for the portfolio choices confronting local investors. In these circumstances the view that the exchange rate and equity returns are likely to be *jointly* determined gains plausibility and the following analysis will adopt this perspective.

The model is an adaptation of the traditional macroeconomic portfolio balance approach to exchange rate determination associated especially with Branson (1976) and Branson *et al.* (1977). For application to the Mexican case, it is assumed that resident investors hold a portfolio of three assets: peso money balances (M), the part of the (fixed) stock of Mexican shares (S) that is not held by foreign investors (with 'holdings' H) and foreign currency (F). It is assumed for simplicity that foreign investors only buy and sell Mexican shares in exchange for foreign currency (they do not hold pesos). The portfolio equilibrium of resident investors may therefore be described in the following system of three equations, a definition and a constraint:

$$M = m(\bar{y}, \bar{r}^*)W, \tag{11.2}$$

$$P(\bar{S} - H) = h(\overset{+}{y}, \bar{r}^*)W, \tag{11.3}$$

$$eF = f(\bar{y}, \overset{+}{r}^*)W, \tag{11.4}$$

$$W = M + P(\bar{S} - H) + eF, \tag{11.5}$$

$$m + k + f = 1. \tag{11.6}$$

The first three equations provide for the equilibrium holding by domestic investors of (peso) money, shares (S) net of foreign holdings (H) at the current market price and foreign exchange accounts measured in pesos (eF). The fourth expression defines the financial wealth of Mexican resident investors in pesos at current market prices. The final expression confirms that all wealth must be held in some combination of the three forms, while the share price (P) is defined as the inverse of the yield (y) on a share paying a dividend of one peso: $P = 1/y$.

The partial derivative signs indicate that the three assets are held in the portfolio as gross substitutes. Money is assumed to receive no (or fixed) interest, suggesting that its position in the portfolio will be influenced negatively by an improvement in the equity yield or in the return on foreign currency (r*). While the demand to hold shares is also influenced negatively by the return on foreign currency, an improved dividend yield has a positive effect on equity demand. Symmetrically, the demand to hold foreign currency is weakened by an improvement in equity yields but strengthened by a rise in its own rate of return. While further detail on the model is provided in the Appendix, its present relevance relates to the exchange rate sensitivity of equity returns observed in the Mexican context.

The requirement that increased holdings of Mexican equities by international investors must translate into an equivalent increase in foreign assets in the portfolios of residents permits the impact on equity returns and the exchange rate to be determined. Assuming a wealth-neutral exchange, the following expression linking the percentage changes in share prices and the exchange rate may be derived from the slope of the monetary equilibrium schedule specified in the Appendix:

$$
\overset{0}{P} = \left[\frac{eF}{\dfrac{m_y}{m} \dfrac{W}{P} - P(S - H)} \right] \overset{0}{e}.
\tag{11.7}
$$

With m_y representing the marginal impact of a change in equity yields on the desired proportion of money deposits in the portfolio, the elasticity 'coefficient' linking equity returns and exchange rate fluctuations in equation (11.7) is unambiguously negative: share prices fall when the peso weakens. Moreover, the absolute size of this term tends to increase when the (initial) proportion of foreign assets to domestic shares held in the portfolios of residents rises. That is, increased 'internationalization' of resident portfolios may be associated (at least until full market integration is achieved) with enhanced apparent sensitivity of equity returns to exchange rate movements. Intuitively, a given absolute change in foreign holdings will have a greater proportional impact on the quantity of shares that must be absorbed into domestic portfolios while relatively small exchange rate adjustments could help substantially to rebalance a comparatively large foreign asset component of the portfolio in peso terms.

Although the extensive data requirements for testing portfolio models constitute a widely recognized weakness, this interpretation has some consistency with the increased vulnerability of Mexican equities to fluctuations in international sentiment as the 'weight' of foreign investors on the exchange has grown.

BMV estimates suggest that international holdings represented about 35.5 per cent of capitalization in 1998. In 1999, they rose to 43.4 per cent and, after dipping slightly in 2000 (41.3 per cent), had approximately the same value in 2001 (BMV, 2001).

One further implication of equation (11.7) is that an increase in exchange rate sensitivity of equity returns could arise through a decrease in the relative attraction of equities to domestic investors (captured by a fall in the value of the equity yield-sensitivity of money holdings, m_y, in the formula). While domestic and foreign investors will tend to share bullish or bearish sentiment about equities as information becomes available, a further application of the portfolio framework highlights a macroeconomic connection between the two groups that appears to have been important in the Mexican case.

With the adoption of a floating peso, monetary policy has been conducted with varying degrees of reference to the exchange rate, especially when policy makers expect a high degree of uncertainty in the foreign exchange market. During periods of solid demand for the peso, an associated policy goal is for the Bank of Mexico to enhance purchases of dollars, via options and the contingent dollars sales scheme, in order to foster the accumulation of reserves and to reduce exchange rate volatility. In general, the objective of reducing both inflation and the probability of depreciation has been attained at the expense of increasing interest rate variability. Monetary policy was particularly influenced by exchange rate considerations in the months of 1998 leading up to the Russian default and the authorities have increasingly acknowledged the objective of smoothing exchange rate movements (Carstens and Werner, 1999).

The importance of this monetary policy orientation for the share price–exchange rate relationship is depicted in Figure 11.2. The shifted (dashed) S and F schedules represent the effect of a fall in shareholdings by foreign investors (H) and the resulting need for them to be absorbed by residents. A monetary policy reaction seeking to mitigate the exchange rate consequences of the shift would entail a backward movement of the M schedule, with consequences indicated by the thinner arrows. The smaller peso depreciation is 'bought' at the expense of a larger equity price correction.

Whereas attention has already been drawn to the internationalization of holdings on the BMV, the following section presents two varieties of evidence that are consistent with the perspective presented here. The role of (anticipations of) monetary policy changes in influencing overall equity valuations will be considered before examining the enterprise characteristics to which investors appear to have been particularly sensitive during the international turbulence of the later 1990s.

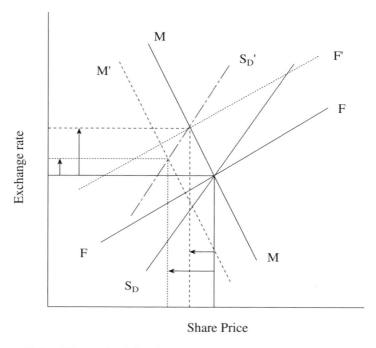

Figure 11.2   Effects of a fall in holdings by foreign investors

MONETARY POLICY, EQUITY VALUATION AND FIRM INDEBTEDNESS

A central implication of the portfolio model was that a monetary policy stance designed to stabilize the exchange rate would be likely to lead to greater variation in equity prices than otherwise. To develop an empirical test of this relationship, it will be assumed that the proposed connection would come to be anticipated by market participants. A weakening of the peso would signal a tightening response on the part of the monetary authorities whereas a strengthening of the currency, *ceteris paribus*, would suggest a subsequent easing of monetary policy. A new variable defined as the change in the monthly interest differential favouring Cetes (Mexican Treasury Bills) over US Treasury Bills is therefore added to the basic estimating equation (11.1) with a one-month *lead*. If exchange rate changes imply the suggested response of interest rate policy, two empirical consequences would be expected. The estimated coefficient for the new variable would be negative since an anticipated easing/tightening of monetary policy would have positive/negative consequences for equity prices.

Moreover, because current exchange rate changes help to produce these anticipations, the exchange rate coefficient in the original relationship would be expected to decline with the introduction of the new variable. The 28-day Cetes rate is chosen as the most representative interest rate in Mexico and the nearest comparable rate for three-month US bills. With $(r - r^*)$ referring to the monthly differential favouring Cetes, the relationship estimated is therefore

$$R_{\text{Sector}} = \alpha + \beta_1 R_{\text{SP500}} + \beta_2 \Delta e_{\text{Pesos/\$}} + \beta_3 \Delta (r - r^*)_{t+1} + \gamma. \qquad (11.8)$$

The estimated coefficients for this relationship are reported in Table 11.6. The period chosen, with the exception of the retail and transport and communication sectors, is from May 1997. Corresponding to the initial evidence presented in Table 11.4, the starting date for the retail sector has been set at August 1997 and that for transport and communications at August 1998. The results in Table 11.6, therefore, may be compared directly with those in the second half of Table 11.4.

Table 11.6   *Monetary policy responses to exchange rate changes: anticipation in equity returns (1997:05 to 2001:07) (equation (11.8))*

Sector	β_1	β_2	β_3	Adj. R^2	D.W.
IBMV	1.01	−0.353	−0.151	0.66	1.92
N = 51	(5.66)***	(−0.86)	(−3.12)***		
Construction	0.715	−1.102	−0.156	0.58	1.96
N = 51	(3.43)***	(−2.25)**	(−2.76)***		
Manufacturing	0.663	−0.623	−0.038	0.52	2.2
N = 51	(4.76)***	(1.91)*	(−1.01)		
Other	1.01	−1.18	−0.122	0.62	2.25
N = 51	(4.81)***	(−2.41)**	(−2.15)**		
Retail	0.793	−1.32	−0.057	0.44	2.33
N = 48	(3.17)***	(−2.32)**	(−0.85)		
Services	0.967	−1.94	−0.166	0.63	1.82
N = 51	(3.76)***	(3.22)***	(−2.38)**		
Transport and	1.106	1.55	−0.263	0.63	1.8
Communication	(4.17)***	(2.51)***	(−3.84)***		
N = 36					

Note: *t*-ratios are in parentheses.

When these results are compared with the findings reported in Table 11.4, the predicted effects of the new variable (captured in β_3) receive some support. With the exception of manufacturing and retail, a negative and significant coefficient is observed on the lead interest differential term. Moreover, its inclusion depresses the magnitude of the exchange rate coefficient in all cases. For the IBMV as a whole, the exchange rate influence is no longer significant, and only weakly so for manufacturing. The effects on the magnitude of the exchange rate coefficient in construction, 'other' and services are especially noteworthy. Construction has a strong domestic orientation and high exposure through interest rate fluctuations to the tightening of monetary policy.

Although diminished substantially by inclusion of the new variable, the continuation of high exchange rate sensitivity in services and transport and communications is of interest. Even when subsequent adjustments to monetary policy have been allowed for, it appears that the bank-dominated services sector has remained particularly exposed to exchange rate developments with a 10 per cent strengthening of the peso being associated, *ceteris paribus*, with a 19 per cent improvement in the equity price. Turning to the Telmex-dominated transport sector, inclusion of the new variable confirms that the sector has a strong underlying *positive* exposure to the $US with a weaker peso helping its share price. This result appears to be consistent with the substantial dollar linkage of the telephone company's revenues and its strong balance sheet position.

An immediate objection to the procedure adopted in Table 11.6 is that, if the current period exchange rate movement 'predicts' the subsequent change in interest differentials, the two explanatory variables must be collinear. While this is, indeed, the implication of the hypothesis being tested, it may be noted from the statistical viewpoint that the lead interest differential term is only moderately correlated with the exchange rate variable (adjusted $R^2 \not\subset 0.37$). Additional indicators appear, therefore, to have been relevant in forming market anticipations of interest rate policy. If multicollinearity does not pose a serious difficulty in the interpretation of the results in Table 11.6, the continuing evidence of serial correlation in the reported Durbin-Watson statistics suggested re-estimation with the inclusion of an autoregressive error term (not shown). In no case did the first-order process alter appreciably the values of the estimated coefficients. Experimentation with alternative interest rate 'leads' confirmed that only the one-month case had a significant effect.

The suggestion that exchange rate fluctuations exerted part of their influence on share price movements through the information they provided on likely changes in interest rate policy implies that firms with high exposure to interest rate fluctuations would be likely to exhibit comparatively high exposure to the exchange rate. To examine this inference, monthly data on the share prices of 38 firms were obtained from both *Datastream* and BMV sources with the criterion for selection of the firms being that they comprised the high 'marketability' list of the BMV between October 2001 and March 2002.

Firm-specific exchange rate 'betas' were first computed, using the form of equation (i) for both the full period covered by Table 4 and for the 'turbulent' period identified in the first half of Table 11.5. The 38 computed values then constituted the dependent variable in the following intra-firm regression equation. For ease of interpretation, the sign of the estimated betas was reversed prior to estimation (so that a positive value for the dependent variable implies that share prices rise as the peso strengthens against the dollar):

$$\beta_2 = \alpha + \gamma_1 X/S + \gamma_2 D/E + \gamma_3 D_{\text{Construction}} + \gamma_4 D_{\text{Retail}} + \gamma_5 P/BV + \varepsilon. \quad (11.9)$$

The first two explanatory variables seek to capture operational and contractual exposure, respectively. The exports to total sales ratio (X/S) would be expected to exert a negative effect on the (recalibrated) dependent variable since peso appreciation would tend to undermine export profitability. A high debt–equity ratio (D/E), by contrast, would be expected to generate a positive sign with an appreciating currency acting to improve the position of the firm in two ways: foreign currency debt service would become less onerous while the tendency for lower interest rates to follow a strengthening currency would also ease outflows associated with peso-denominated obligations. As a final firm-specific influence, the price to book value ratio (P/BV) was added. Other things equal, a high price to book value ratio suggests the prospect of earnings growth over time. It is hypothesized that exchange rate sensitivity for such firms may be less than if present earnings are the dominant consideration. The two sector dummies remained after variable deletion tests in which manufacturing was the excluded sector and suggest that firm returns in both the construction and retail sectors exhibited 'excess' sensitivity.

Firm values for the variable *X/S* are derived from data for the full year of 2001, while *D/E* is the ratio at the end of September 2001, and *P/BV* is measured at the end of August 2001. The three ratios are obtained from Banamex (2002) and *Expansión* (2000). The estimated coefficients of equation (11.9) in both the full and high sensitivity subperiods are listed in Table 11.7.

The estimated coefficients in Table 11.7 have the predicted signs. The negative value for γ_1 suggests that peso depreciation improves the trade competitiveness of internationally exposed firms, while the positive value for γ_2 implies that a strengthening peso is valuable for heavily indebted firms. The negative coefficient γ_5 on the P/BV term suggests that, when the share price discounts comparatively high *future* returns, contemporary exchange rate movements are of diminished importance. This variable, however, is only weakly significant over the full period. The primary result is that balance sheet exposure (D/E) becomes the most important determinant of exchange rate sensitivity in the

Table 11.7   Determinants of exchange rate betas, $\beta_2 s$ (equation (11.9))

	Full period		Turbulent period	
	Parameter	t-test	Parameter	t-test
α	1.128	3.727***	1.45	2.604***
γ_1	−0.968	−2.122**	−0.712	−0.849
γ_2	0.155	2.741***	0.590	5.658***
γ_3	0.506	1.656	1.420	2.527***
γ_4	0.510	1.639	1.156	2.02**
γ_5	−0.168	−1.439	−0.276	−1.285
R^2	0.365	—	0.561	—

Notes: Number of observations = 38, *** and ** indicates significance at 2 and 5 per cent; *X/S*, *D/E* and *P/BV* were entered in terms of percentage values.

turbulent period, while the exports to sales ratio as an indicator of operational exposure is significant only in the full period. The turbulent period (May 1997–March 1999) therefore appears to have reflected enhanced investor concern with corporate financial structures and their interaction with the exchange rate. The sector-specific effects for the domestically oriented construction and retail sectors (γ_3 and γ_4, respectively) achieve significance in the later subperiod, suggesting heightened exchange rate sensitivity in their returns as monetary policy targeted the exchange rate.

CONCLUSIONS

The analysis has drawn attention to the high degree of exchange rate sensitivity in equity returns for certain subsectors of the Mexican stock exchange, especially during a period characterized by international financial strain. While this period was, presumably, atypical it helped to identify apparently key factors involved in the exchange rate exposure of equity investments. In addition to the gradual internationalization of the market, attention was drawn to two interrelated influences. When monetary policy attempts, in part, to stabilize the movements of a floating exchange rate, the impact on share prices of fluctuating international investor interest tends to be amplified. The natural explanation, for which evidence was found, is that the high interest rates needed to 'defend' the peso also act to damage the prospects of heavily indebted firms. Moreover, the relevant debt indicator is not only the foreign component: floating interest rate domestic debt is a key factor in the process.

From the perspective of encouraging the growth of equity financing, especially as a means for reducing excessive leverage, this conclusion is troubling. For domestic investors whose wealth may be substantially oriented to domestic (real and financial) assets, the tendency for the pattern of equity returns to amplify fluctuations in the international value of the peso is unlikely to be an attractive feature. At least unless average returns on domestic securities are comparatively high, increased exposure to foreign assets would seem to be the natural diversification choice. The paradoxical implication would be that, whereas firms may wish to retire debt through the proceeds of new issues, domestic investors may only emerge after the debt exposure has been substantially reduced.

It is in this context that the emphasis often placed on the market reforms needed to attract foreign investors would seem to be especially important. Such investors would normally have a diversification interest in acquiring Mexican assets, provided that an acceptable market framework could be assured. While accumulating evidence suggests that foreign investors are hardly consistent in their appetite for emerging market equities, the support they may be able to supply for share prices could improve the prospects for a shift in the capital structure of domestic firms away from debt and towards equity.

NOTES

1. These figures do not include some issues of intermediate and small firms: three in 1996 and seven in 1997.
2. This is a capitalization-based index computed as follows:

$$I_t = I_{t-1} \left(\Sigma P_{it} Q_{it} / \Sigma P_{it-1} Q_{it-1} \right) F_{it}$$

Thus the index on day t, I_t adjusts (multiplies) its value on the previous day by (one plus) the growth in the capitalization of the constituent shares (where Q_{it} is the number of shares of issuer i on day t and F_{it} is an adjustment factor for rights issues). The IBMV is therefore weighted in the same manner as the US Standard & Poors 500 index used in the following comparison.
3. Embotelladoras Argos (mainly a Coca Cola franchise) made an initial public offer in 1998 with the gearing ratio declining from 52 to 45 per cent in 1999. Grupo Bimbo (baking) made a primary issue in 1999 with a decline in gearing to 50 per cent in that year. Corporacion Interamericana de Entretenimiento (a holding company covering entertainment and real estate) also made a primary issue in 1999, with the gearing ratio declining from 100 in 1998 to 86.19 per cent in 1999 according to the *Expansión* (2000) figures.

REFERENCES

Banco de México (2002), 'Indicadores Económicos y Financieros', Cuadernos de Información Económica, accessed at www.banxico.org.mx.

Banco Nacional de México (2002), 'La Semana Bursátil, Indicadores Bursátiles Nacionales', accessed at www.banamex.com.

Becker, R., G. Gelos and A. Richards (2002), 'Devaluation expectations and the stock market – the case of Mexico in 1994/95', *International Journal of Finance and Economics*, **7** (3) (August), 195–214.

BMV (2001), *Annual Report 2001*.

BMV (2002), 'Indicadores Bursátiles', accessed at www.bmv.com.mx.

Branson, W.H. (1976), 'Asset markets and relative prices in exchange rate determination', Institute for International Economic Studies seminar paper no. 66, Stockholm.

Branson, W.H., H. Halttunen and P. Mason (1977), 'Exchange rates in the short run: some further results', *European Economic Review*, **12**, 345–402.

Carstens, A. and A.M. Werner (1999), 'Mexico's monetary policy framework under a floating exchange rate regime', Banco de México research paper 9905, Banco de México.

DataStream (2002), Program DataStream: Equities (900b).

Domínguez, K.M.E. and L.L. Tesar (2001), 'A re-examination of exchange rate exposure', National Bureau of Economic Research working paper W8128, Washington, DC.

Expansión (2000), 'Las 500 Empresas Más Grandes de México', (CD-ROM).

Solnik, B.H. (1974), 'The international pricing of risk: an empirical investigation of the world capital market structure', *The Journal of Finance*, **29** (4), 365–78.

APPENDIX: THE PORTFOLIO MODEL

Stock demand and supply equilibrium for each of the three assets is depicted in Figure 11.2, relating the exchange rate to the price of shares. The slopes of the (peso) money market (M), domestic shares (S-H) and foreign currency (F) schedules are as follows:

Peso Money Market

$$\frac{\partial e}{\partial P} = \frac{\left[\frac{W}{P^2}\bar{m}_y - m(\bar{S} - H)\right]}{mF} \langle 0.$$

This schedule is negatively sloped in view of the negative impact on money demand at the margin when equity yields rise.

Domestic Equity Market

$$\frac{\partial e}{\partial P} = \frac{\left[(1-k)(\bar{S} - H) + \frac{W}{P^2}\overset{+}{k}_y\right]}{kF} \rangle 0.$$

The positive slope in this case is guaranteed by the positive impact on the demand to hold shares of a rise in their yield.

Foreign Exchange Market

Finally, the slope of the foreign exchange market schedule is:

$$\frac{\partial e}{\partial P} = \frac{\left[f(\bar{S} - H) - \frac{W}{P^2}\overset{-}{f}_y\right]}{(1-f)F} \rangle 0.$$

As the proportions of the portfolio comprising the three assets, m, k and f must sum to unity, the slope of the equity equilibrium schedule must exceed that of the foreign exchange market. This reflects the gross substitutes assumption by which share demand responds more to the (own) equity yield than does the demand to hold foreign currency ($k_y > |f_y|$). Figure 11.2 depicts the effect on the equilibrium position of a given reduction in foreign holdings of domestic firms.

The reduction in foreign holdings of equities requires that the portfolios of domestic investors must absorb the extra shares at the expense of an equivalent (by value) reduction in foreign exchange balances. The leftward shift of the equity schedule depicted in the figure represents the reduction in share prices (higher yield) that will be required (at any given exchange rate) to reconcile domestic investors to this change. The schedule for foreign exchange must also shift to the left as its reduced availability would require a rise in the yield on equities (or an exchange rate depreciation) to re-establish domestic portfolio balance. Since the exchange of equities for foreign currency implies no wealth effect other than that arising from the change in share prices and the exchange rate, the (peso) money schedule will remain in the same position.

12. The evolution of financial systems: the development of the new member states of the European Union

Elisabeth Springler

INTRODUCTION

Since 1 May 2004 the European Union has ten new member states, a circumstance which has been heavily discussed even before the enlargement.[1] The macroeconomic as well as the structural and institutional situation of the accession countries had to be examined. The focus of attention in this chapter is on the eight transformation countries, which had to go through a substantial restructuring and developing process in the previous decade to be able to join the European Union. These eight transition countries (Estonia, Czech Republic, Hungary, Latvia, Lithuania, Slovenia, Poland and Slovakia) performed well in macroeconomic terms. In 2002, growth rates reached between 1.4 per cent in Poland and 6.1 per cent in Latvia after a decade of high volatility. At the same time inflation decreased remarkably, reaching between 7.5 per cent in Slovenia and 0.3 per cent in Lithuania in 2002, compared to 32.3 per cent in Slovenia respectively 410.2 per cent in Lithuania in 1993. Unemployment showed a slight increase in the last decade and in 2002 varied between 5.8 per cent in Hungary, which, exceptionally, saw a decrease in unemployment, from 11.9 per cent in 1993, and Poland, with 18.1 per cent, which represents an increase of 1.7 percentage points compared to 1993 (OeNB, 1/2003). These data show that differences in performance are observable despite the fact that the accession countries follow the same trend. Countries with a closer geographical and, in many cases, also historical relationship with Central Europe developed more quickly in the mid-1990s, whereas the Baltic states improved tremendously in the late 1990s. Also the countries which have developed more quickly still suffer from institutional and structural problems due to regional disparities. Taking one of the transformation countries with the highest development in GDP growth and institutional settings, Hungary, one can see that large disparities in GDP per head exist. According to the Community Support Framework for Hungary, the country accounted for 54.8 per cent of GDP per head of EU25 in 2000.

Measured on a regional level, central Hungary, with the capital, Budapest, accounted for 83.8 per cent of EU25 GDP per head in 2000, whereas the figure for the poorest region, the Northern Great Plain, stood at only 34.7 per cent, and for Northern Hungary at 35.4 per cent.

Apart from these general trends in economic development numerous studies (among others, Arestis *et al.*, 2001; Gibson and Tsakalotos, 2003) have shown the importance of the financial sector for economic development of an economy have come to the conclusion that, for less developed countries, the establishment of credit-based finance–industry relationships, which lead to bank-based national financial systems, has a stronger positive impact on economic development and growth than market-based financial systems have. The right institutional setting seems therefore to be one of the most important factors for economic development. Given these facts, this chapter analyses the financial systems of eight transition countries out of the ten new member states of the European Union. Three questions, considered below, emerge out of the analysis:

Can Banking Evolution be Observed in the New Member States?

First the stage of banking evolution has to be detected, since no financial system existed at the beginning of the transformation process. If no development had taken place the analysis of the right financial system for economic development in underdeveloped countries was redundant. In the case where an evolution of the banking system is observable, the following question has to be asked.

Which Financial System do the New Member States Follow?

As mentioned above, the research hypothesis of this chapter is that a bank-based system promotes better economic development for emerging countries than a market-based financial system would do. Furthermore, trends for the future development of financial systems have to be discussed. As comparative studies (see, among others, Amable, 2004) point out, trends in European financial systems – especially in the member states of the European Union – for a transformation towards a market-based financial system can be detected. The third question therefore follows.

Is a Trend towards a Market-based Financial System Observable in Transformation Countries?

The causal argumentation for this research question– as a follow-up from the hypothesis of the second question – would be that a convergence towards a market-based financial system leads to negative effects on future growth and economic development of the new member states.

The chapter proceeds as follows: first the Post Keynesian aspects of banking evolution and national financial systems are analysed, which means that the first two questions mentioned above are going to be discussed simultaneously. Thus, the chapter provides a theoretical overview of the Post Keynesian background and investigates in the following the stage of banking evolution and financial systems on an empirical basis for the new member states. The classification into a bank or market-based financial system first follows a purely quantitative data set of the World Bank. This quantitative approach is enriched by qualitative measures such as institutional features in banking regulation and incorporated in the third question, which will be at the centre of argumentation in the second section of this chapter.

The chapter contributes critically to the ongoing debate as to which financial system might promote economic growth and development better than another and discusses the facts from a heterodox point of view.

BANKING EVOLUTION AND FINANCIAL SYSTEMS IN THE NEW MEMBER STATES

Post Keynesian theory provides several causal mechanisms related to the question of the development of financial systems, which contribute to the research question of this chapter. To analyse national financial systems in transition countries, and the future trends, two fields of Post Keynesian analysis are of special interest. First the five-stage setting of banking evolution introduced by Chick (1992) and Chick and Dow (1988) allows us to classify transition economies into certain development stages. Although the various stages of banking evolution cannot be sharply distinguished, as Chick (1992) points out, this framework enables us to consider banks according to different number, size and function. Throughout the stages a reduction in the number of banks (especially in stages one and two) can be observed, whereas the size of the remaining banks continuously increases. Additionally, the functions of banks develop. Banks work, as Chick (1992) calls it, as '*direct-lending*' institutions in the first stage of banking development, which includes savings preceding any investments. As the evolution process emerges the savings precedence diminishes and the theory of endogenous money starts working for the banking sector in stage four. Before reaching this stage banks are subject to exogenous money and the money multiplier is the main feature of money creation with banks' restraint of reserves. Apart from this, also interbank mechanisms develop, as well as the function of the Central Bank as lender of last resort within stage three. In the highest stage, banks are characterized by – as Chick calls it (1992, p. 198) – 'the absence of passivity regarding any part of the banks' balance sheet'. Therefore this stage of evolution can be interpreted as an enlargement of Moore's theory on horizontal money supply under the assumption of endogenous money (see, for example, Moore, 1988, 1989), where central banks play a passive role in fulfilling the demand of loans without opposing visible restrictions, such as credit rationing or credit constraint on firms. Rochon's (1999) approach of firm restrictions and active balance sheet activities of commercial banks contributes to the linkage between Post Keynesian monetary and banking theory. The gap between models of banking theory and monetary theory in Post Keynesian economics has already been criticized, in 1987, by Dymski. Rochon's (1999) approach can therefore be cited as an attempt to close this gap.

While research is undertaken in this area of monetary economics the aspect of banking in relation to financial systems with respect to economic development does not seem to have developed recently, although this linkage is highly relevant in a globalized world. Therefore the second important theoretical feature of Post Keynesian theory for the research question of this chapter is the analysis of the contribution of financial systems to economic growth. The question that has been asked in this respect in numerous studies is whether one national financial system promotes economic growth better and more sustainably than another. The overall conclusion that can be made (although one or the other author might support a different opinion) is that neither bank-based nor credit-based, nor market-based financial systems contribute better to economic growth (see, among others, Demirgüc-Kunt and Levine, 1999; Levine, 2000; Levine and Zervos, 1998). Post-Keynesian theory nevertheless provides clear causalities, which lead to the conclusion that developing countries should prefer bank-based financial systems. Dymski (2003, p. 2) points out clearly that market-driven or market-based financial structures are not able to enhance growth and reduce inequality, especially in less developed countries, from an heterodox point of view, since increasing competition between financial institutions will not lead, as argued by neoclassical economists, to the setting up of financial institutions which aim to serve all economic classes. In this respect the question of which financial system is to be set up in developing countries is strongly interrelated with effects of financial liberalization.

These effects have been discussed by, among others, Dymski (2003), who has shown that the market-supporting strategies claimed by financial market liberalization theorists do harm economic development in less developed countries. Similarly, Gibson and Tsakalotos (2003, p. 140) conclude in their survey of trends in financial systems that 'financial markets come up with their own particular dynamics, which can drive the behaviour of institutions (banks) and make for less desirable outcomes than a situation where markets do not have such a large role to play'. Their argumentation is based on an analysis of aims in the European Union to foster market elements of national financial systems in the member states of the European Union by introducing the Financial Service Actions Plan. The argumentation of Gibson and Tsakalotos is different to that of Dymski. They do not analyse the McKinnon and Shaw model of financial deepening as a starting point but discuss directly the information problems linked to financial markets, and conclude that, using the approach of Stiglitz, banks can overcome the direct problems of asymmetric information more easily by screening the potential creditor. Although other features of asymmetric information might be relevant for the banking sector, as Mishkin (1996) discusses when looking at the second-stage problems of asymmetric information of the banking system that occur between commercial banks and central banks, they might have not only a growth-reducing effect but also a destabilizing one for the financial system itself. It seems nevertheless that the setting up of a bank-based financial system has a better impact on economic development in less developed countries.

The empirical evidence of banking evolution and the question of which financial system emerged in the new member states will be discussed simultaneously, thanks to the strong interrelations of these questions, as mentioned above.

Question 1 Can Banking Evolution be Observed in the New Member States?

Since financial systems simply did not exist before the transformation process started in the late 1980s, banking transformation as well as banking consolidation proved to be of great importance for the setting up of a national financial system and for leading these countries out of 'financial repression', as McKinnon (1973) and Shaw (1973) would have called it. In the case of transformation countries, their term, 'fragmented economy', where the state intervenes heavily with the result of qualitative and quantitative distortions, might apply. Qualitative and quantitative distortions account for credit misallocations due to state interventions. This means that a system of administrative distributed loans leads to a promotion of debtors with investment projects of low returns and a general lower level of distributed loans due to administrative costs. The conclusion of McKinnon and Shaw that financial liberalization is the best way to promote stability and development in these countries is misleading. All transformation countries have suffered from banking instabilities, as Table 12.1 shows, followed by banking crises in the light of financial liberalization and economic transformation.

Apart from the differences in the costs arising from banking crises all systemic crises in the new member states followed the same progression. After new banks opened business in the early 1990s, several of them had to be shut down, were merged or had their licences revoked (see Table 12.1) owing to an increasing amount of non-performing loans, which were a leftover from administrative credit allocation mechanisms. This can also be seen as a result of the generous licencing of new private banks in the course of the transformation process in

Table 12.1 Banking crises and consolidation

Country	Date of crises	Reason	Measures to offset crises	Losses or costs
Czech Rep.	1991–?	38% of non-performing loans (1994–5)	Banks closing	1994: 12% of GDP to bank support
Estonia	1992–1995	Insolvent banks: 41% of financial system assets	Banks mergers and licences revoked	1993: 1.4% of GDP
Hungary	1991–1995	1993: insolvent banks: 25% of financial system assets		10% of GDP
Latvia	1995–present		1994–9: 35 bank licences revoked	1995: 7% of GDP 1998: 3% of GDP
Lithuania	1995–1996		1995: 12 banking liquidations	
Poland	1990s	1991: 7 banks' solvency problems (90% of credit)		1993: 2% of GDP
Slovakia	1991–present	1997: 31% of loans unrecoverable		
Slovenia	1992–1994		3 banks were restructured	Recapitalization: $1.3 billion

Source: Caprio (2003, pp. 2, 3).

236

the early 1990s as Klein (2003, p. 16) states. As can be seen in Table 12.1, 1995 was a year in which banking consolidations in many transitions countries took place. Therefore Table 12.2 compares the number of nationally-owned commercial banks operating in the transition countries in 1995 and 2000. It becomes evident that, on the one hand, the number of nationally-owned commercial banks decreased significantly in all transition countries and that, on the other hand, the ratio of state dependence in all countries except for Slovenia and the Czech Republic also decreased.

Table 12.2   Number of commercial banks, 1995 and 2000

Country	No. (1995)	State ratio (1995)	No. (2000)	State ratio (2000)
Czech Rep.	32	17.6	14	28.2
Estonia	14	9.5	3	0.0
Hungary	22	49.0	9	7.7
Latvia	31	9.9	9	2.9
Lithuania	15	61.8	7	38.9
Poland	63	71.7	27	23.9
Slovakia	15	61.2	10	49.1
Slovenia	33	41.7	22	42.2

Source: Klein (2002, p. 301, annex 11); own calculations.

Comparing these stylized facts of the accession countries with the five-stage setting of Post Keynesian theory, which posits that the number of banks should first increase as the evolution process starts and decrease again in the following since small private banks are going to be consolidated in stage two of the process, it becomes evident that the accession countries have at least reached stage two of the banking evolution process. Interbank activities enable the discussion of even further development in banking. As described by the banking evolution setting, a rise in interbank activities would account for stage three and four. Therefore interbank claims of residential commercial banks on a national and international level are investigated. Figure 12.1a shows the results of interbank claims in percentage changes of millions of national currency from 1998 to 2003 for Hungary and the Baltic States. These countries are selected as representative of the two different cohorts of economic development mentioned above to secure the results of banking evolution against differences in economic development in the different cohorts. Hungary shows much more stable data on interbank activities than the Baltic States do. Therefore the trend-line for Hungary is less steep than the trend-lines of the other states of the sample. Looking at the total

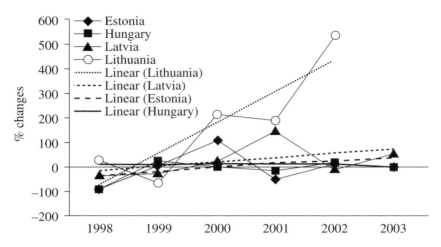

Online-Data sources: Statistical research of Estonia Central Bank, Hungary Central Bank, Latvia
Central Bank, Lithuania Central Bank.

*Figure 12.1   Interbank activities: development of claims of national
            commercial banks*

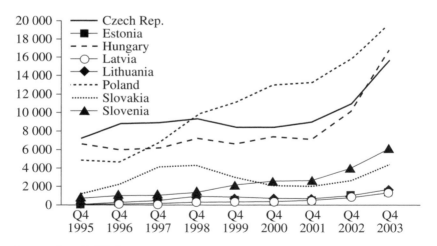

Source: Dymski (2004)

*Figure 12.2   Interbank activities: international claims and deposits: external
            loans of reporting Banks vis-à-vis individual countries
            (millions US dollars)*

amount of interbank claims, Hungary shows the highest level of activity. Despite these differences in the total amount of interbank claims, all countries show a rising trend-line, which leads to the conclusion that interbank activities were increasing. Negative changes of national interbank claims might be observed due to bank mergers that have taken place. Therefore the trend-line is more important for the argument than the results for an individual year.

Figure 12.1 gives an overview of the degree of international banking integration of the accession countries and shows a similar picture as Figure 12.2. Also on an international level interbank activities were increasing. This leads to the conclusion that the banking evolution process has reached stage three to four. Since all transition countries, except for the Czech Republic, are considered to have an underdeveloped financial structure, when measuring the level of loans provided to the private non-financial sector and the degree of market capitalization of the stock exchange, it is concluded in this chapter that stage five of banking evolution has not yet been reached.

Table 12.3 and Annex 1 show the results of measuring development of financial structures of the 'old' and 'new' member states of the European Union. Whenever the results for a country are less than the mean of the ratio of loans provided to the private non-financial sector to GDP, and less than the mean of market capitalization of the stock exchange, it is regarded as underdeveloped. The method used to conduct this measure was taken from Demirgüç-Kunt and Levine (1999). As it is obvious that the results might depend on the level of development of the countries in the sample, Table 12.3 shows the results for all European Countries ('whole sample') for which data were available, EU25 ('new' and 'old' member states), EU south ('old' southern European member states and the accession countries), EU central ('old' central European member states and the accession countries), EU north ('old' northern European member states and the accession countries) and Eastern Europe (accession countries).

Using different samples can partly but not fully avoid the problem of sample dependence, since the specific country ratio is still conducted by removing the mean of the whole country sample. Therefore the country-specific averages presented in Annex 1 still incorporate samples dependence. Nevertheless, Table 12.3 analyses the relation in terms of development of the new member states vis-à-vis the existing member states. All accession countries, except for the Czech Republic, are regarded as underdeveloped in all samples which include some 'old' member states of the European Union. Apart from the fact that the results of Table 12.3 and the underlying data presented in Annex 1 show that stage five of banking evolution is not reached, the necessity of investigating the financial system that emerged throughout the banking evolution process becomes evident, since the sample for Eastern Europe shows us that Hungary, Poland and the Slovak Republic are regarded as developed within this sample

Table 12.3　Development of financial structure

	Whole sample	EU25	EU south	EU central	EU north	Eastern Europe
Czech Rep.	D	d	d	d	d	d
Hungary	U	u	u	u	u	**d**
Latvia	U	u	u	u	u	u
Lithuania	U	u	u	u	u	u
Poland	U	u	u	u	u	**d**
Slovak Rep.	U	u	u	u	u	**d**
Slovenia	U	u	u	u	u	u

Source:　For data, see Annex 1.

thanks to their amount of market capitalization. Since a high level of market capitalization is an indicator of a potential market-based financial system, the investigation of the national financial system becomes even more important.

Question 2　Which National Financial System do the New Member States Follow?

The financing method alone does not give a proper answer to the question of which financial system might be in use, as numerous studies (see, among others, Mayer, 1988) on financial structure have shown. Financial flows measured by quantitative methods accompanied by qualitative factors, which show the relationship between money debtor and lender and the importance of the financial institution, seem to provide a better tool for the classification of financial systems. This chapter will follow that dual approach and rely on the work of Demirgüç-Kunt and Levine (1999) in method and data for the quantitative classification and on methods of banking regulation to present the institutional setting of the financial system on a qualitative basis.

Quantitative approach
The quantitative approach introduced by researchers of the World Bank offers a broad data set covering all 25 member states of the European Union, except Estonia. The classification into bank-based or market-based financial systems is undertaken according to three ratios: 'bank v. capitalization', 'bank credit v. trading' and 'trading v. overhead costs'. With this approach not only financial flows (represented by 'banks v. capitalization') but also the efficiency (represented by 'trading v. overhead costs') and the development (measured by 'bank credit v. trading') of the two financial intermediaries (banks and stock exchange)

are covered in the analysis. This chapter follows the method of Demirgüc-Kunt and Levine and uses the data set of the World Bank (Demirgüc-Kunt and Levine, 1999b) to classify the new member states of the European Union, which have all been missing from the work of Demirgüc-Kunt and Levine (1999a). Each country's specific ratios are calculated from the individual time series (in this case 1993–2002) after removing the mean of the country sample. In the following, a *structure index* is composed as the sum of the individual ratios. If the value of the structure index is above the mean of the sample, the country is regarded as market-based. A problem that immediately arises when using the structure index is the sample dependence of the outcome. Data for the analysis in Annexes 2(1) and 2(2) show that adding a single country to the sample – in this case Norway – leads to changes in country classifications. Austria, for example, is classified as market-based in Annex 2(1) although numerous other studies (see, among others, Allen and Gale, 2001) as well as data in Annex 2 show that the country can be regarded as bank-based. Therefore the financial systems of the transitions countries in this chapter are analysed by using different country samples. To show the relationship of these new member states towards the existing ones the structure index is composed for EU25 (no data for Malta and Estonia), EU south (including Cyprus, Greece, Italy, Spain) and the transition countries, EU central (including Austria, Belgium, France, Germany, Ireland, Luxembourg, Netherlands, United Kingdom) and the transition countries, EU north (including Denmark, Finland, Sweden) and the transition countries as well as for the transition countries alone. Table 12.4 presents the outcomes of the various samples and shows whether the transition countries can be regarded as market (m) or bank (b) based according to this quantitative approach.

The results for Czech Republic, Hungary, Latvia, Lithuania and Poland are the same in all samples used including some or all member states of EU15 and

Table 12.4 Structure index of the new member states

	EU25	EU south	EU central	EU north	EE
Czech Rep.	B	b	b	b	M
Hungary	B	b	b	b	B
Latvia	B	b	b	b	M
Lithuania	B	b	b	b	B
Poland	B	b	b	b	B
Slovak Rep.	b	m	b	m	M
Slovenia	b	m	b	b	M

Source: For data, see Annex 2.

classify them as bank-based. For Slovakia and Slovenia, the results differ according to the sample used. When using bigger country samples like EU25 or EU central also these countries can be regarded as bank-based, whereas smaller samples can make them appear as market-based. It has to be noted that in the case of EU south and EU north country members of EU15 are in the sample which show strong bank-based data when comparing EU25 as can be seen in Annex 2(2). This might lead to a sample bias and to the result that Slovakia and Slovenia, which are definitely less bank-based than other transition countries, are regarded as market-based.

Concluding from the quantitative data, the following ranking in country groups from more bank-based to less bank-based can be set up, where purely market-based financial systems seem to be unlikely:

Hungary, Lithuania, Poland	⟶	very strong bank-based financial systems
Czech Republic, Latvia	⟶	strong bank-based financial systems
Slovakia, Slovenia	⟶	weak bank-based financial systems

Qualitative approach

As mentioned above, a purely quantitative approach is insufficient in determining financial systems, but qualitative factors have to be added which show the institutional setting and are responsible for the relationship between creditor and debtor. The problem that arises is how to grasp this relationship and how to find comparable factors between countries. To solve this problem, this chapter will rely on methods of banking supervision. As Eller (1999) points out, different systems of banking supervision can be defined. Strong direct influences on the financial intermediary and protective measures which implement a significant role of the state can be distinguished from indirect measures, which do not imply strong institutional influences but are based on preventive measures like legal frameworks. Deposit insurance systems are defined as protective measures in banking supervision and are regarded as a symbol for strong institutions which are necessary for bank-based financial systems and their close relationship between creditors and debtors. Table 12.5 gives an overview of the various methods of deposit insurance in the new member states. Two elements become obvious at first sight. First, except for Slovenia all new member states have an explicit deposit insurance system, which is compulsory. Second, all these systems were established in the middle of the 90s after banking crises occurred. This is in line with the observations made in the first part of this chapter, where it was noted that banking evolution and institutional development started in the middle of the 90s.

Furthermore it is observable that the Baltic States introduced their deposit insurance systems later than overall transition countries with a closer geographic connection to Central Europe. Differences in the implementation of the deposit

Table 12.5 *Deposit insurance systems*

Countries	type explicit = 1 implicit = 0	Date enacted/revised	Administration official = 1 joint = 2 private = 3	Membership compulsory = 1 voluntary = 0	Permanent fund funded = 1 unfunded = 0	Source of funding 0 = Private funding 1 = Joint funding 2 = Public funding
Czech Republic	1	1994	1	1	1	1
Estonia	1	1998	2	1	1	1
Hungary	1	1993	2	1	1	1
Latvia	1	1998	1	1	1	1
Lithuania	1	1996	1	1	1	1
Poland	1	1995	1	1	1	1
Slovakia	1	1996	2	1	1	1
Slovenia	0	—	—	—	—	—

Source: Demirgüc-Kunt and Sobaci (2000).

insurance system can be detected in the covered amount and the roles of the state in administration and funding. The strongest possible interference of the state would occur in the case of an official administration joined with a public source of funding. Since all countries have chosen an official or joint administration with joint funding, the role of the state in banking supervision cannot be neglected. These results confirm the conclusions drawn from quantitative analysis. Only Slovenia, which also from the quantitative data has proved to be less bank based, does not have an explicit deposit insurance system.

The conclusion that can be drawn so far is that the banking systems in transition countries have undergone a remarkable evolution after the banking crises in the mid-1990s and have improved their institutional setting. All countries can be regarded as bank-based, which would suggest further economic development in the future according to the assumptions made. Only Slovenia showed a weaker appearance in qualitative and quantitative terms and might not be fully in line with the other economies in terms of institutional settings. This leads us to the third question of the chapter, since changes in the European financial system, which might have a negative effect on development in the new member states, are suggested.

Question 3   Convergence towards a Market based Financial System?

In addition to the current stage of banking development and national financial system, also the question of future trends of national financial systems especially in the European Union is worth discussing. Several studies (Gibson and Tsakalotos, 2003; Amable, 2004; Ernst, 2004) have shown that national financial systems in the European Union tend to converge to a more market-based financial system. Three main factors are promoting these changes. Gibson and Tsakalotos (2003) see the driving force in the establishment of the Financial Services Action Plan, which aims to promote a single wholesale market and additionally open and secure retail markets, as well as the setting up of state-of-the-art prudential rules for supervision. The authors claim that especially the reinforcement of a single wholesale market will introduce strong market-based incentives into bank-based structures. Additionally the introduction of the Basel II agreements as well as changes in corporate governance structures are mentioned as further factors that might foster the element of change. Amable (2004) as well as Ernst (2004) conclude in their econometric analyses that corporate governance structures are a significant factor of change in national financial systems. Unfortunately, no specific elements are analysed within the rather broad system of corporate governance structures and Basel II elements in their research. Before analysing tendencies for convergence towards a market-based financial system in the transition countries the causalities between Basel II and corporate governance have to be clarified first.

The Basel II framework consists of three pillars (BIS, 2001). The main pillar aims to provide an adequate minimum capital ratio to reduce the risk of default. Additionally, guidelines for improved standards of prudential supervision, which should enhance the transparency of the market, are given. Market disclosure as the third pillar aims to increase information about individual banks and companies as well as bank groups. Out of the measures undertaken in the second pillar (prudential supervision) similar causal relations to the ones presented when analysing the methods of banking regulation in the qualitative approach of classifying financial systems can be presented. It can be investigated whether the introduction of Basel II guidelines led to a shift in banking supervision from protective to preventive measures. If a shift is observable one can conclude that the Basel II framework will lead to a reduction in institutional importance in a specific financial system and therefore to a shift towards a market-based system.

The interrelations between corporate governance structures and financial systems' convergence focus as well on the role of institutions for banking regulation. In general, three different meanings of corporate governance can be distinguished in the economics literature. In the most narrow definition, corporate governance and its structure is investigated at the firm level and deals mainly with shareholder rights, as, among others, Zingales (1997) and Shleifer and Vishny (1996) discuss. A broader definition of corporate governance investigates the structure of ownership on a more aggregate level within a national financial system (see Allen and Gale, 2001; Prevezer and Ricketts, 1994). Corporate Governance Codes, which aim to increase reputation and confidence in the financial system via self-regulation mechanisms (Martinek, 2002) serve as a further definition of corporate governance structures. In this case financial stability will be achieved by market forces, whereas institutional regulations are diminished. Therefore it can be argued that the introduction of Corporate Governance Codes in connection with the aim to replace institutional regulation by self-regulation mechanisms promotes a shift from a bank-based financial system with strong institutions to a more market-based financial system.

EVIDENCE FOR TRANSFORMATION COUNTRIES

Most of the transitional countries introduced Laws of Banking Supervision in the mid or late 1990s, as Würz and Müller (1998) state, giving the examples of Poland in 1998, the Czech Republic in 1994, with changes in 1998, Hungary in 1997 and Slovenia in 1998/9. All new member states, except for Lithuania, for which no data were available, adopted minimum capital asset ratios which are in line with the Basel I agreements. Furthermore, measures of banking supervision do seem to support the national financial system, since strong direct

Table 12.6 *Banking supervision*

Country	Minimum capital–asset ratio	Actual risk-adjusted capital ratio	Risk-weight in line with Basel guidelines	Discipline – direct interventions
Czech Republic	8%	10.60%	Yes	Yes
Estonia	10%	16%	Yes	Yes
Hungary	8%	16.70%	Yes	Yes*
Latvia	10%	16%	Yes	Yes*
Lithuania	–	–	–	only provisions to cover actual losses
Poland	8%**	14.20%	Yes	Yes
Slovakia	8%	Yes	Yes	None
Slovenia	8%	14.50%	Yes	Yes

Note: * direct interventions have not been undertaken in the last 5 years; ** first year 15%, second year 12%.

Data source: Database Banking Supervision, World Bank.

Table 12.7   Corporate governance in the transition countries

Country	Compliance with OECD standards[1]	Introduction of corporate Governance Code[2]
Czech Republic	medium compliance	February 2001
Estonia	medium compliance	—
Hungary	high compliance	—
Latvia	high compliance	—
Lithuania	high compliance	2004
Poland	high compliance	June 2002
Slovak Republic	medium compliance	September 2002
Slovenia	medium compliance	March 2004

Notes:
[1] Chen (2004).
[2] Diverse country reports: Czech Securities Commission (2001); National Stock Exchange of Lithuania (2004); The Gdansk Institute for Market Economies (2002); Bratislava Stock Exchange (2002); Ljubljana Stock Exchange (2004).

or protective measures in addition to deposit insurances (see Table 12.6) can be detected. This evidence leads to the conclusion that, although Basel I agreements are already implemented in the transition countries and Basel II will also be implemented, no shifts in banking supervision towards less protective measures has occurred so far. Therefore a shift in financial systems seems to be unlikely according to the argumentation given above.

Similar to the introduction of the Basel agreements a high or medium level of compliance with the OECD Principles of Corporate Governance has also been reached. Table 12.7 shows the level of compliance and the date of introduction of national Corporate Governance Codes.

Five out of the eight transition countries have already set up national Corporate Governance Codes, which aim to implement compliance with OECD principles. All introduced Corporate Governance Codes count only for companies listed on the stock exchange. This is a major difference from the aims of the introduction of Corporate Governance Codes of EU15, which want to achieve higher transparency and self-regulation of the system by introducing these principles for all companies, not only the listed ones. Only when firms which finance their investment projects via the credit channel also participate in the new system will a self-regulation mechanism and market discipline be able to offset the power of institutions. Since this tendency is not observable in the transition countries and their major goal is to set up guidelines in coordination with international standards and to increase efficiency, the existence of Corporate Governance Codes cannot be quoted as a shift towards a self-regulation system. High compliance with international standards is even achieved without the existence of explicit Corporate Governance Codes, as the cases of Hungary and Lithuania show.

CONCLUSION

Although the transformation process started as early as the late 1980s, substantial changes and developments in banking evolution have only been observable following the banking crises of the mid-1990s. Together with banking evolution the setting up of national financial systems took place. According to quantitative and qualitative factors of research, all eight transition countries have introduced a bank-based system, although Slovenia and the Slovak Republic are the most market-based out of the transition countries. This leads to the conclusion that financial systems in the new member states are ready to promote further economic development and therefore help these countries to catch up with EU15 in economic terms. When looking at future trends in financial systems, no signs of convergence towards a more market-based financial system are observable, although the transition countries introduced the factors conducive to a shift: elements of Basel II banking supervision and Corporate Governance Codes. The argumentation of implementation is different to that of EU15. Promotion of market regulation is not the final goal, but the necessary increase in transparency and efficiency achieved by implementing international financial standards. Financial deepening is currently taking place and, although institutional transformation processes are not under discussion at the moment, it has to be noted that also the new member states might tend towards more market-based systems once the national financial systems are regarded as developed. Evidence for this can already be found in the fact that those countries which have a higher degree of financial development when we compare the eight transition countries achieve that status thanks to high market capitalization and not to high levels of banking intermediation.

NOTE

1. I would especially like to thank Gary Dymski, Karl Petrick and Steve Pressman for their suggestions, ideas and contributions during the 8th Post-Keynesian Workshop and Conference, 2004.

REFERENCES

Amable, Bruno (2004), 'An overview of financial systems' diversity', in *The Transformation of the European Financial System. Where Do we go? Where should we go?*, Oesterreichische Nationalbank proceedings for OeNB workshop no. 1, pp. 23–53.

Anonymous, 'Community Support Framework 2004–2006, Republic of Hungary, Objective 1 of the Structural Funds', CCI No: 2003 HU 16 1 CC001, downloadable (http://www.nfh.hu/doc/nft/OP/CSF_final.pdf).

Arestis Philip, Panicos O. Demetriades and Kul B. Luintel (2001), 'Financial development and economic growth: the role of stock markets', *Journal of Money, Credit and Banking*, 33 (1), 16–41.

Bank for International Settlements (BIS) (2001), The New Basel Capital Accord: An Explanatory Note, Basel: BIS.

Bratislava Stock Exchange (2002), 'Corporate Governance Code', downloadable from the European Corporate Governance Institute (http://www.ecgi.org/codes/all_codes.htm); accessed July 2004.

Caprio, Gerard (2003), 'Episodes of systemic and borderline financial crises', Dataset World Bank.

Chen, Hsianmin (2004), 'Corporate governance sector assessment project, report on the 2003 assessment results', European Bank of Reconstruction and Development (EBRD).

Chick, Victoria and Sheila Dow (1988), 'Post-Keynesian perspective on the relation between Banking & Regional Development', Thames Poly., School of Social Sciences.

Chick, Victoria (1992), 'The evolution of the banking system and the Theory of Saving, Investment and Interest', in Philip Arestis and Sheila Dow (eds), *On Money, Method and Keynes*, New York: St Martin's Press, pp. 193–205.

Czech Securities Commission (2004), *Corporate Governance Code based on the OECD Principles*, Prague: Czech Securities Commission.

Demirgüc-Kunt, Asli and Ross Levine (1999a), 'Bank-based and market-based financial systems: cross country comparison', World Bank research policy working paper 2143.

Demirgüc-Kunt, Asli and Ross Levine (1999b), 'A new data base on financial development and structure, World Bank downloadable, accessed at www.worldbank.org/research/projects/finstructure/structure_database.xls.

Demirgüc-Kunt Asli and Tolga Sobaci (2000), 'Deposit insurance around the world: a database', World Bank, downloadable, accessed at www.worldbank.org/research/interest/confs/upcoming/deposit_insurance/dataset2.xls.

Dymski, Gary (2003), 'Banking in transformation: financing development, overcoming poverty', unpublished manuscript.

Dymski, Gary (2004), 'Credit rationing and financial exclusion in the age of globalization', presented at the 8th Post Keynesian Summer School, Center for Full Employment and Price Stability, University of Missouri – Kansas City.

Eller, Roland (1999), *Handbuch Bankenaufsicht und interne Steuerungsmöglichkeiten: Quantifizierung und Analyse von Risiken mit bankinternen Modellen, bankaufsichtliche Anforderungen*, Stuttgart: Schäffer-Poeschel.

Ernst, Ekkehard (2004), 'Financial systems, industrial relations, and industry specialization: an econometric analysis of market interaction', in *The Transformation of the European Financial System. Where Do we go? Where should we go?*, Oesterreichische Nationalbank proceedings for OeNB workshop no. 1, Vienna, pp. 60–95.

Gibson, Heather and Euclid Tsakalotos (2003), 'Finance–industry relationships in Europe and the prospects for growth and convergence', in P. Arestis, M. Baddeley and J. McCombie (eds), *Globalization, Regionalism and Economic Activity*, Cheltenham, UK and Northampton, MA, USA: Edward Elgar, pp. 127–50.

Klein, Dietmar K.R. (2002), *Die Bankensysteme in Mittel- und Osteuropa.*

Levine, Ross (2000), 'Bank based or market based financial systems: Which is better?', World Bank, working paper.

Levine, Ross and Sara Zervos (1998), 'Stock markets, banks and economic development', *American Economic Review*, **88** (3), 537–58.

Ljubljana Stock Exchange (2004), 'Corporate Governance Code', downloadable from the European Corporate Governance Institute (http://www.ecgi.org/codes/all_codes.htm), accessed 20 July 2004.

Martinek, Thomas (2002), 'Nur Freiheit schafft Vertrauen', *Trend-Manager*, no. 2.

Mayer, Colin (1988), 'New issues in corporate finance', *European Economic Review*, **32**, 1167–89.

McKinnon, Ronald (1973), *Money and Capital in Economic Development*, Washington, DC: Brookings Institution.

Mishkin, Frederic S. (1996), 'Understanding financial crises: a developing country perspective', NBER working paper, no. 5600.

Moore, Basil (1988), *Horizontalists and Verticalists: The macroeconomics of credit Money*, Cambridge, MA: Cambridge University Press.

Moore, Basil (1989), 'A simple model of bank intermediation', *Journal of Post Keynesian Economics*, **XII** (1), 10–28.

National Stock Exchange of Lithuania (2004), 'The Corporate Governance Code of the Companies listed on the Stock Exchange of Lithuania', downloadable from the European Corporate Governance Institute (http://www.ecgi.org/codes/all_codes.htm); accessed 30 July 2004.

Oesterreichische Nationalbank, 'Focus on transition', 1/2003.

Prevezer Martha and Martin Ricketts (1994), 'Corporate governance: the UK compared with Germany and Japan', in Nicholas Dimsdale and Martha Prevezer (eds), *Capital Markets and Corporate Governance*, New York: Oxford University Press, pp. 237–56.

Rochon, Louis-Philippe (1999), 'The creation and circulation of endogenous money: a circuit dynamique approach', *Journal of Economic Issues*, **33** (1), 1–22.

Shaw, Edward S. (1973), *Financial Deepening in Economic Development*, New York: Oxford University Press.

Shleifer Andrei and Robert Vishny (1996), 'A survey of corporate governance', NBER working paper, no. 5554.

The Gdansk Institute for Market Economies (2002), 'The Corporate Governance Code of Polish Listed Companies', downloadable from the European Corporate Governance Institute (http://www.ecgi.org/codes/all_codes.htm), accessed 2004.

Würz, Michael and Wolfgang Müller (1998), 'Prudential supervision in Central and Eastern Europe: a Status report on the Czech Republic, Hungary, Poland, and Slovenia', *OeNB Focus on Transition*, **2**, 80–95.

Zingales, Luigi (1997), 'Corporate governance', NBER working paper, no. 6309.

Online-Data Central Bank Statistical Research: last accessed 31 July, 2004

Estonia: http://www.bankofestonia.info/pub/en/dokumendid/statistika/pangandusstatistika/tabelid/.

Hungary: http://english.mnb.hu/engine.aspx?page=mnben_statisztikai_idosorok.
Latvia: http://www.bank.lv/eng/main/statistics/?PHPSESSID=5ec55689de8ca5c6d4443
  bfb91dca60b.
Lithuania: http://www.lbank.lt/eng/statistic/index.html.

APPENDIX

Annex 1   Developed and underdeveloped financial systems

Country	Private credit by deposit money banks to GDP	Stock market total value traded to GDP
Austria	0.96	0.06
Belgium	0.74	0.12
Bulgaria	0.09	0.41
Croatia	0.33	0.01
Cyprus	0.82	0.24
Czech Republic	0.64	0.09
Denmark	0.49	0.28
Finland	0.64	0.54
France	0.88	0.38
Germany	1.07	0.35
Greece	0.37	0.35
Hungary	0.26	0.12
Ireland	0.69	0.26
Italy	0.62	0.26
Latvia	0.13	0.02
Lithuania	0.12	0.02
Luxembourg	1.05	0.04
Netherlands	1.00	1.01
Norway	0.60	0.22
Poland	0.21	0.05
Portugal	0.84	0.20
Romania	0.08	0.01
Slovak Republic	0.30	0.05
Slovenia	0.27	0.03
Spain	0.82	0.72
Sweden	0.40	0.74
Switzerland	1.65	1.44
United Kingdom	1.16	0.81
Mean whole sample	0.62	0.31
Mean EU 25	0.63	0.29
Mean EU south (incl. Cyprus) and new member states	0.45	0.18
Mean EU central and new member states EE	0.63	0.23
Mean EU north and new member states EE	0.35	0.19
New member states/Eastern Europe	0.28	0.05

Annex 2   Structure indexes

Structure index EU25 and Norway (1)

Country	Bank v. capitalization	Trading v. overhead	Bank credit v. trading	Structure
Austria	4.22	−11.74	7.60	0.08
Belgium	−0.76	−8.64	0.58	−8.82
Cyprus	−0.98	−7.81	−1.27	−10.05
Czech Republic	0.62	−10.88	1.69	−8.56
Denmark	−1.47	−6.19	−2.79	−10.45
Finland	−2.22	12.65	−3.26	7.17
France	−1.30	−3.61	−2.62	−7.54
Germany	0.42	−3.04	−1.17	−3.79
Greece	−1.27	−3.74	−3.36	−8.37
Hungary	0.83	−11.31	−2.30	−12.78
Ireland	−1.30	35.39	−1.07	33.02
Italy	−0.88	−7.26	−2.05	−10.19
Latvia	1.65	−13.56	7.03	−4.88
Lithuania	−0.76	−13.54	2.14	−12.17
Luxembourg	−2.39	−10.50	10.66	−2.23
Netherlands	−1.84	63.60	−3.63	58.13
Norway	−0.61	−3.47	−1.68	−5.76
Poland	2.82	−12.58	−0.11	−9.87
Portugal	0.17	−5.19	−0.11	−5.13
Slovak Republic	7.94	−12.63	1.21	−3.48
Slovenia	2.51	−13.01	4.83	−5.66
Spain	−1.11	10.37	−3.30	5.96
Sweden	−2.30	21.36	−3.95	15.11
United Kingdom	−1.99	15.35	−3.07	10.28
			Mean	0.00

Structure index EU25 (2)

Country	Bank v. capitalization	Trading v. overhead	Bank credit v. trading	Structure
Austria	4.19	−11.89	7.52	−0.17
Belgium	−0.79	−8.79	0.51	−9.07
Cyprus	−1.00	−7.96	−1.34	−10.30
Czech Republic	0.59	−11.03	1.62	−8.81
Denmark	−1.49	−6.34	−2.87	−10.70
Finland	−2.25	12.50	−3.33	6.92
France	−1.33	−3.77	−2.69	−7.79
Germany	0.39	−3.19	−1.24	−4.04
Greece	−1.30	−3.89	−3.43	−8.62
Hungary	0.80	−11.46	−2.37	−13.03
Ireland	−1.33	35.24	−1.14	32.77
Italy	−0.90	−7.42	−2.12	−10.44
Latvia	1.62	−13.71	6.96	−5.13
Lithuania	−0.79	−13.70	2.06	−12.42
Luxembourg	−2.42	−10.65	10.59	−2.48
Netherlands	−1.86	63.44	−3.70	57.88
Poland	2.80	−12.74	−0.18	−10.12
Portugal	0.14	−5.34	−0.18	−5.39
Slovak Republic	7.91	−12.78	1.13	−3.73
Slovenia	2.48	−13.16	4.76	−5.91
Spain	−1.14	10.22	−3.37	5.71
Sweden	−2.33	21.21	−4.03	14.86
United Kingdom	−2.02	15.20	−3.15	10.03
			Mean	0.00

Structure index Central EU and EE (3)

Country	Banks v. capitalization	Bank credit v. trading	Trading v. overhead	Index
Austria	3.51	8.28	−10.92	0.87
Belgium	−1.47	−0.90	−7.83	−10.20
Czech Republic	−0.09	0.05	−10.06	−10.10
France	−2.02	−4.64	−2.80	−9.45
Germany	−0.29	−3.91	−2.22	−6.43
Hungary	0.12	−4.85	−10.50	−15.23
Ireland	−2.01	−4.26	36.21	29.93
Latvia	0.94	1.61	−12.74	−10.19
Lithuania	−1.48	0.85	−12.73	−13.35
Luxembourg	−3.10	20.32	−9.68	7.54
Netherlands	−2.55	−5.98	64.41	55.89
Poland	2.11	−2.33	−11.77	−11.98
Slovak Republic	7.23	−1.35	−11.59	−5.71
Slovenia	1.80	2.65	−12.37	−7.92
United Kingdom	−2.70	−5.54	14.57	6.32
			Mean	0.00

Structure index EU south EE (4)

Country	Banks v. capitalization	Bank credit v. trading	Trading v. overhead	Index
Cyprus	−1.94	−1.31	0.63	−2.62
Czech Republic	−0.34	2.23	−2.44	−0.55
Greece	−2.24	−3.73	4.70	−1.27
Hungary	−0.13	−2.67	−2.88	−5.68
Italy	−1.84	−2.44	1.17	−3.11
Latvia	0.69	3.79	−5.12	−0.64
Lithuania	−1.73	3.03	−5.11	−3.81
Poland	1.86	−0.15	−4.15	−2.43
Portugal	−0.79	−0.75	3.25	1.70
Slovak Republic	6.98	0.83	−3.97	3.84
Slovenia	1.55	4.83	−4.75	1.63
Spain	−2.07	−3.66	18.66	12.93
			Mean	0.00

Structure index EU north EE (5)

Country	Banks v. capitalization	Bank credit v. trading	Trading v. overhead	Index
Czech Republic	−0.34	2.13	−4.69	−2.89
Denmark	−2.43	−3.15	0.00	−5.58
Finland	−3.18	−3.71	18.84	11.95
Hungary	−0.13	−2.77	−5.12	−8.02
Latvia	0.69	3.70	−7.37	−2.98
Lithuania	−1.73	2.93	−7.35	−6.15
Poland	1.86	−0.24	−6.39	−4.78
Slovak Republic	6.98	0.74	−6.22	1.49
Slovenia	1.55	4.73	−6.99	−0.71
Sweden	−3.26	−4.35	25.30	17.68
			Mean	0.00

Structure index EE (6)

Country	Banks v. capitalization	Bank credit v. trading	Trading v. overhead	Index
Czech Republic	−1.61	0.53	1.62	0.54
Hungary	−1.40	−4.37	1.18	−4.59
Latvia	−0.58	2.10	−1.06	0.45
Lithuania	−2.99	1.33	−1.05	−2.72
Poland	0.59	−1.85	−0.09	−1.34
Slovak Republic	5.71	−0.86	0.09	4.93
Slovenia	0.28	3.13	−0.69	2.72
			Mean	0.00

Index

ADF test 128, 140
adjustment
  automatic 138
  of exchange rates 11–12, 19, 174, 178,
    187, 193, 220, 224
  to external imbalance 11–12
  of interest rates 153, 160
  of GNP 131, 133, 135
  lending 11–12, 14–15, 19
  of prices 12, 21, 123, 145
  of salaries 195, 198
  structural 171, 180, 184, 186
  symmetrical 20
agent
  heterogeneous 27, 29, 70, 72, 75
  and institutions 95–7
  limitations of computational abilities
    87, 88
  rational maximizing 134
  representative 26–9, 63
  and uncertainty 87–91
aggregate demand
  and anti-inflationary policy 195–201,
    205
  and credit expansion 161
  determinants of 135
  and economic crisis 174
  and full employment 111
  and GDP model 40–54, 56
  and growth 186
  and inflation 188, 193
  and interest rates 38–55
    fluctuations of 132
  and landlords 124
  and long-run equilibrium 134
  and monetary factors 138
  and restrictive monetary policy 174
  shocks of 132
Aglietta, M. and Orlean, A. 81
Akerlof, G., Dickens, W. and Perry, G. 81
allocation 181, 184, 189

Alzheimer's strikes 26
Amable, B. 232, 244
analysis
  dynamic 40, 44, 46–51, 56
  static 42, 44–7, 49–51, 53
Andolfatto, D. and Gomme, P. 70
anti-inflationary policy
  and exchange rate stabilization 193–4,
    200
  effects of 194–5, 197, 199–201
Arestis, P. 94, 232
Arestis, P. and Demetriades, P. 94, 188
Arestis, P. and Eichner, A. 144
Arestis, P. and Sawyer, M. 72
Arrow securities 26
Asian economies 15, 17, 19–21, 175,
  188
asset
  financial 17–18, 20
  inflation of prices, see inflation
Auctioneer, Divine 26
austerity 38
Austrian Economics 85, 88

Backhouse, R. and Salanti, A. 129
Backus, D. and Drifill, J. 60
Baglioni, A. 150
balance
  of payments 21, 160, 198, 200, 205
  of trade 15, 19–20, 197–8, 185, 187,
    205
balance sheet 17, 106–8, 112–13, 118,
  120, 123, 148, 151, 178–80, 184,
  233–4
Baliño T., Bennett, A. and Borensztein,
  E. 174
Ball, L. and Sheridan, N. 72, 76
bank
  as 'circuit starter' 189
  commercial see commercial bank
  versus capitalization 253–6

see also credit supply
Bank of England 29
Bank of Mexico 210–11, 221
banking system 12–13, 90–91, 108, 179,
    181
    evolution of *see* evolution
    fragility of 178, 191
    oligopsony in 148–51, 154, 161, 170
bankruptcy 12–13, 113, 203
Barber, W. 99
Barro,. R. 33, 138
Barro, R. and Gordon, D. 24, 60–62
Basel agreements 244–8
Bateman, B. 98
Becker, R. 213
behavior
    cybernetic models of 56
    and economic experiments 22
    and institutions 96–7
    organizational 56
    rule following 58
benchmark 63, 76, 84
Bernarke, B. 24, 68, 72–4
Bernarke, B. and Mishkin, F. 73, 81
beta (exchange rate) 212, 215–17, 223,
    225–6
bias
    inflationary 64–5, 73, 77–8, 80
Biefang-Frisancho Mariscal, I. and
    Howells, P. 73
Blinder, A 62, 68, 81
Bolsa Mexicana de Valores (BMV)
    208–12, 221
    IBMV 210, 214, 219, 227
Bonds, B. 21
Boskin effect 74
Bossone, B. and Abdourahmane, S. 189
Bouhaili, A. and Nafa, N. 99
Branson, W. 219
Bray, M. 24
Brazelton, R. 99
Bretton Woods 11–12
Bridge loan 11–12, 14
Bruno, M. and Easterly, W. 188
Bryant, J. 81
bubbles
    financial 108, 112, 118, 120–21, 123
Buira, A 21
business cycle 122, 125–6, 128–9,
    131–3, 136, 138

Calvo pricing mechanism 24
Campbell, J. and Mankiw, G. 132
capacity
    idle 194–8
capital
    controls of 173, 175, 178, 183, 186,
        187
    flight of 173, 177, 182, 185, 205
    flow of 12–20, 21, 175, 177–8, 192–8,
        208
    see also net transfer of resources
    gains in 106, 108–9, 115, 117–21,
        123–4
    marginal efficiency of 135
    markets of 192, 206
    requirements 29, 36
capital asset pricing model (CAPM) 212,
    219
capital factor services
    balance of 18–19
capitalist economies 18, 89, 93, 95, 98–9,
    134
capitalization
    international financial 194, 199, 201,
        204
    of the market 209–10, 211–12, 221,
        227, 236, 239–40, 248, 253–5
Carstens, A. 21
Carstens, A. and Werner, A. 221
Carvalho, F. 97
Casseti, M. 199
Central Bank
    accountability of 59, 62, 66–8, 71,
        76–7, 79–80
    communication strategy of 67–9, 72, 74
    confidence framework of 58–9, 65,
        67–72, 74, 80
    credibility framework of 58–65, 67–8,
        70, 72–4, 80
    dual mandate of 66, 70, 72–6, 79
    and economic agents 58–60, 63, 66–9,
        71, 74
    hierarchical mandate of 61, 63, 72–3,
        75, 77, 79
    independence of 65, 67, 70–71, 80
    legitimacy of 70–71
    as a lender of last resort 91, 137, 179,
        233
    openness of 59, 66–71, 75–7, 79
    transparency of 59, 67–8, 74–6, 79–80

change
structural 87
Chenery, H. and Srout, A. 172, 180
Chick, V. 233
Chick, V. and Dow, S. 233
China 181, 184–6
Christiano, L. and Eichenbaum, M. 138
circuit
monetary 141
circular flow model 104, 112
Claims
interbank 133, 137, 238–9
Coase, R. 85
Coase's transaction costs 85
collateral 28, 121
collusive behavior
in banking 141, 149, 160
commercial bank 141–61, 235–8
and liability management 145–6,
148–9
and oligopolistic competition 141,
144, 149–50
and oligopsony in deposit market 141,
149, 161
and profit maximization 141, 148, 150,
160–61
common currency 29
common knowledge 68, 73, 80
common understanding 68
Commons, J. 85, 92–4
and Keynes 92–3, 99
communism 33
competition
between currencies 173, 181–2, 184,
187, 188
in trade 11, 193–201, 205
confidence strategy *see* Central Bank
construction sector (Mexico) 210–11,
214, 215–18, 223–7
consumption 37–8, 40, 42, 104–5
function of 42
out of income 116, 118
marginal propensity to 37–8, 42,
109–10
contagion 29
contracts
exposure 218, 225
forward 91
incomplete 26
legal 91

money-denominated 91
money-wage 91
optimal incentive 62, 65
replacing rules 62
conventional wisdom 37–8
cooperation 85
coordination 85
Cornwall, J. 95
creativity 87–8
credibility
framework *see* Central Bank
institutional design for 61, 62
versus flexibility dilemma 73, 76
credit
risks 144–6, 150, 157
supply of 28, 179–81, 202, 205–6
credit supply curve
slope of 150
horizontal 143–4
upward-sloping 145
creditor 13–14, 21, 37–9, 111, 202–4,
235, 242
creditworthiness 13, 28
Cribari-Neto, F. 138
crisis
in banking 177, 235–6, 242, 244, 248
of currency 214, 217, 221
financial 11, 15–16, 18, 21, 31, 175,
177, 182, 188, 198, 206
Cross, R. 126, 138
Crotty, J. 96
Cukierman, A. and Hercowitz, Z. 148
currency
competition 173, 181–2, 184, 187, 188
Czech Republic 175, 231, 237, 239,
241–3, 245–7, 252–6

Davidson, P. 87, 89, 91, 134, 185, 189
Dalziel, P. 80, 81
debt
crisis 11, 15–17
and crowding out of investment 109,
112, 115, 117, 120, 122–3
deflation 111–12, 115–16, 119–23
and equity 209, 211–12, 225, 227, 230
foreign 172–3, 175–8, 182, 185, 187,
188, 191, 194, 196, 204–6, 208
and interest rates 12–13, 18, 20
leveraging of 111–12, 117, 119, 122,
124, 202, 204

public 40, 42–5, 47, 53–5, 56
ratio to GDP 39, 42–3, 51–4
relief in HIPC 177
repayment profiles of 17–20, 21
restructuring of 12–13
service of 17– 20, 26–7, 42, 44–7,
        54–5, 109, 111–13, 115–17,
        120–23, 175, 201, 204–5, 208
debtor 37–39, 111, 202–4, 206, 235, 240,
        242
deficit
    of current account 175– 8, 182, 185,
        186, 188, 192, 198, 200, 204
    fiscal 17, 38, 54, 104, 160, 169–70
    of trade 13, 20, 24, 194–5, 197–200,
        205
deindustrialization 195, 203
delegation
    strategic 61–2, 65, 77
demand
    aggregate *see* aggregate demand
    for credit , 141, 143–50, 157, 160–61,
        202–3
    of consumers 111–12, 122, 161
    for current bank accounts 157
    for deposits 141, 150–51, 161
    effective 111, 119
    for equity 209, 220, 229
    fall in 196, 198–200, 205
    and fall in wages 15, 174, 199
    for financial capital 197, 200
    for foreign currency 209, 213
    inflation pressures of 188, 201, 205
    for money 23, 32, 63, 99, 229
Demirgüç-Kunt, A. and Levine, R. 234,
        239–41, 243
Demirgüç-Kunt, A. and Sobaci, T. 243
democratic dilemma 75
deposit demand
    interest elasticity of 141, 150, 157
deposit insurance system 242–4, 247
deposit markets 150
    oligopsony in 141, 149, 161
    free competition in 143
deposit rate
    and interbank rate 146, 148
    in Mexico 154, 157, 160
    setting by commercial banks 144–5,
        148, 151
Dequech, D. 97

Deriet, M. and Seccareccia, M. 161
developing countries
    and current account problems 178,
        185–6
    and domestic currency 179, 182, 184,
        188
    and economic growth 195, 205
    employment in 14–15
    and exchange rates 177–8
    and foreign debt 12–20, 21, 172,
        178
    and inflation 174, 188
    and interest rates 177
    lending to 11–20, 21
    see also dollarization
development 15, 20, 180, 184–6, 232–40,
        242, 244, 248
Diaz-Alejandro, C. 149
dichotomy
    classical 34, 63, 72, 74, 78, 80
Dickey, D. and Fuller, W. 138
Diebold, F. and Rudebusch, G. 138
Dillard, D. 99
discretion
    monetary 58, 60, 74, 76
dividend 109–10
Dixon, R. 95
dollarization 173–4, 179, 182–3, 185
Domar E. 19–20, 21, 172
Domar's stability conditions 20
Domínguez, K. and Tesar, L. 213
Dornbusch, R. 183
Dornbusch, R. and Fischer, S. 188
Dow, A. and Dow, S. 145
Dow, S. and Rodrigues-Fuentes, C. 147,
        232
Dubey, P., Geanakoplos, J. and Shubik,
        M. 35
Dudley, D. 94
Dunn, S. 99
Dutt, A. 138
Dutt, A. and Ross, J. 137
Dymski, G. 234–5, 238, 248
dynamics
    industrial 40, 56
    see also system dynamics

earnings
    retained 105, 111–12
Easterly, W. 189

economics
  heterodox 37
  mainstream 87, 126, 129
Eichengreen, B. 187
Eichengreen, B. and Hausmann, R. 175
Eichengreen, B., Hausmann, R. and
  Richardo, P. 175
Eichner, A. 92, 94, 143, 157
Eller, R. 242
Ely, R. 93
employment 112
  in developing countries 14–15
  full 11, 75, 111, 113
Enders, W. 138
Enron 118, 119
equilibrium
  of the balance of payments 145, 171,
    187
  in banking 148
  general 26, 31, 87
  of DGP and aggregate demand 41, 56
  monetary 220
  multiple 65, 81, 132, 134–5
  natural long-term 60, 62–6, 78, 80,
    134–6
  of portfolio 219, 229–30
    see also portfolio balance
  reputational 60, 62
  shifting 47, 135–6, 138
  short-term 188
  temporary 42, 47
  with underemployment 137
  unique predetermined 59, 69, 78, 134
equity finance 117, 119, 208–9, 211
equity returns
  and exchange rates 212–21
  and monetary policy 221, 223–4
ergodic hypothesis/ergodic process 87,
  89
Ernst, E. 244
Estonia 231, 236–8, 240–41, 243, 246–7
Euro system 29–31
European Central Bank (ECB) 71, 80
European Commission 30
European Constitution 31
European Union 231–2, 234, 239–48
  accession/transition countries of
    231–3, 237, 239, 241– 5, 247–8,
    256
Evans, G., and Honkapojha, S. 81

evolution
  in banking 232–3, 235, 237, 239, 242,
    244, 248
exchange rate
  adjustment of 12, 19, 174, 178, 187,
    193, 220, 224
  appreciation of 11, 193–201, 204–5
  devaluation of 11, 174–5, 179, 204
  exposure 213, 216–18, 221, 224–6
  flexible 12–13, 38, 174, 208–9, 212–3,
    218–9, 221, 216
  managed 209, 218
  in Mexico 151–6, 160, 164, 167,
    169–70
  and monetary policy 221–3
  pegged 208, 213, 230
  stability of 11–12, 192–3, 199, 205–6
  stabilization policy of 193–200
expectations
  adaptive 25
  anchorage 58–9, 61, 63, 66, 68, 73–4,
    76, 78
  formation of 27, 66, 70, 72, 74
  inflationary 193, 205
  of insolvency 202–3
  rational 22–7, 58, 60, 63–4, 66,
    69–70
  self-fulfilling 78

Faust , J. and Henderson, D. 75
Fazzari, S., Ferri, P. and Greenberg, E.
  138
Fazzari, S. and Variato, A. 197
Federal Reserve (Fed) 38, 43, 59, 67–8,
  71–2, 76, 80
Federal Saving and Loan Insurance
  Corporation (FSLIC) 123
'Fedspeak' 68
feedback 56
  control systems 40
  effects 41, 50
  loops 40–41
Felix, D. 204
Ferguson, R. 68
finance, insurance and real estate (FIRE)
  106, 108, 110, 117
finance
  hedge 17–18, 21
  Ponzi 18–20, 21, 112
  speculative 18

financial system 108, 115, 174, 177–84, 188–9, 232, 234, 241–8
   international 11–12, 18–19, 20
   bank-based 232, 234, 240–45, 248
   market-based 232–4, 240–45, 248
firm 195–8, 201–5
   degree of monopolization 195–6, 198, 199–200
fiscal policy 17, 30–31, 38
   restrictive 13, 193–4, 197, 201
Fischer, S., Sahay, R., and Végh, C. 174
forecasting 135–6
focal point 59, 66, 70, 72, 74, 79–80
Fontana, G. and Palacio-Vera, A. 81
Forder, J. 81
foreign exchange
   excess demand for 11, 13
   markets of 12–13
Forrester, J. 39–40
Friedman, M. 60, 68, 198
Friedman-Lucas model 68, 72, 78, 84
Fry, M. 143

Galbraith, J. K. 37–8, 95
Galbis, V. 149
Game theory 69
Geanakoplos, J. and Polemarchakis, H. 28
General Theory of Employment, Interest and Money 66, 87–8, 92–4, 105, 107, 110, 112–13
Ghigliazza, S. 149
Gibson, H. and Tsakalotos, E. 232, 234, 244
globalization 196, 204
GNP data series *see* unit roots
Goodhart, C. 63
Goodhart, C., Sunirand, P., and Tsomocos, D. 29
Goodhart, C. and Vinals, J. 65
governance structure 32–4, 59, 66–7, 70–71, 76, 79–80
   corporate 244–5, 247–9
government spending 17
   excessive 11
Great Depression 105, 108, 112
Greenspan, A. 37, 67–8, 71, 76, 118
growth
   of domestic demand 15
   and demestic policy 16

real 14–16
and holding of reserves 17, 19, 20, 172, 180–81, 192–201, 205, 231–5
Gruchy, A. 93
Gurley, J. and Shaw, E. 149

Habermas, J. 81
Hahn, F. and Solow, R. 134
Hamilton, W. 99
Herr, H. and Priewe, J. 175, 181, 186, 188, 189
Hibbs, D. 61
Hicks, J. 88, 94
Highly indebted poor countries (HIPC) 177
Hodgson, G. 85, 99
Holt, R. and Pressman, S. 92
Honohan, P. and Shi, A. 179
Hudson, M. 32
Huerta, A. 161
Humphrey-Hawkins procedure 71
Hungary 231–2, 236–47, 252–6
hysteresis
   in labor markets 134

ignorance 89
imagination 87–8
imbalance
   external 11–13, 16
indebtedness
   of developing countries 12, 14
International Monetary Fund (IMF) 137, 171, 179
   adjustment lending 11–12, 15–16, 19
   conditional lending ('seal of approval') 14–20, 21
   Independent Evaluation Office of 14, 21
immutable reality models/ immutability 87–8
imports 193–201, 204
   competition with 194, 198–201
   and domestic workers 198–9, 201
income 105, 107–12
   disposable 37, 40, 42, 47, 50
   distribution of 198, 204
   diversion to debt service 109, 111–3, 115–6, 120–22, 204
   multiplier of 118

national 40–42, 44
inflation
  in developing countries 11, 14, 21
  of asset prices 108, 111, 115–18, 122
  bias 64–5, 73, 77–8, 80
  cost-push 173–4
  and exchange rate appreciation 193–4,
    200
  New-Keynesian view 58, 72, 74
  reduction in 192–5, 197, 199–201,
    204–5
  targeting of 24, 58–64, 67, 71–80,
    174
  by 'surprise' 24, 76
information
  asymmetrical 62, 235
  imperfect 26, 62, 97, 219
  problems of 26, 34, 35
innovations
  financial 26, 36
insolvency 202–3, 206
instability 87–90, 98
  financial 12, 17, 19, 21, 206
  Wicksellian 23
institutions 85–6, 90–91, 96–7, 184–5,
    187, 188
  building of 180, 184, 186
  defined 96, 99
  and economic behavior 96–7
  financial 17, 21, 109–10
  formal 95–6, 100
  in Post-Keynesian theory 91–2
  informal 96
  informational-cognitive function of 97
  micro-foundations for Post-Keynesian
    economics 97–8
  of property 109
  restrictive functions of 96–7
  teleological functions of 97
Institutionalism
  Historical 85
  New 85–6
interest rates
  and aggregate demand 37–9, 44–7, 51,
    54–5
  and debt 12–13, 15, 17–18, 20, 37–56,
    108, 111, 113–123, 173–187,
    188, 193–4, 198, 205
  on deposits 151–2, 154–60, 164–7,
    170

differential (Mexico-USA) 216, 222–4
elasticity of investment 37, 39, 41, 46,
    49
exogenous 143, 145–6
interbank 16–17, 141–2, 144–57,
    160–61
on loans 164–8
perverse effects of 37–40, 53–4
intermediary
  financial 26–9, 105, 142, 242, 249
investment
  crowding out of 107, 109, 112, 115,
    117–23
  and external debt 175, 179
  fall in 109, 112, 124, 201–6
  financing of 18, 28, 90–91, 111, 180,
    247
  and growth 112, 180–84, 189
  interest rate elasticity of 37, 39, 41, 42,
    43, 54
  Keynes's view on 98, 110
  with negative return 17
  into tangible capital 105–12, 118–19,
    123
  and uncertainty 135, 137
IS curve 22
Isard, P. 188
Issing, O. 30
Ize, A. and Parrado, E. 174

Jeanne, O. and Zettelmeyer, J. 177
job creation 205
Journal of Economic Studies 124
Journal of Post Keynesian Economics 95

Kaldor, N. 143
Kalecki, M. 195, 198, 205
Kaleckian principle of increasing risk
    144
Kamin, S. 149
Kaminsky, G. and Reinhart, C. 177
Kaminsky, G. and Reinhatt, C.M. 188
Keller, R. 99
Keynes, J. M.
  and Commons, J. 92, 93
  and consumption 112
  and inflation 16, 188
  and econometrics 94
  and equilibrium 135
  and expectations 93, 135

and euthanasia of the rentier 111, 116,
118
and *General Theory* 66, 87–8, 92–4,
105, 107, 110, 112–13
and Great Depression 108, 112
and hoarding 116
and income multiplier 118
and inflation 16, 188
and instability 89
and institutions 92–6
and investment 110, 112
and Keynes's Clearing Union 20, 185,
189
and Malthus, T. 124
and monetary theory of production 94,
189
and money 80, 91
and non-ergodicity 88
proposal for surplus countries 189
and rationality 95
and saving 104, 106–13, 115–16
and Say's Law 112
and shifting equilibrium 135–6, 138
and socialization of public investment
98
and Townshend, H. 95
and *Treatise on Probability* 86
and *Treatise on Money* 90
and uncertainty 86–7, 89, 92–3, 135–6
King, M. 24, 195, 198
Kiytaki, N. and Wright, R. 31
Klein, D. 37
knowledge
lack of 87
Kohn, D. 76
Kregel, J. 11, 87, 135–6
Kuczynski, P. and Williamson, J. 188
Kydland, F. and Prescott, E. 24, 60, 70,
80, 81

labor
employment of 105, 115
propensity to save of 110
spending power of 108
tax burden of 119–20
unit costs of 183–5, 188, 187, 193
lags 25
land 105, 118
Larson, S. 98
Laski, K. 206

Latin-American economies 15, 17, 19,
171, 181, 192
Latvia 231, 236–8, 240–43, 246–8,
252–6
Latzer, M. and Schmitz, S. 31
Lavoie, M. 144
Lawson, Tony 95
adaptive 68, 73, 78
interactional 66, 68, 78
legitimacy 65–7, 70, 71, 77
le Heron, E. 72
lending
and inflation of asset-prices 111,
115–23
interbank rate of 17, 38, 144, 148–9,
151
and interest rates 12, 18, 20, 208
of International Monetary Fund (IMF)
see IMF
private 12–17
Levine, R. 234
Levine, R. and Zervos, S. 234
liberalization
economic 171–2, 197, 199, 205
of interest rates 149, 155, 157
financial 161, 172–3, 175, 178, 180,
182–3, 187, 189, 192, 206
of trade 94, 188
liquidity 17, 20, 90, 201–2
preference for 16, 18–20, 135, 141,
145
and banking 143–4, 147–8, 161
trap of 74
Lithuania 231–48, 252–6
loan
out of accrual of interest 109–10,
116–17, 123
exponential growth of 115–7, 119–20,
122
for purchase of existing assets 107–8,
116, 119, 120, 122
as recycled savings 108–11, 116–7,
119
syndicated 12
Lohmann, S. 61
Lopez, J. 161
Lucas, R. 68, 138
Lucasian
critique 27–8, 87
counterrevolution 22–3, 34

misperception 132, 138

Macroeconomic models 22–5
  logical consistency of 27–8
  micro foundations of 22, 26, 28, 34
  of multiple equilibria 132, 134–5
Malthus, T. 113, 124
Mankiw, G. 132
manufacturing sector (Mexico) 210,
  214–15, 217–18, 223–5, 230
mark-up on loan rates
  estimation by commercial banks 141,
    143, 144–8, 150–51, 154
market
  financial 20, 26–9, 117, 119, 192, 205
Marshall – Lerner conditions 175
Martinek, T. 245
Martinez, L. 154
Matthews, R. 99
McCallum, B. 24, 64–5, 81, 129, 131–2,
  138
McKinnon, R. 235
Means, G. 93, 94
Mehta, J. 81
Meltzer, A. 34
Menger, C. 31
Meyer, L. 71–3, 76, 81, 240
Meyer, L., Swanson, E., and Wieland, W.
  81
Minsky, H. 17–18, 21, 87, 89–91, 95, 99,
  137, 202–3
Mishkin, F. 73, 234
Mitchell, W. 85
monetary policy
  and demand for liquidity 145, 157
  dual mandate of 66, 72–4, 76, 79
  and credit supply 144, 154, 161
  and exchange rate stabilization 221–6
  hierarchical mandate of 61, 63, 72–3,
    75, 77, 79
  and interest rates 143–5, 157
  link with fiscal policy 30–34
  regime of 58–9, 62–3, 67–8, 72, 74,
    76, 80
  restrictive 11–13, 194, 197, 201–2,
    205
  see also anti-inflationary policy
  of stabilization 37–8, 53, 136–7
  of sterilization 16–17
  and regional imbalances 30

unique mandate of 61, 66, 77, 79
  see also New Consensus, Central Bank
monetary targeting 23, 61, 66, 73, 77, 79
  monetary theory
  Mengerian 31, 80
  chartalist 32
  of production 92, 94–5
money
  electronic 150, 157
  endogenous 11, 70, 72, 78, 91, 141–5,
    148, 233–4
  exogenous 64, 145, 233
  functions of 31–2, 80, 90
  horizontal approach to 142–6
  multiplier 23, 233
  neutrality of 63, 80, 130
  non-neutrality of 67, 72, 90, 126,
    136–7
  structuralist approach to 145–7
Moore, B. 143, 161, 202, 233–4
Mortgage 119–20
Mosler, W. 199
Mott, T. 196, 205
Mussa, M. 30

Nafa, N. 99
nation state 30
National income and product accounts
  (NIPA) 104, 106, 110–12
Ndikumana, L. 201–2
Nelson, C. and Plosser, C. 125, 128–32,
  134, 136–7, 138
Neo-classical synthesis 94
Neo-merchantilist strategy 184
net transfer of resources 15–16, 18–20,
  21
  negative 15–17, 20
net worth
  growth in 107, 115–16, 144
new classical economics 58, 62, 80, 138
New Deal 93, 99
*A New Guide to Post Keynesian Econom-
  ics* 92
new-Keynesian economics
  and economic reality 88
  and expectations formation 66
  and inflation 67, 72, 74
  and monetary policy 58, 65–6, 79–80
  and uncertainty 80
  and unit roots 131, 134

New Theories of the Firm 85
Niggle, C. 144
Nobel prize 85
nominal anchor 174, 187
non-ergodicity/non-ergodic process
        88–91, 134
Nordhaus, W. 61
North, D. 85, 99

Oligopoly *see* commercial bank
open market operations 144, 147, 149,
        151, 153, 157, 159, 161
opportunity cost
    marginal 26
Optimal Control Theory (OCT) 60
Optimal Currency Area (OCA) theory
        29–30
original sin 175
Orlean, A. 81
Orphadines, A. and Williams, J., 73, 81
output
    fluctuations in 138
    gap in 73, 75, 77, 154
    growth in 72
    long-run natural rate of 132–3
    spending on 108, 116
override procedure 61, 66, 77

Padoa-Schioppa, T. 143
Palley, T. 141, 148
path dependence 134, 137, 138
pecuniary 36
Perron, P. 138
Persson, T. and Tabellini, G. 61, 81
peso 208, 210–26
Petrick, K. 248
Phillips curve 22, 73, 75
    augmented 60
Poland 231, 236–43, 245, 247, 252–6
Pollin, R. 145
Ponzi finance 18–21, 112
portfolio
    balance of 212–14, 219–22, 229–30
    internationalization of 220–21, 226
    investment 160–61, 172, 188
post-Keynesian economics
    and credit supply curve 142, 161
    and expectations formation 66
    and financial system 233–4, 237
    and historical time 92, 135–6

and institutions 86, 90–95, 98–9
and institutionalism 86, 94–5, 98–9
and monetary theory 88, 90–91
and non-ergodicity 87, 89, 95, 135
and persistence of shocks 136, 138
and uncertainty 87, 89, 92, 95, 99, 135
and unit roots 134–7
pragmatism 94
Pressman, S. 248
Prevezer, M. and Rickets, M. 245
Price , R. 113, 122
price
    stability 24, 65, 67, 71, 73, 74–6, 173
    stickiness 24–5, 36, 91
prisoner dilemma 69
privatization 206
process
    difference-stationary 127–32, 138
    ergodic 87, 89
    non-ergodic 88–91, 134
    trend -stationary 127–32, 138
producers domestic
    and foreign imports 193–8
    degree of monopolization of 195–9
productive capacity
    idle 196–7
productivity 193–5, 205
profits 144, 147–51, 192–3, 201–6
    falling margins of 194–9
profitability
    of exports 144, 150
Public Choice 85
public preferences 75
purchasing power 112
    parity of 188

random walk 125–7, 133, 137, 138
rationality
    bounded 88
Radzicki, M. 40
de Rato, Rodrigues 13, 21
real estate 118, 121–2
    see also FIRE
Real Bills theory 34
Real Business Cycle (RBC) 126, 128–9,
        136, 138
rentier
    income of 105–6, 110, 204
    property of 105–6, 111
    euthanasia of 111, 116, 118

reputation 60, 62, 68–9, 77, 79
reserves
    of foreign exchange 12–13, 15–17, 19,
        21
response
    hump-shaped 25
Richardson, G. 56
risk
    assessment of 28
    in banking 142, 145–51, 202
    of a currency crisis 178–9, 182
    of a current account deficit 175–8
    of default 245
    differentiated 148, 151
    and investment 111, 202–3, 188
    Kaleckian principle of increasing risk
        144
    of a liquidity trap 74
    premium for 28, 177, 182, 188
    reduction in 90, 178
    and uncertainty 89
    unhedgeable 26
Roberts, E. 40
Robinson, J. 96, 184
Rochon, L.-.P. 143–5, 160, 161, 234–5,
        238, 248
Rodrik, D. 161, 172, 186, 188
Rogoff, K. 61–2, 75
Rojas, E. and Rodriguez, P. 145
Rojas-Suarez, L. 174
Rudebusch, G. 138
rule
    instrumental 62, 67, 73, 77
    monetary 58–9
    targeting 62, 64, 77, 79
    Taylor 64, 80
    versus discretion 58, 76
Russian bond default 216

Sachs, J. 186
Samuels, W. and Medema, S. 94
Sargent, T. and Wallace, N. 23
Sarr, A. 150
Savage's expected utility theory 88
saving
    and debt creation 106, 108–11, 113–16
    forced 107, 113
    gross 107, 110, 115
    growth of through accrual of interest
        110, 112–20, 123

Keynes's view on 108–9, 111–12, 116
    out of income 108–9
    and lending of 109–19, 121, 123
    marginal propensity to 107, 109–10,
        116
    net saving 107, 110–11, 114–15, 123
Sawyer, M. 198, 203
Say's Law 11, 112
scarcity 91, 146
Schelling, T. 66, 81
Schelling salience 66
Schotter, A. 99
Schumpeter, J. 180, 189
Schwartz, M. 144
Seccareccia 161
secular flow
    of spending 104, 111–12
securities
    financial 107, 109, 110–11
services sector (Mexico) 210–11,
        214–18, 223–4, 230
servomechanisms 40
Setterfield, M. 138
Shackle G. L. S. 86–8
Shaw, E. 235
Sherman, H. 203
Shleifer, A. 33, 245
Shleifer, A. and Vishny, R. 245
Shubik, M. 28
Shubik School 29
Shubik and Wilson, 35
signal
    extraction problem 70
Simon, H. 56
Slovakia 231, 236–8, 242–3, 246, 256
Slovenia 231, 236–8, 240–48, 252–6
Smithin, J. 98, 143
Solnik, B. 212
sovereignty 30
Spanos, A. 151
speculation
    financial 119, 192, 202, 205
spending
    propensity to 39, 54, 55
stability
    financial 18–21, 29–30, 32
    macroeconomic 184, 187
stabilization policy 64–5, 93, 96, 98, 193,
        197, 199, 201
stagnation 195–6, 205–6

Steindl, J. 195–6, 201, 203
Stigler, G. 26
Stiglitz, J. 28, 172, 187, 189, 234
Stiglitz, J. and Weiss, A. 28
Stoneman, W. 99
Streissler, E. 31
stress tests 29
Strout 172, 180
structure index 241, 253–6
Sunirand, T. 29
supervision
    in banking 242, 244–8
surplus 11, 104
    of current account 179–80, 183–5,
        187, 189
    of trade 15, 19, 172, 180
Svensson, L. 24, 62, 73, 81
Svensson, L. and Woodford, M. 81
system dynamics 39, 40, 41, 56
    see also feedback

tax rates
    on capital gains 119, 122
    on wages and profits 122
    on direct investment 119
Taylor, J. 24, 134
Taylor
    rule 64, 80
    reaction function 22
technological shocks 129
    and GDP fluctuations 134, 136
    see also real business cycle
Telmex 211, 214, 224
Tequila Crisis 209–10, 214
Thornton, H. 28, 75
time
    historical 89, 94, 134
    irreversibility of 137
    scarce 27
    inconsistency of 60, 64–5, 68, 76, 78,
        81
Tinbergen, J. 94
Tobin effect 130
Townshend, H. 95
Toporowski, J. 161
trade
    competition in 11, 193–201, 205, 225
    foreign 111, 194–5
    liberalization in *see* liberalization
    tariffs on 193–5

unions in 198
traded (non-traded sectors) 211, 226,
    230
transaction costs
    Coaseian 26–7, 85
    in market exchange 31
transfer payments 11, 39–42
transmutability/ transmutable process
    87–8
transversality condition 27–8
transparency 59, 67–8, 74–6, 79–80
Treasury bill rate 151–4, 157–61, 164,
    167–70
A Treatise of Money 90
A Treatise on Probability 86
'true' model of the economy 60, 63,
    65–9, 78–9, 80
trust 85
Tsomocos, D. 29
Tugwell, R. 93

uncertainty
    and credit supply 202
    and exchange rate stabilization 192,
        206
    and expectations 73–4, 80, 91, 95, 135
    in foreign exchange markets 221
    fundamental 72, 89–92, 95, 98
    and inflation targeting 73–4, 77
    and institutions 92–3, 95, 98–9
    Knight's theory of 88
    and monetary policy 66, 68, 70, 73–4,
        80
    and money 90–91
    probabilistic 78
    and speculative practices 205
underdevelopment 137, 181–5
unemployment 201
    involuntary 133, 135
    natural rate of 60, 134, 136
unit roots 125–37, 138
utility function
    quadratic 24

Vandenbroucke, F. 184
VAR model, Mexico 151–2
Veblen, T. 85, 99

wage 195, 198–9
    stickiness of 24–5, 91

anchor of 174, 183, 187
wage price spiral 174
Wal-Mart (Walmex) 211, 214
Walsh, C. 62
Washington consensus 171–87, 188, 189
wealth 107
    disparities of 116–17, 122
West , K. 133, 138
Wicksellian model 62
Wieland, W. 81
Wiener, N. 56
Williamson, J. 171–3, 187, 188
Williamson, O. 86, 99

Winkler, B. 69
Wolfson, M. 35, 143, 146–7, 197–8,
    203–4
Wong, K. 161
Woodford, M. 24, 62, 80
workers
    negotiating power of 198–9
World Bank 171, 179–80, 233, 241
Wray, L. R. 21, 145, 157, 203

Yellen, J. 24

Zingales, L. 245